JOHN A COSTELLO
1891 - 1976

COMPROMISE TAOISEACH

ANTHONY J JORDAN

John Aloysious Costello

Acknowledgements

I would like to thank the following libraries' staffs for kind assistance. National Archives: (Eileen Tracey, Tom Gilsenan) National Library, RDS, (Mary Kelligher and Gerard Whelan), Royal Irish Academy; Pembroke; Ringsend; IIAC; Security staff at Dáil Éireann, Gilbert Library (Maire Kennedy, Padraic O'Brien, Eithne Massey, Eithne Sharkey, Leo Maguire), Mary Clarke of Dublin City Council Archives, Ged Walsh, Ruairi Quinn TD, Patrick Lynch, Brendan Keane, Tom Delanty, Mary Rieke Murphy, Stephan Moran, T M Healy, Gerard Hogan. I thank Mr. Liam Cosgrave for identifying the members of both inter-party Governments on pages 88 and 118. I would also like to thank Michael O'Connor, Bernice Curly, Seán Donnelly, and David Lowe of The Central Remedial Clinic's Desktop Publishing Training Unit, for their help and commitment.
And to my wife Maura for living with one more character.
Also to the inestimable Mr. Murphy, whom I love dearly.

ISBN: 978-0952444787

Editor: Judith M. Jordan

Westport Books, Gilford Road, Dublin 4.
westportbooks@yahoo.co.uk

Design & Print Reproduction
by
The Central Remedial Clinic
Desktop Publishing Training Unit,
Vernon Avenue
Clontarf,
Dublin 3.
Tel: 805 7400

This book is dedicated to my siblings

Paddy, Josephine, Tommy, Bernadette and Jimmy.

CONTENTS

	INTRODUCTION	6
Ch 1.	COMPROMISE TAOISEACH	9
Ch 2.	YOUNG JOHN COSTELLO	17
Ch 3.	ATTORNEY GENERAL	21
Ch 4.	ORDER OF ST PATRICK	33
Ch 5.	ELECTION DEFEAT, 1932	35
Ch 6.	CONSTITUTIONAL AFFAIRS, 1936-7	41
Ch 7.	1943 GENERAL ELECTION	47
Ch 8.	POLITICAL PARTIES IN 1940'S	51
Ch 9.	FIANNA FÁIL DEFEAT IN 1948	55
Ch 10.	THE CENOTAPH: COSTELLO'S FOLLY?	59
Ch 11.	TAOISEACH	65
Ch 12.	DECLARATION OF REPUBLIC	73
Ch 13.	MOTHER AND CHILD DEBACLE	89
Ch 14.	ELECTION DEFEAT, 1951	99
Ch 15.	PATRICK KAVANAGH'S LIBEL CASE	105
Ch 16.	SECOND INTER-PARTY GOVERNMENT, 1954-57	113
Ch 17.	COSTELLO REBUKES HIERARCHY	119
Ch 18.	HUGH LANE PICTURES - ARTS COUNCIL	129
Ch 19.	AMERICAN STATE VISIT	139
Ch 20.	FATEFUL YEAR OF 1956	143
Ch 21.	IRA TROUBLE RE-SURFACES	149
Ch 22.	FINE GAEL DOLDRUMS, 1957-1973	157
Ch 23.	COSTELLO INTERVIEWED 1967	171
Ch 24.	FREEMAN OF DUBLIN WITH deVALERA, 1976	175
	FOOTNOTES	181
	SELECTED BIBLIOGRAPHY	191
	INDEX	192

INTRODUCTION

It is striking how scarcely anything has been written about the two Fine Gael politicians who led Irish governments in the first part of the 20th century, WT Cosgrave [1922-1932] and John A Costello [1948-1951 and [1954-1957]. When I discovered this anomaly some years ago, I decided to fill that gap by writing a book about each man. I was not unduly surprised to discover, despite his pivotal role in establishing the State, that there was a general ignorance about WT Cosgrave, considering that his leadership of government ended in 1932.[1] I was surprised that there was also a great ignorance about Costello, considering how comparatively recently his leadership of two governments had been. There are probably many reasons for this situation. Both were modest men who, in the Fine Gael tradition, did not seek to project themselves as iconic leaders. Of course since Fianna Fáil have held the reins of power for such long periods, its interpretation of history and its role therein have received most attention from historians and biographers.

When John A Costello is remembered, it is usually for being chosen by a variety of political party leaders as a compromise candidate they could coalesce under as Taoiseach, to form the first Inter Party Government in 1948. He is seen as someone who was plucked, almost out of nowhere, to undertake this extraordinary role. There is further amazement and almost incredulity that as Brian Feeney writes "Costello announced out of the blue during a visit to Canada in September 1948 that he intended to declare a republic", and take Ireland out of the Commonwealth and refuse to join NATO[2]. But of course that is to ignore Costello's long pedigree of State service, both in the Attorney General's office during the crucial years from 1921-1932 and as a frontbencher of the Fine Gael party from 1933 onwards. Costello has said that the result of the Pact Election of 1922, when the people voted for the Treaty, was the crucial moment for him in throwing in his lot with the pro -Treaty people[3]. Costello's early formidable record is almost unknown, but a careful study of those years certainly reveals clear signals that he may in fact have been one of the better prepared politicians to undertake the role of government leader, since the foundation of the State. He had built a very successful career at the Bar and was happy to combine that, in the Fine Gael tradition, with his membership of Dáil Éireann. He was a major contributor to Dáil debates on constitutional measures. He opposed the Bill repealing the External Relations Act in 1936 deeming it "a political monstrosity the like of which has been unknown to political legal theory". Opposing the draft Constitution Bill in 1937 he said, "This draft as it stands offers its Framer as a whole burnt offerings to feminists and feminist associations". He lost his Dáil seat in 1943 but regained it in 1944.

Costello's satisfying life was rudely shattered when all the diverse political parties and Independents combined to oust Fianna Fáil from sixteen years of continuous rule. The only point of contention was the leadership of General Richard Mulcahy in Fine Gael, whose harsh measures during the Civil War had made him unacceptable as Taoiseach for the Republican Clann na Poblachta, and some others. The name of John A Costello, untarnished by Civil War involvement, emerged as a compromise Taoiseach acceptable to all. His robust backing for the Army Comrades Association and the Blueshirts, in response to IRA attacks on Fine Gael meetings in the early 1930's, was overlooked. The emergence of his name as an agreed candidate for Taoiseach came as a shock to him and he was reluctant to contemplate leaving his legal career and disrupting his family life. Costello was essentially a very reserved family man, though well skilled in adopting the role of friend or foe as his legal expertise demanded. However, he was advised by friends that he had little choice but to accept the offer.

It had been a canon of Fianna Fáil faith that coalition government was bad and could not work. Costello disproved this theory and demonstrated that in fact coalition government could be more democratic than single party government. As Taoiseach he acted more in the role of a chairman than a chief. Nevertheless he embarked on constitutional change and stole Fianna Fáil's clothes by declaring a Republic and exiting from the British Commonwealth. Internal party differences in Clann na Poblachta, between Sean MacBride and Noel Browne, contributed greatly to the demise of Costello's first government. However, the split in the Labour Party was healed during this period. After his defeat Costello returned to the Bar where his most famous case was as defence counsel for 'The Leader' in Patrick Kavanagh's libel case. The aftermath of their court jousting provides an interesting case study of the contemporary relative positions of an establishment figure and a poverty stricken artist.

Costello's second period as Taoiseach saw him adopt further Keynesian economic policies, which laid the basis for future radical development. This government was remarkable for Costello's little known, stinging rebuke to the Catholic Bishops in 1955 defending his intention to include Trinity College Dublin as an integral part of the Agricultural Institute. Poor economic circumstances caused by international upheavals and a renewal of an IRA offensive in the North led to the fall of the government.

The 1957 defeat of the Second Inter - Party government led to much soul searching within Fine Gael and Labour. There was speculation of realignment between like minds within both parties and even talk of an amalgamation of the two parties. Costello himself favoured major changes. In the event another unbroken period of sixteen years of Fianna Fáil rule followed.

Costello continued to lead the Fine Gael party within the Dáil and resumed his legal practice. His refusal to become a full-time party leader in 1959 saw James Dillon take that post. Among the achievements that he was most proud of accomplishing in government were; the Declaration of the Republic; founding the Industrial Development Authority; setting up the Arts Council; 'recovering' the Lane Pictures; introducing economic planning. He was made a Freeman of Dublin in 1975 alongside Eamon deValera.

Michael McInerney wrote of Costello in 1967, "Costello, who was closely associated with the early Free State Government, although not in a leading way, was not one of the great, but he will hold a special place in history. Costello today is 76, white haired and full of energy. He neither looks nor sounds his age. Hardly ever taking a holiday, he is kept busy by his profession and his politics. Impressive with a resonant and slightly Dublin accent, of sturdy build and with a rough charm, he has the same qualities that caused him to be selected in 1948 as Taoiseach. He has none of the charisma of a Pearse, a Griffith or a deValera and without any real philosophy, except the desire to secure better social services for the people"[4].

W.T Cosgrave

CHAPTER 1

THE COMPROMISE TAOISEACH

John Aloysious Costello was an eminent barrister and a part-time Fine Gael politician, who had been a long time member of the Dáil, when a complicated set of results in the general election of 1948, catapulted him into the office of Taoiseach. Fianna Fáil had been in unbroken government for sixteen years since 1932. It had been recently challenged by a new republican party, Clann na Poblachta, which believed that Fianna Fáil, the so-called republican party, had betrayed its earlier republican ideals and was just another partition - minded party. The Clann had sensationally defeated Fianna Fáil in a series of by-elections in 1947. The Machiavellian leader of Fianna Fáil, Eamon deValera, decided that his best strategy was to call an early general election before the new party could organise effectively nationwide. The resulting election in February threw up a most complicated set of results, which offered the possibility of ending Fianna Fáil's term in office. However the obstacles that lay in the way were formidable. Little did John A Costello contemplate that the final *coup de grace* for deValera would rest on his shoulders.

The final results of the election were:
Fianna Fáil – 68
Fine Gael – 31
Labour 14
National Labour – 5
Clann na Poblachta - 10
Clann na Talmhan – 7
Independents -12

At first it appeared that Fianna Fáil would have little difficulty in returning to office with the help of National Labour and some Independents. The details of what exactly happened next come from several sources including Richard Mulcahy and Sean MacBride. Mulcahy responded to Costello's urgent request in 1967 as the latter prepared for an interview with Michael McInerney of the *Irish Times*. As Costello had not been involved in the earliest manoeuvers, it was only natural that he was hazy on what exactly had happened, prior to his being invited to become a candidate for Taoiseach. He wrote to Mulcahy saying, "My recollection is that the suggestion originally came from Sean MacBride but I am not sure whether the suggestion of an Inter-Party government came from him or from you or from Bill Norton"[1]. In reply to Costello, Mulcahy recounted how he had originally 'consulted' Dan Morrissey, a frontbench colleague, on the possibility of contacting the other leaders of parties about a concerted effort to oust Fianna Fáil. Morrissey's response was positive but he reckoned that such a government would only last six months. Morrissey emphasised that Mulcahy would have to contact the other leaders himself.[2] Mulcahy then issued a statement saying that Fine Gael would resist the return of deValera and that his party would cooperate with others on a common platform to form an administration[3]. This was echoed the next day by Sean MacBride, the leader of Clann na Poblachta, who said that there was a mandate from the electorate to "put them out"[4]. Subsequently Mulcahy contacted all the other party leaders inviting them to a meeting in Leinster House.[5] Each attended on Friday 13th, except for the National Labour Party, which was strongly expected to back Fianna Fáil. At the Leinster House meeting, the thorny issue of civil war politics raised its head around the person of Richard Mulcahy. He had been leader of the national army in the civil war, and in the circumstances had no option but to prosecute it in a harsh and terrible way. The wounds were still visible particularly in Clann na Poblachta, where an alliance with Fine Gael would be unthinkable for many and the idea of serving under General Mulcahy as Taoiseach untenable. The feeling would be mutual for many in Fine Gael. This episode was naturally a very delicate matter for Mulcahy to write to Costello about, even so many years later. He dealt with it by writing, "Norton intimated that he did not think that his party would agree to serve in a government under the leadership of one who had been the leader of another party"[7]. Mulcahy, a long-time dedicated patriot on so many earlier occasions, did not demur and a discussion arose over who in Fine Gael, the largest party, would be acceptable as Taoiseach. The higher echelons of the Fine Gael party had always been composed of competing princes. Noel Browne has pointed out that even in cabinet, Mulcahy was "treated with a mixture of levity and contempt by his party colleagues"[8]. Sir John Esmonde from Wexford and Sean MacEoin of Longford were mentioned. Sean MacBride says that he suggested Sir Anthony Esmonde, "who apparently was not acceptable to most of the leadership of Fine Gael". MacBride proposed Esmonde because he believed that he had been somewhat understanding of republicans. MacBride says referring to Fine Gael, "They then suggested Jack Costello. I knew Jack Costello well from the Law Library. I had great respect for him: he was business-like and capable. He had not really been much involved in bitter civil war politics. In addition his son was also progressively minded and useful"[9]. Noel Browne wrote that Costello's "hands were clean of bloodletting"[10]. However, both Mulcahy and Costello himself have agreed that it was William Norton who first mentioned Costello's name for Taoiseach, while Patrick Lynch believed it to have been Sean MacBride [11.].

Costello was TD for Dublin South East and a frontbench spokesman for Fine Gael on External Affairs for the previous fifteen years[12]. As a Barrister he had been senior counsel to the Irish Trade Union movement for a long time[13]. He remained oblivious to these proceedings as the Friday meeting of the Party leaders went on to consider policy matters. MacBride looked for higher public investment, reforestation and Hospital Trust funds to build hospitals and sanatoria and a major increase in social welfare. MacBride was adroit enough not to seek assurances on two of his party's policies, the release of political prisoners and the repeal of the External Relations Act.

He termed the new arrangement as Inter-Party Government rather than a coalition, and envisaged many matters being left to a free vote in the Dáil. Each party would retain its own individuality and freedom.

The various parties and a group of Independents, including James Dillon, Alfie Byrne and Oliver J. Flanagan, agreed to meet met on the Saturday to consider accepting the proposals. Mulcahy's account to Costello then says, "Norton had asked that if I could bring you along particularly for the purpose of your advice and help. There was a general feeling that you should be so asked and I had no difficulty in assuring them that you would be there". Mulcahy saw Costello that same Friday night and "reported the position" to him. On the Saturday Mulcahy and Costello visited McGilligan and "discussed the situation with him". The party leaders met in the Mansion House that Saturday evening at the invitation of the Lord Mayor, where final agreement on the distribution of the ministries was made. As Mulcahy wrote to Costello, "You were then invited to become Taoiseach. It was arranged that we would meet again on Sunday night to hear your decision".[14] This invitation was a shock for Costello, who was quite content with his lucrative law practice and his Dáil membership. It was clear that he had some hard thinking to do.

Sean MacBride regarded the meeting as historical and quite interesting from his point of view. He wrote, "While I had been in close touch for a long time with Jack Costello and Paddy McGilligan at the Bar, and very occasionally with Sean MacEoin, I hadn't met many of the Fine Gael leaders since the Civil War, when I met them under different circumstances. I must say it was an extremely friendly meeting"[15]. Costello later said, "I never wanted to be Taoiseach. I was appalled at the idea. I think my resolve was shaken mainly by the appeals made to me next day by O'Higgins at Mulcahy's home. At the Mansion House I met the others and for the first time met Dr. Noel Browne. I also met Jim Larkin".[16] He told Patrick Lynch that he was not even interested in becoming Attorney General or a Minister[17]. Mulcahy acknowledged that Costello had 24 hours to leave all that his life had meant to him, professionally and personally[18].

As usual, and despite matters of State, Costello played his regular fourball round of golf on the Sunday morning at Portmarnock, with his constant partners, Seamus O'Connor, the Dublin City Sheriff, RF Browne of the ESB, and Dick Roche from the Taxation Office[18a]. On that fateful Sunday he called on a close legal colleague Arthur Cox, who had married the widow of the assassinated Minister for Justice, Kevin O'Higgins. Costello wrote, "I also determined to consult my old friend Mr Arthur Cox and arranged to meet him at 5 o'clock on Sunday afternoon in his office. I attended at the office with my friends the late Mr. Richard Browne and Mr Richard Rice and I put the position to Mr Cox, who when after hearing all the points of view gave it as his firm opinion that there was no way out for me but to accept nomination. We had remained friends since our college days and were professionally associated. I valued his advice and secretly hoped that he would advise me against it. But he was logical. Had he advised against, I would have been tempted to stay in the law"[19].

However, Cox told him, "You have been in politics for 30 years, and you cannot refuse the top post. If you play with fire you must expect to get burned some time"[20]. Costello made the fateful decision and accepted the nomination to the post that same Sunday at the reconvened meeting at the Mansion House[21].

Costello's next job was to meet National Labour, which was very willing to cooperate. He recalled, "I promised them a fair deal, no more. James Everett was the hero of the Inter - Party Government, he was under such pressure to support Fianna Fáil"[22]. In his 1967 reply to Costello's urgent request for a refresher course on the details of these events, Mulcahy graciously reminded Costello, "I am sure you don't forget that their experience under you caused them to become a united Labour Party"[23].

However it was not at all certain that Fianna Fáil would be forced into opposition. Up to the day before the new Dáil met, it was being confidentially forecast that the five National Labour Party TD's and some Independents would return Fianna Fáil to government[24]. The Congress of Trade Unions, dominated by the ITGWU instructed those five TD's on 13 February to support Fianna Fáil[25]. However, the National Party leader James Everett and Dan Spring refused and informed Mulcahy that their five members would support a new government. As Fianna Fáil had ruled out coalition government, this was the only way Everett could become a government minister. That same day 17[th]Feb, Mulcahy announced an agreed ten-point policy between the various parties and Independents, " in view of the defeat of the Fianna Fáil party in the general election, and desirous of offering the people an alternative government on an inter-party basis".

The agreed points were:
  Increased agricultural and industrial production.
  Immediate all-out drive to provide houses for the working and middle-classes at reasonable rates. Luxury buildings to be rigidly controlled.
  Reduction in the cost of living.
  Taxation of all unreasonable profit-making.
  Introduction of a comprehensive social security plan
  to provide insurance against old age, illness, blindness,
  widowhood, un-employment, etc.
  Removal of recent taxes on cigarettes, tobacco, beer and cinema seats.
  Immediate steps to provide facilities for the treatment of sufferers of tuberculosis.
  Establishment of a Council of Education.
  Immediate steps to launch a National Drainage Plan.
  Modification of means test as at present applied to old age,
  widows, and orphans, and blind pensions[26].

DeValera's nomination as Taoiseach was defeated in the Dáil by 76 voted to 75 on 18 April. Richard Mulcahy then proposed John A Costello as Taoiseach. In doing so, he said that Costello had been selected by a number of groups in Parliament. His selection has not been a question of bargaining, but a manifestation of that spirit which is deep in our tradition and deep in our faith, "I do beseech those who challenge us in various ways that we cannot work together to hold their judgements. Criticise us in any way you can and show us the better ways of doing things but we are asking you to give us Deputy John Costello as Taoiseach".

Other party leaders then followed, though essentially outlining briefly their own party's position. James Dillon of the Independents said that Costello was a decent man who came from a decent family. Sean MacBride declared that his party's essential policy called for the repeal of the External Relations Act and the declaration of an independent republic. However he recognised that the mandate they got from the electorate did not allow them to demand that measure. He considered "Deputy Costello as the best, most suitable and fitting candidate for the position of Taoiseach". Just before the actual vote, Young Jim Larkin was overheard saying to Costello, "Don't you know that we would do anything for you"[27]. The nomination was approved by 75 votes to 68. The new Taoiseach was cheered heartily by his supporters who clapped and congratulated him on his victory. Fianna Fáil was furious with the outcome, feeling cheated and betrayed by the National Labour Party and Clann na Poblachta. Tom Derrig described the former as "opportunists" and the latter as "so-called republicans"[28]. Sean Lemass who spoke bitterly and long, shouted across the chamber "We are leaving you this country in good shape. Make sure you hand it back that way". deValera later described the new Government as "a fraud against democracy"[29].

Mr Costello was then escorted to the Taoiseach's room where he had a brief meeting with Mr. deValera. He then went to Áras an Uachtárain, accompanied by his son-in-law, Alexis Fitzgerald, to be appointed as Taoiseach by President Sean T O'Kelly. Terry deValera, Eamon's son, [born 1922] writes that as a young solicitor in the office of Patrick Ruttledge, " Alexis Fitzgerald was a senior solicitor on the staff and for practical purposes, he ran and managed the office. I always found him most courteous, friendly, understanding and willing to help and guide where this proved necessary. He had married Grace, the eldest daughter of John A Costello, who tragically died young"[30] .

On his return to the Dáil at seven o'clock, Costello told the members "The President confirmed me as Taoiseach".

Then he announced his Ministers;
Tánaiste and Minister for Social Welfare, Mr. William Norton (Lab.)
Minister for Education, General Richard Mulcahy (F.G.)
Minister for External Affairs, Mr. Sean MacBride (C. na P.)
Minister for Lands, Mr. Joseph Blowick (C. na T.)
Minister for Posts and Telegraphs, Mr. James Everett (Nat. Lab.)

Minister for Agriculture, Mr. James Dillon (Ind.)
Minister for Finance, Mr. Patrick McGilligan (F.G.)
Minister for Justice, General Sean MacEoin (F.G.)
Minister for Defence, Dr. Thomas F. O'Higgins (F.G)
Minister for Industry and Commerce, Mr. D. Morrissey (F.G.)
Minister for Local Government, Mr. T.J. Murphy (Lab.)
Minister for Health, Dr. Noel C. Browne (C. na P.)
Attorney General – Designate, Mr. Cecil Lavery S.C.

The new Government contained two additional Ministers. In the previous Government, the Taoiseach also held the External Affairs ministry. James Ryan had held the ministries of both Social Welfare and Health. Eithne MacDermott has pointed out that Fine Gael's disproportionate number of powerful ministries can be put down most probably to the other party's reaction to Mulcahy's magnaminity in agreeing to cede the role of Taoiseach to Costello at their request[31].

In replying to the debate Costello said that he was not going to respond to Sean Lemass' bitter criticisms. He said that he did not want to play party politics. "I am not here to get any advantage out of political office. The only reason I consented to act is because there is a group of patriotic Irishmen, working on democratic lines, agreeing to do what they believe is necessary to be done and what was not done by the last Government". He announced that a full statement on the policy of the new Government would be announced in about a fortnight, and would be based on the fullest data to be provided by each of the Ministers. The new Cabinet members would meet to discuss general policy and to appoint new Parliamentary Secretaries. The new Ministers would take up their duties immediately. A special survey would be made of each Department for special reports to the Cabinet to enable it to arrive at a general comprehensive policy for the entire country. "We have been elected as a representative Government," he said, "and our policy will be national rather than a party one. Our first concern will be directed to agriculture, in an effort to increase production and to raise the standard of living of the rural community". He said that he believed that the new Government would develop the friendliest of relations with the British Government and people and would do all possible to increase trade between the two countries. A policy of special care for the development of Irish industry would be pursued, but the Government would not allow inefficiency or excess profits to hide behind tariffs. Reduced living costs would be the aim of this Government. When complete information was available the Government would apply itself to the problem of reducing the adverse trade balance and by encouraging industrial expansion and national public works schemes, would endeavour to reduce emigration. Mr. Costello said that the improved social services announced, could be financed from economies, which, he was sure, could be effected in many departments, including the Department of Defence, and by the restriction of luxury building and spending.

The only post within the cabinet to which Costello made the nomination was that of Attorney General. However in this exercise he demonstrated his ability to exert his will and his own ideas on a civil service which was used to having its 'advice' followed. He choose Cecil Lavery for the post but made some unusual changes in the operation of the post, which could be seen as featherbedding his own kind. Costello himself had agreed to take a large reduction in his own income by accepting his new role. Lavery was doing the same thing. Costello increased Lavery's salary to that of his own £3,000 per annum. He also allowed him to treat fees paid to the AG for the performance of his professional duties as his own. Costello went further and allowed Lavery to continue his own private legal practice, "in his discretion, he might deem not to be incompatible with the duties of his office"[32]. Costello also got the Chief Justice to formally welcome Lavery as the leader of the Bar, as he himself had been, as Attorney General.

Thus completed an extraordinary journey by a man who had not sought the office and only very reluctantly accepted it. He was the head of a government made up of several parties, whose leaders had already agreed on the composition of the cabinet and who intended to pursue their own party's interests in government. Each party choose portfolios in which it had a particular interest. The three Parliamentary Secretaries were also later divided out according to the same criteria. Brendan Corish of Labour became Parliamentary Secretary at Local Government; Michael Donnelan of Clann na Talmhan at Finance; Liam Cosgrave of Fine Gael was appointed at Industry and Commerce and to the Department of the Taoiseach; Patrick Hogan of Labour got the post of Leas Cheann Comhairle. The Dáil approved the new cabinet by 75 votes to 65.

Costello addressed the nation on Radio Éireann. He said, "The groups that comprise the government have their own separate policies and individuality which they will continue to maintain. Over a wide field of action they are in complete agreement"[33].

The general expectation was that the new Taoiseach and his government could not remain long in office. It was a marriage of convenience, prompted by hatred for Fianna Fáil, and the lust for power, presided over by a Chairman chosen by his disparate Ministers as their compromise Taoiseach. However that Government was to preside over some of the most fundamental decisions of State, which still reverberate in today's 21st century Ireland.

While Costello was a compromise 'outsider' as choice for Taoiseach, he was also not such an integral part of the Fine Gael party apparatus, as can be seen from its officer board in 1949, which read:
President – General Richard Mulcahy TD
Vice Presidents – Dr. TF O'Higgina TD. General Sean MacEoin TD
Hon. Secretaries – Senator Michael Hayes MA., Liam Cosgrave BL, TD
Trustees
General Richard Mulcahy TD
Dr. TF O'Higgins TD

Standing Committee:
Sean Collins BL, TD
Senator James Crosbie BL
Alan P Dempsey
J Harold Douglas TC
Patrick McGill SC TD
MJ O'Higgins Solr. TD
John O'Leary BL
Gerard Sweetman Solr. TD
General Secretary –
Liam Burke[34].

Lord Rugby wrote in a patronising fashion to his government indicating that Costello was a nondescript politician. He wrote, "I gather from my conversation with him that he retains a friendly memory of the Lord Chancellor. I do not suppose that the Lord Chancellor remembers the new Taoiseach"[35].

Former home of John A. Costello ot Herbert Road, Dublin.

CHAPTER 2

YOUNG JACK COSTELLO

John A Costello was born on the 20th of June 1891 to a Dublin middle- class Catholic family which was pro-Parnell. He was the younger son of John Costello, and Rose Callaghan of Rathdown Road. His father was a public servant, who had served for several years as a member of Dublin Corporation[1] and had been a friend of James Larkin. John A received his primary and secondary education at the Christian Brothers O'Connell's Schools, in the heart of the city. There he was well versed in the four 'Rs', as he said, Reading, 'Riting', 'Rithmetic' and Rebellion[2].

The Irish Universities Act of 1908 abolished the Royal University, replacing it with Queen's University and the National University of Ireland, which catered essentially for Catholics, with constituent colleges in Dublin, Cork and Galway. This move was heartily supported by the Irish Parliamentary Party. UCD replaced the Jesuit university which had operated at the same address for the previous 25 years.

John A Costello was one of the first class of students who enrolled there from 1909 to 1913. These were exciting times in Ireland as two general elections took place in 1910 leaving the IPP holding the balance of power at Westminster. Home Rule was passed in the Commons but rejected in the House of Lords. The Ulster and Irish Volunteers were formed in 1913, the same year as the Great Dublin Lock-Out. The students at UCD were confident that they would soon be playing a major role in a Home Rule Ireland.

Costello was a brilliant student. He studied modern languages, Irish and law, winning the Barton Prize and several scholarships. Fellow students who would later play prominent political roles in the Irish Free State were Kevin O'Higgins, Paddy McGilligan, Hugh Kennedy, Patrick Hogan, Thomas Bodkin, Conor Maguire, Cecil Lavery, Jim Magennis, Denis and Aubrey Gwynn, Cahir Davitt, Ginger O'Connell, Edward Freeman, and George O'Brien. Among the students John A Costello vied with in examinations and debating societies at university, was his close friend Arthur Cox. The most prestigious historical student body at UCD and the centre of social life was the Literary and Historical Society, the famous 'L and H'. Women were not allowed to become members despite several attempts to change the rules. When on 10 December 1910 a motion to allow women in was passed, Costello and Cox opposed it and tried unsuccessfully to filibuster proceedings[3]. Women did not become members at TCD's Historical society for another 60 years. The most ambitious and brilliant students always challenged for the post of auditor. Previous incumbents had been John Dillon [1874/5] and Tom Kettle [1898/90]. James Joyce was a defeated candidate in 1900. In the academic year 1911/12, Cox was proposed by a Belvederean school colleague, George O'Brien, and Costello by Conor Maguire. Each had his own election agents. Cox was victorious by 112 votes to 63.

Costello later recalled, "My closest friend and rival in college was Arthur Cox. But compared to Cox I was the complete amateur. He knew every trick in the bag and always defeated me. At that time my only ambition was to get to the top of the legal profession and then a backbencher. Cox's was to get to the top of the legal profession and then become Prime Minister"[4].

George O'Brien later wrote of this election; "If anybody had ventured to predict that one of the parties in this 1912 contest for the auditor of the L & H would have become Prime Minister of an Irish Republic, his prophecy would have been received with some scepticism. If a hearer had chosen to believe that the prophecy would come true and had been asked to say which of the candidates was destined for this distinction, he would have unhesitatingly chosen Arthur Cox. I do not think that anybody would have chosen Costello, who matured late and whose elevation was the result of unforeseen political circumstances". O'Brien continued, "In normal times there is a very gradual and indeterminate transition from the lower to the higher ranks of professional and political life. But when a revolution succeeds, a new generation suddenly takes the place of the old. In Ireland the Treaty produced such a revolution." However, George O'Brien was never at ease with John Costello, possibly because Costello was the favourite pupil of the prominent Professor Arthur Clery. O'Brien wrote, "We were few enough to get to know each other very well, even if some of us did not like each other very much. Indeed, some of the developments in the political history of Ireland in the years since the Treaty grew out of the affinities and dislikes of my contemporaries. Old alliances and old quarrels re-appeared in the wider field of public life. We were a band of brothers, even if the family was rather disunited"[5]. The finals of the LLB examination were due in June 1913. Cox wrote in his diary, "O'Brien and Costello are working like blazes". O'Brien later withdrew from the examination. Cox then got first place with Costello second, both securing First Class Honours[6].

After university Costello entered the King's Inns where he won the Victoria Prize and was called to the Bar in 1914. Women were not allowed to become members of the legal profession until the Removal of the Sex Disqualification Act in 1919. The Free State saw its first woman solicitor admitted in 1923.

EGAN VERSUS GENERAL MACREADY

As a young barrister Costello was involved as a junior counsel in some famous cases. Among these was the *habeas corpus* case of John J Egan from county Clare, versus General Macready in 1921. Macready was the officer commanding the British forces in Ireland, which were then trying to defeat an Irish insurrection. This case was important on a fundamental legal basis but also because it later led to *habeas corpus* becoming as an important legal principle in the Irish Constitution. Egan was a soldier in the British army who was arrested on 26 May 1921 in Clare and charged with being improperly in possession of unauthorised ammunition. He was tried before a military court, convicted and sentenced to death. Egan then awaited execution in Limerick prison.

However Egan's legal team, including Costello, sought a *habeas corpus* on the basis that the military had overstepped their power under the Restoration of Order in Ireland Act 1920. Egan, they argued, had, at a minimum, the right to trial by court-martial and his detention was unlawful and he should be released. Counsel for the military argued that due to the state of open rebellion pervailing in Ireland, which aimed to overthrow the King's Government, a state of war existed. Their Counsel argued that the powers of the military derived from the prerogative of the Crown. The judge, Sir Charles O'Connor, said that the Defence of the Realm Act 1914 dealt with the state of war and had to be read in conjunction with the Restoration of Order Act. He accepted that a state of war existed. However, he held that it was clear that under the Restoration of Order Act, an offence punishable by death must be tried by a properly-constituted Court-martial and not the military court, that had been involved in Egan's trial. The judge said that the tribunal of a Court-martial had always been regarded as absolutely fair and impartial. He therefore issued the writ of *habeas corpus*. In conclusion, the judge enunciated the first principle of British law, that every subject of the King is at least entitled to be legally tried and legally convicted.

He ended by quoting Cockburn C.J, "There are considerations more important than even shortening the temporary duration of an insurrection. Among them are the eternal and immutable principles of justice, without lasting detriment to the true interest and well-being of a civilized community". General Macready refused to obey the court ruling and produce Egan before the Court. The Court then made a ruling directing Macready to show cause why he should not be attached for contempt. Macready defied that order also, and threatened to arrest anybody seeking to enforce the writs. Though the British Government agreed with Macready that the judgement smacked of appeasement in the war in Ireland, the Irish Lord Chancellor, Sir John Ross, prevailed upon the Government to release Egan.

Egan later became a Lieutenant in the Irish army[7]. Costello was also involved in the Wigg and Cochrane litigation, and the Mrs Croker and Fr. O'Donnell cases.

The Incorporated Law Society supported the World War and it expressed its "abhorrence and condemnation" of the 1916 Rising. The new State set up the 'Republican Courts' and the new situation created much work for the legal profession. John A worked in those new embryonic courts which functioned successfully for a brief period before succumbing to political events[8]. When WT Cosgrave introduced the new Courts of Justice Bill in 1923, he discovered quite quickly how the lawyers retained such a powerful position in civil society, despite the recent revolutionary struggle.

ALLIES HIMSELF WITH FREE STATE

Costello supported the Treaty side believing that in the deValera-Collins Pact election of 1922, the people overrode that political fudge and voted for the Treaty. He gave lavish praise to the Labour Party for entering the Dáil and playing a democratic role in the emerging Irish Free State. Even WT Cosgrave, the President of the Executive Council often did not appear to give due credit to the Labour Party in this regard. Costello said, "If Labour had stayed out there would have been no Government and no Parliament. Those Labour Deputies came in despite pressure and threats to their lives and some of them at least, were threatened with the gun if they entered the Dáil. They formed a grand Opposition, critical, yet constructive, intelligent and knowledgeable". Costello added, that in an area that he himself played a vital part in, "the Labour Party helped also if critically, to have law and order maintained. Parliamentary Institutions were established and some effort was made to ameliorate the great economic and social distress in the country"[9]. This influenced John A greatly in his decision to accept re-appointment to a part-time post in the office of the Attorney General. He realised that the Treaty also offered great potential for the development of the international status of the new State. It would be in this field that Costello would work assiduously and successfully for over the next ten years.

One task he received early in his career, as a solicitor in the Attorney General's office was to write a memorandum on "The Right of Public Meetings". He compiled a study of the law on free assembly. He found that "there was no such specific right under British law. Interference with a lawful assembly was only illegal insofar as it was a violation of the rights of the individual concerned. There were no specific places where free assembly was protected. An unlawful assembly was normally defined as a group which intended to commit a crime, or which gave a firm and courageous person reason to believe a breach of the peace was likely. Having a lawful object did not in itself make a gathering lawful. While lawful meetings could not be prohibited just because of the action of a few wrongdoers, the authorities could prevent even a peaceful assembly to prevent a breach of the peace"[10].

Costello married Ida Mary O'Malley in 1919. She was a daughter of Dr. David O'Malley of Glenamaddy Co. Galway. At the time of their marriage, she was a teacher at the Dominican College for Girls at Eccles St Dublin. The couple had five children. He regarded his primary responsibility as providing for the welfare of his family in an environment as conducive as possible to their personal and professional betterment.

*****

CHAPTER 3

ATTORNEY GENERAL
1926-1932

Hugh Kennedy had been one of the chief legal advisors of the first Cosgrave Government of the Irish Free State. He later became Attorney General. When in 1926 Kennedy was appointed to the Supreme Court as Chief Justice, John A Costello was appointed Attorney General. As a backroom operator Costello's work was seldom 'mentioned in dispatches' in relation to the enormous volume of work that he put in as legal advisor to the governments. However it is possible on occasion to hear directly from him, or through others, of his presence on important occasions.

Sean MacBride accepted that during those early years there were a number of people in Cumann na nGaedheal who wanted to assert the rule of law and the legal system, and have them function effectively. He adds that, " The Free State government was not willing to do anything without necessary legal powers. They passed all these various Acts. But the purpose of the Acts was to suspend the ordinary rule of law. These Acts were usually passed at the instance of the Attorney General. I think Jack Costello, who was Attorney General for a time, was responsible for getting these acts passed in order to avoid the rule of law from being disregarded completely"[1].

TRANSFER OF DOCUMENTATION TO NORTHERN STATE

When the Northern authorities established a Public Records Office in Belfast in 1926, CH Blackmore, the Cabinet Secretary, came to Dublin and sought the release of documentation concerning the six counties. This request came to Michael McDunphy, the Assistant Secretary in the office of the President of the Executive Council. It was known that in 1922 Michael Collins had embargoed such a transfer. It transpired that later, in 1923, Land Registry deeds were transferred at the request of the British Government. However subject to the outcome of the Boundary Commission Report, all further transfer was embargoed. McDunphy gleaned from Blackmore that a reciprocal agreement was then in place with various Departments. This surprised McDunphy and the Executive Council, which had no knowledge of it. The matter was then referred to the Attorney General for his opinion. Costello reported that the Northern Ireland Government had no legal ground under the Government of Ireland Act on which to base a claim, and that, the Irish Free State had no legal authority to make such transfers[2]. The Executive Council adopted the advice and issued a Memorandum saying "It is proposed to take no further action in this matter". Both McDunphy and Diarmaid O'Hegarty, secretary to the Executive Council, disagreed with Costello's advice, saying that the Government had already committed itself to such transfers over a six-year period[3].

TERRITORIAL DISPUTE

Another issue with the North arose on a territorial waters dispute affecting Lough Foyle. Costello advised, in 1927, that Northern Ireland was limited to six parliamentary counties and did not encompass their territorial waters. He said that the Irish Free State had a strong and clear cut claim to ownership of the whole Lough. But since the Free State could not enforce its claim the matter proved somewhat academic. However Donegal County Council wanted the claim enforced[4].

The fishing rights on the Foyle had been held by the London-based organisation, the Honourable Irish Society. Donegal fishermen successfully challenged this in a 48-day High Court hearing in 1948. An appeal was imminent when the Northern Attorney General Major Lancelot Curran wrote to Cecil Lavery suggesting that both jurisdictions discuss the matter of the Foyle. In 1950 both jurisdictions agreed to buy the fishing rights and set up a joint authority to manage them. This was one of the first measures of cooperation between North and South[4a]. Costello commented that this, together with co-operation on the Northern River Erne and the Great Nothern Railway, "have given grounds for the belief that friendly relations can do much to achieve eventual unity more certainly than threats of bloody warfare"[4b]. On the last occasion he attended Geneva with Kevin O'Higgins in July 1927, we catch a happy glimpse of them both with Joseph Walshe, as O'Higgins wrote the final letter of his life to his wife, "I rout out Walshe and Costello at 6.45 every morning and we swim in the lake before breakfast"[4c].

SUMMARY OF DIPLOMATIC ADVANCES BY IRISH FREE STATE

Though Costello only became Attorney General in the decisive year of 1926, he had been involved in that office almost from the beginning. The Dáil had bitter memory of the failure of the post-war Peace Conference to give it a hearing. It also knew that the League of Nations gave no support to Sein Féin's claims for international recognition for Ireland as an independent entity. The fact that successive governments had a portfolio of External Affairs indicated how important they viewed the matter of international relations. Lloyd George had told Arthur Griffith on 13 December 1921, that the British were ready to support Ireland's membership of the League, once a new constitution was agreed, The Constitution came into effect on 6 December 1922. The Government again made overtures for membership during 1922. Alfred Cope, the assistant Irish Secretary, had told WT Cosgrave during 1921 that any application to the League would be referred to the British Government for adjudication on the State's status as defined under Article 1 of the Covenant of the League. Cope had later reiterated Lloyd George's position to Cosgrave, when Ireland would become a fully self-governing Dominion[4d]. In early1923, Cosgrave told Desmond Fitzgerald Minister for External Affairs that, "this question of our entry to the League of Nations ought to be definitely decided. Unless the state of war interferes or prejudices our application, we ought to apply in my opinion"[5].

As usual, Cosgrave then delegated the matter to his Minister. The Irish Free State joined the League and set up a permanent presence in Geneva. It was the first Dominion country to do so, though Canada followed in 1924. In general, Ireland and Canada were keen to establish their international freedom of movement, independent from Great Britain. Cosgrave led the eight man Irish delegation to its first meeting of the League in September 1923. He addressed the assembly, first in Irish, to inform his audience that Ireland had its own language. He spoke at length about Ireland's heritage and her historical links as a European country. He concluded by saying, "Ireland comes amongst you as an independent Nation, and as a co-equal member of the Community of Nations known as the British Commonwealth, resolved to play her part in making much of this great institution for peace as complete and efficient as possible". Ireland gave a new impetus to the League as in 1923, the Dominions were an unknown factor in international law[6]. Cumann na nGaedheal organised a celebratory banquet at the Metropole in Dublin to mark both the 13th centenary celebrations of St Columbanus at Bobbio, which Cosgrave had attended, and the triumph at Geneva of 14 September 1923[7]. The *Irish Independent* of 15 September reported Cosgrave saying at the elaborate ceremonies, which welcomed him home, "Ireland has formally taken her place in the League of Nations. Her sister States received her with cordial and enthusiastic welcome. We come back from Geneva more than ever proud of our country: more than ever determined to work for the well-being of her people and we hope that the whole Irish people will see to it that the high esteem in which our country is held shall be justified". The *Irish Times* of the same day said in an editorial: "In the interval between the election of 1922 and that of this year, President Cosgrave and his colleagues had, under difficulties such as rarely confronted any new government, to face the task of establishing peace and order and ensuring security for life and property. They not only succeeded in accomplishing that work but they also carried through many legislative reforms. The crowning achievement was the admission of the Free State as a member of the League of Nations. This is a demonstration to the other nations of the world of the independent status which the Free State enjoys under the Anglo-Irish Treaty". Lionel Curtis has written that Cosgrave was most keen to return to Dublin, as the results of the August general election were coming through and placed a great strain on his already poor health. Curtis thought Cosgrave "might crack at any moment, a change of leadership at this moment would be most disconcerting"[8]. Ireland appointed a High Commissioner in London in 1923, and in 1924 one to the United States. Gradually, appointments were made to Tokyo, Paris, Geneva, Ottawa, Berlin, and the Vatican. Ireland attended its first Imperial Conference in 1923, as a newcomer and observer. On 11 July 1924 it registered the Anglo-Irish Treaty with the League of Nations, Treaty Bureau. This led to an objection from the British, who regarded the Treaty as an inter-Commonwealth agreement, and not allowed to be registered, under Article 18 of the League. For Ireland, the precedent of registration would imply sovereignty from Britain, on the basis of an international treaty and copper fastened the legitimacy of the Irish Free State at home and abroad.

During sensitive negotiations on 3 October, Cosgrave was asked an embarrassing parliamentary question on the matter. He replied that "the subject of the question is one which must obviously receive its consideration in due course and proper time"[9]. On June 1924 Cosgrave received a letter from Alfred O'Rahilly in Geneva, urging the immediate registration of the Treaty. Michael Kennedy writes, "Cosgrave took centre stage and took the decision on his own initiative, surprisingly, when Fitzgerald was in London. Cosgrave also consulted Attorney General Hugh Kennedy". Monday 23 June was the key date for registration. Cosgrave took the decision to go ahead, Kennedy cautiously agreed; and finally Joe Walshe gave his perspective. "Never before in Irish League policy, had decisions been taken at such speed. Cosgrave's desire to implement the registration policy on his own initiative and with Fitzgerald out of the country, are two actions not in line with the accepted view of Cosgrave's character"[10]. The registration of the Treaty was a major accomplishment of the Government. Over the next two years Ireland joined Canada and South Africa in developing the Commonwealth into an association of equals. The Imperial Conference of 1926 laid down principles, in the Balfour Declaration, which allowed the development to remove all restriction remaining on the absolute co-equality of the member states of the British Commonwealth with Great Britain[11]. Costello said of this Conference, "General Hertzog of South Africa wanted to get the right to secede from the Commonwealth. I told him that this was a dangerous line to pursue just like that, as it seemed illogical and inconsistent to demand equality just for the purpose of secession. I was convinced that the British would go far on co-equality but not that far. Our single Irish aim was to secure the full the rights and procedures granted in the Anglo-Irish Treaty of 1921-2 and to put those rights into principle. We wanted them applied as concrete facts. But in the event Hertzog and O'Higgins achieved ultimately the same result although working along different lines. Although we did not obtain the right to secede we did get the establishment of the subsequent conference and of an expert Committee to deal with the practical matters of constitutional procedure and practice" He quotes O'Higgins as saying, "It's a long game and I'd like to see the end of it". Costello adds "It did end in the Statute of Westminster and the Republic of Ireland Act, though O'Higgins was then dead". Costello mentions particularly MacKenzie-King of Canada as a great friend of his and of Ireland. He also mentions Mr. O.D. Skelton of Canada who "was of great help to Ireland in a subsequent conference in Canada. While maintaining his position on Canada and Quebec fully, he also gave Ireland fullest support"[12]. At the League of Nations Council in March 1927, Austen Chamberlain sought to claw back some British prestige by implying that only Britain could represent the Dominions on the Council. Ireland played a major role in organising the election of Canada to the Council in September. Cosgrave signed the Renunciation of War Pact on 27 August 1928[13]. He introduced it to the Dáil, as an "international instrument of very considerable importance". Fianna Fáil argued and voted against the measure, despite the fact that it was such a breakthrough, being the first time a Dominion State had signed an international agreement independently of Britain[14].

Indeed Britain had refused to sign it and no Commonwealth country had yet signed it. Paddy McGilligan summed up the Pact as acknowledging.that "the time has come when a frank renunciation of war as an instrument of national policy should be made, to the end that the peaceful and friendly relations now existing between their peoples may be perpetuated; convinced that all changes in their relations with one another should be sought only by pacific means and be the result of a peaceful and orderly process". Fianna Fáil deemed it a pact for the 'haves' against the 'have-nots'. The matter was passed by 84 votes to 60 in the Dáil.

In 1929 the Free State became a signatory to an agreement on submitting disputes to the permanent Court of International Justice at Geneva. In September 1930 the State was elected to a non-permanent seat on the Council of the League of Nations. in succession to Canada, and through the good offices of Australia[15].

CODIFICATION OF INTERNATIONAL LAW

Another area Costello was involved in was that of codification of international law, with the aim of making it clearer and unified. The Irish Free State felt that it would allow the League to develop by letting the Permanent Court act definitively in international disputes. This would automatically provide the Dominions with a body superior to the Privy Council. This could be used on cases between the Dominions. In 1927 the Assembly had suggested three areas a codification conference might consider, nationality, responsibility for damage suffered by foreigners in League states and territorial waters. The conference that took place in 1930 was not productive. The League then requested that codification continue. The Free State was in favour of this. However, at the committee meeting, Britain, Germany, France, Italy and Greece sought to have the matter shelved indefinitely. Costello, who was leading the Free State delegation, argued against this saying that it "could mean nothing else except that all projects of codification were to be shelved for all time. Such a course would be unthinkable as it would abandon or postpone indefinitely the work of progressive codification". Costello realised that the large States' proposals suited them but the smaller states would have a different interests.

He went on; "The codification must embrace the formulation of new rules, and the modification of existing rules. The experts concerned in the preparatory work must be under constant political guidance. The work of codification must be continuous- new efforts must be continually made to define new subjects for codification. Account must be taken of the fact that under modern conditions international law is in a state of flux and evolution: for that reason, the code of international law, should contain revision Clauses. Codification should be continued and directed in a manner most likely to produce the best possible results". He suggested that a new committee would report to the Assembly in 1931. The Polish delegation supported the Irish position and a joint resolution was presented to the Assembly, which attracted the support of the smaller states, with the larger ones not objecting[16].

In summing up the Free State's involvement with the League of Nations, Michael Kennedy writes, "The state was not just acting to enhance her own prestige or international position. Ireland was not playing to the gallery, but trying in a limited manner to prevent another war breaking out". Kennedy projecting forward to Costello's second term as Taoiseach, adds, "The legacy of Ireland's years in the League of Nations can be seen in her United Nations policy between 1955 and 1969. Boland and Costello, both League of Nations veterans were involved in the development of United Nations policy, where Ireland's policy of a belief in international law and order and need to safeguard the small against the powerful remained"[17].

STATUTE OF WESTMINSTER

The biggest breakthrough diplomatically which lent credence to the Treaty being a stepping stone to greater independence from Britain, came in 1930-1, when Ireland was to the fore in having the Statute of Westminster enacted. This laid down that no law passed by the Parliament in Great Britain could apply to any of the Dominions, without their own request and agreement. The Colonial Laws Validity Act of 1856 was repealed in its application to the Dominions. The key passage of the Statute of Westminster provided that- "No Act of Parliament of the United Kingdom passed after the commencement of this Act, shall extend or be deemed to extend, to a Dominion as part of the law of that Dominion, unless it is expressly declared in that Act, that Dominion has requested, and consented to the enactment thereof. No law and no provision of any law made after the commencement of this Act by the Parliament of a Dominion, shall be void or inoperative on the ground that it is repugnant to the law of England, or to the provisions of any existing or future Act of Parliament of the United Kingdom, or to any order, rule, or regulation made under any such Act, and the powers of the Parliament of a Dominion shall include the power to repeal or amend any such Act, rule or regulation in so far as the same is part of the law of the Dominion".

Sean MacBride wrote that "The real architect in the negotiations with regard to the Statute of Westminster was Paddy McGilligan, with the help of Jack Costello and Hugh Kennedy"[18].

The Cosgrave government could possibly have made more of this major political advance, were it not for the fact that it did not wish to unduly upset its unionist citizens. The reality then was that the Irish Free State emerged, in constitutional theory as well as in actual practice, as a completely autonomous nation; so that the sole link between it and Great Britain was the King. But the King was to function entirely, so far as Irish affairs were concerned, at the will of the Irish Government[19]. However, once more Fianna Fáil opposed this measure in the Dail[20].

The fundamental nature of this Act in relation to Ireland was highlighted, when on 20 November 1931, Winston Churchill opposed it on the Second Reading debate in the Commons, where it referred to Ireland. He had resigned from Baldwin's Shadow Cabinet earlier on the issue of giving Dominion Status to India.

In 1931 Baldwin and Ramsay MacDonald had combined to form a national government, in which there was no office for Churchill. He sought in 1931 to have the Irish Free State omitted from the Statute, "as this Bill confers upon the Irish Free State, full legal power to abolish the Irish Treaty. It would be open to the Dáil to repudiate the Oath of Allegiance, they could repudiate the right of the Imperial Government to utilize for instance, the harbour facilities at Berehaven and Queenstown". He sought to introduce an amendment to the Bill saying "nothing in this Act shall be deemed to authorise the Legislature of the Irish Free State to repeal, or alter the Irish Free State Agreement Act 1922, or so much of the Government of Ireland Act 1920, as continues to be in force in Northern Ireland". Mr. Amery, who had been first Lord of the Admiralty and Secretary of State for the Dominions, said that he had extended to his colleagues from the Irish Free State the same complete confidence, loyalty, and whole-hearted welcome that he had extended to any other statesmen of any other Dominion. He added, "If you give, you must give generously, and without looking back"[21].

After the debate, Austen Chamberlain understood Churchill had been reassured that Cosgrave would give a declaration about future action However, two days later Churchill wrote to Chamberlain saying that he did not think that an assurance by Cosgrave would be any substitute for the amendment he proposed. He continued, "It is at best even money that deValera will have control of the Irish government very soon, and the mere fact that Cosgrave made this declaration would only spur him on all the more to stultify it. Pray, therefore, do not assume me placable by any such assurances"[22].

Cosgrave wrote to Stanley Baldwin after the Second Reading. Baldwin read the letter to the Commons. It said, "I need scarcely impress upon you that the maintenance of the happy relations which now exist between our two countries is absolutely dependent upon the continued acceptance by each of us of the good faith of the other. The situation has been constantly present to our minds, and we have reiterated time and again, that the Treaty is an agreement, which can only be altered by consent. I maintain this particularly, because there seems to be a mistaken view in some quarters, that the solemnity of this instrument in our eyes could derive any additional strength from a parliamentary law. So far from this being the case, any attempt to erect a Statute of the British Parliament into a safeguard of the Treaty would have quite the opposite effect here, and would rather tend to give rise in the minds of our people to a doubt as to the sanctity of this instrument"[23]. Cosgrave added that the Statute was an agreement between all the Governments of the Commonwealth, which had been considered at great length by the Irish representatives at the Imperial Conference and endorsed, as it stood, by Dáil and Senate. He declared that any amendment of the nature then suggested, would be a departure from the terms of the Imperial Conference Report and would be wholly unacceptable to them. "The interests of the peoples of the Commonwealth as a whole must be put before the prejudices of the small reactionary elements in these islands", he said. Baldwin rejected Churchill's attempt, saying, "any restrictive clause would offend not only the Irish Free State, not only Irishmen all over the world, but other Dominions as well. The Statute of Westminster has to be an act of faith, or it was nothing". The Act became law on 11 December 1931. It included the governments of the United Kingdom, Canada, Australia, New Zealand, South Africa, The Irish Free State, and Newfoundland. Each was to be completely self-governing, but united by allegiances to the monarchy, the succession to which, each Dominion would have a say". The Commons passed the Bill by 360 votes to 50.

Churchill later acknowledged that the whole case of the freedom of manoeuvre for the Irish Free State rested on solid legal ground in the Statute of Westminster[24]. This latter measure was to prove of the utmost import to Ireland, as ironically, it was to be used by deValera during the abdication crisis of King Edward VII in 1937, to remove all monarchical language from the Constitution of the Free State. Another Dominion, which would also later become a republic, South Africa, had its Parliament formally "approve" the King's decision.

Desmond Fitzgerald wrote, "Knowing the history of these last few years, as I do, I am amazed at the way we have changed the situation. By accepting the Treaty we certainly are getting all that the most fervid supporters were claiming for it – and more"[25]. Michael Collins' prophetic words on the Treaty as providing stepping stones, were realised first by the Cosgrave government, then by the deValera government, and later by the First Inter-Party Government. In the last case, the State was declared a Republic, by John A Costello, with a son of Major John MacBride, the Minister for External Affairs, and a son of WT Cosgrave, Parliamentary Secretary, Chief Whip and Secretary to the Government. As Frank Pakenham said in *Peace by Ordeal*," from the Statute onwards, it would be hard to name a single respect in which *qua* Dominion she was prevented from enjoying full practical autonomy".

Eamon deValera himself recognised the diplomatic advances made by the State, when speaking in the Senate in June 1932, on the motion to abolish the oath of allegiance, he acknowledged to Senator Milroy:

"I thought for one, at any rate, that the Twenty-six Counties here, as a result of the 1926 and 1930 conferences, had practically got into the position—with the sole exception that instead of being a Republic it was a monarchy—that I was aiming at in 1921 for the whole of Ireland. I am quite willing to give to Senator Milroy or anybody else, any credit that can be got for the policy they aimed at, and I am prepared to confess that there have been advances made, that I did not believe would be made at the time. I am quite willing to confess it"[26]. .

Costello said, "the Statute of Westminister justified all the arguments that Collins and Griffith had put forward in the Treaty Debates. It received the fullest implementation in the Republic of Ireland Act which enabled us to clear out of the British Commonwealth"[27] .

Kevin O'Higgins

Winston Churchill

Eamonn deValera

W.T Cosgrave

COMMONWEALTH SUPPORT

Costello was very aware of the debt Ireland owed to the support it received from the Commonwealth countries. He explained it thus;
"Kevin O'Higgins was assisted in his work by the representatives of Canada and South Africa, not to mention any of the others. Deputy McGilligan was helped in his very arduous task in 1929 by General Beyers on behalf of South Africa, by the representatives of Canada and by the representatives of Australia. In 1930 we had reached the position, as the result of the prestige that had been gained for this country by their representatives at Imperial Conferences in 1926, 1929 and 1930, that every single one of the representatives of every Dominion, of every State member of the British Commonwealth of Nations, ranged themselves behind the representatives of the Irish Free State and demanded that their rights should be granted, and they were granted finally and for ever. We took on, in return for that co-operation and in return for that assistance which we got from the Dominions through the operation of our membership of the British Commonwealth of Nations, obligations, slight obligations, obligations that cost very little, if anything at all"[28].

BRITISH EMPIRE

On the British Empire Costello said: "It existed before 1926 and 1929. In 1926, Kevin O'Higgins laid the foundation stone of the new structure of an independent nation. Deputy McGilligan put the copingstone on that structure in 1930: the British Empire no longer existed. The King was no longer King in the way he reigned in 1925. He was the symbol of our freedom. He exercised any functions that he did exercise internationally and nationally merely as the mouthpiece of the Irish people. The British Empire had ceased to exist and had become an association of independent free States, completely and independently sovereign. The Imperial Parliament no longer controlled them from Downing Street. All that was swept away. The entire fabric of the British Empire was changed and we became a completely free nation exercising our freedom and our sovereignty in any way that we pleased. It is in that sense that we stand for the Crown as the symbol of our freedom, as the mouthpiece through which the Executive Council acts in certain international affairs and as the fiction through which the executive authority of the Irish Free State acts in our internal affairs. There is no essential difference between the functions exercised by the King in our international affairs and the functions exercised by him in our national affairs."[29].

Costello's view of the Statute of Westminster was that it was decisive. He said, "Ramsay MacDonald, though acting as Chairman was no longer Prime Minster but representing the National government of Labour, Conservatives and Liberals. Canada had a Conservative government and was represented by Mr. Bennett. Australia had a Labour government and represented by Mr. Scullen. The Attorney General was Mr. Brennan. MacDonald tried to row back in connection to Ireland but lost out. Ireland got great support from Canada again. Mr. Guthrie of Canada insisted that Ireland and Canada had similar status. MacDonald had no option but to concede this. The Statute was the Charter of Equality. Anything that the British can do, we can do and we were free to pass our own legislation. The Privy Council did not exist any more in effect. The Statute provided for everything that deValera did afterwards or at least helped him to execute his policy and to make constitutional changes in the 1930's and indeed in 1948. The Statute justified all that Griffith and Collins put forward in the Treaty Debates. It received the fullest implementation in the Republic of Ireland Act, which enabled us to clear out of the Commonwealth in a lawful manner".

Costello added that Patrick McGilligan wrote the final draft of the future Statute which became law a year later in a famous Bill in the House of Commons, 'McGilligan's Charter'. Churchill opposed it but the Bill passed. Six weeks later the Dáil was dissolved and deValera was victorious.

Costello recalled an amusing moment of diplomacy when Ireland was seeking to establish the right to nominate WT Cosgrave as President of the League of Nations without any assistance from Britain. They gave a dinner for delegates from South America. Disaster struck when a waiter dropped a plate of soup on the lap of the wife of the Argentinian delegate and diplomacy had to be aborted

He recalled a particular problem concerning establishing direct access to the King for Irish Ministers, which other Commonwealth members had. Even the republicans backed this. The protocol was to apply through Whitehall and wait. Eventually he says, Patrick McGilligan decided to take direct action. He adorned himself in the correct mode of dress and presented himself at Buckingham Palace and was received graciously by King George V, who was quite content that Ireland should be able to meet him without formalities[30].

While Costello worked essentially with constitutional and foreign affairs, he was quite happy that the Government also made important social and economic advances. He instanced the Land Acts of Patrick Hogan as "revolutionary: fundamental progress of vesting of land in Irish tenant farmers or the giving of land to the landless farm labourer". Hogan lay down the foundation for the great cattle trade and his sugar beet scheme in Carlow was of great significance. He instanced the Local Government Acts as preparing the way for the initiatives in local government. However the best example in Costello's opinion was, McGilligan's Shannon electrification scheme. He said that some newspapers, businessmen, financiers and Department officials opposed it. "We were denounced as 'latter day pirates' and 'young men in a hurry'. We were pioneers in the Shannon Scheme, as WT Cosgrave, Mr. Blythe and many other 'conservatives' stood up to the assault and put the scheme through in spite of the uproar".

Costello's view of WT Cosgrave was "He was very determined and showed great skill in uniting the several brilliant and tense Ministers who were with him. But the more one got to know him the more impressed and amazed one became of his knowledge and judgement. One of his attributes and perhaps this was the secret of his success, was his ease of manner; his great capacity for relaxation even at difficult times. There was a time when tension was almost normal for the rest of us. He had a gift for handling, no genius, but he was straight and decent and full of integrity. But he was very conservative indeed on financial and economic and social questions. It was an astonishing performance from him to remain as Head of a government through such a terrible time"[31].

Costello regarded Kevin O'Higgins as the most outstanding personality of those days – brilliant and courageous. O'Higgins not unnaturally impressed the British, Canadians and others. His base was the Treaty. Costello said that O'Higgins was the last to agree to the execution of his best man Rory O'Connor and the other three prisoners from the Four Courts garrison. Significantly Costello describes that action, "It was a terrible deed at a terrible time, not equalled even by the execution of Erskine Childers. By this and other deeds the Free State Governments ensured their own ultimate defeat".

About Richard Mulcahy Costello said, "He served his country well but it was not appreciated; he was selfless in public affairs; he had idealistic principles". Patrick McGilligan was a "genius". Costello had no particular heroes from the revolutionary period. He replied, "no, my greatest assets are my friends". He regarded the Boundary Commission a "disaster". When the government faced imminent defeat in 1927, it intended to announce a dissolution of the Dáil. However, Costello advised that such action was not required, that it could await the Dáil vote. In the event, the mysterious absence of John Jinks of Sligo, after being chaperoned in a somewhat inebriated state onto the evening train for Sligo by Bryan Cooper and RS Smylie, saved the government and it held office for another five years.

Costello said that after the government defeat in 1932, they all believed that the deValera government would only last for six months. However the snap election of 1933 saw a heavy defeat of Cumann na nGaedhhal. Ironically the new Dáil saw Costello himself elected to the Dáil for the first time.[33]

❋❋❋❋

CHAPTER 4

ORDER OF ST PATRICK

Another matter Costello was intimately connected with as Attorney General occurred on the controversy over The Order of St Patrick. This also provides a microcosm of the constitutional departure from British hegemony. It remains of some interest as the idea of the Order has been resurrected in recent years as a means of contributing to the smoothing of Anglo-Irish affairs in connection with Northern Ireland. The All Party Committee on the Constitution, which reported in 1998, held that the President should have the power to confer honours on Irish citizens, and an amendment to Article 13 of the 1937 Constitution which deals with the functions of the President to this effect, should be considered. Article 5 of the 1922 Irish Free State Constitution said that "No title of honour in respect of services rendered in or in relation to the Irish Free State may be conferred on any citizen of the Irish Free State, except with the approval or upon the advice of the Executive Council of the State". That situation remained settled. Between 1914 and 1926 seven members of the Order of St Patrick died and existing members from Northern Ireland asked the King to appoint others to ensure the continuation of the Order. The British Government decided that the assent of the Irish Government would be necessary. Bernard Forbes, Earl of Granard, a Senator friend of WT Cosgrave, approached the latter on the matter. Cosgrave referred it to his Attorney General JA Costello for advice in March 1927. In June of that year the monarch made the Prince of Wales the later King Edward VIII and the future Duke of Windsor after his abdication, a Knight of the Order.

The Most Illustrious Order of St Patrick was an order of chivalry associated with Ireland. It began under King George III in 1783 and facilitated the monarch to honour Irish peers and princes. It was blatantly used to secure the Act of Union in 1800. In 1907 the order made international news. Its insignia, known as the Irish Crown Jewels, were stolen from Dublin Castle after a visit there by Edward VII, and never recovered. Under Lloyd George the Order became embroiled in his commercial activities of selling honours to raise cash. Costello reported to the government on 18 May 1928. He found that under the 1926 Imperial Conference the King must be advised in all matters relating to the Dominions by their respective governments. This included the granting of Honours. He added that the Order of St Patrick was intended to be a purely Irish Order. Everything in connection with the Order would be for the Executive Council to decide. He found Northern Ireland to be irrelevant to the Order as it was a part of the United Kingdom[1]. Cosgrave's Government accepted Costello's report and conveyed it to the British.

They demurred and hoped that the Irish would 'come in' at a later stage. They decided that henceforth the Order would be confined to members of the Royal family. In 1934 and 1936 two of their princes were made Knights of the Order of St Patrick.

However the last Knight, the Duke of Gloucester died in 1974 and the Order remains moribund. By a strange coincidence the matter crossed Costello's path again, in 1948, when he had become Taoiseach. The post-hoc news of Gloucester's appointment led to an examination of the file in Dublin. It was then discovered that the King, under the royal sign manual and the seal of the Order, had made appointments to the Order of St Patrick and that the chancery of the Order was kept in the Office of Arms in Dublin Castle. If it was still there, the seal could be refused for any further warrants, thus implementing the 1928 decision of the Executive Council. When the seal was sought in Dublin it was discovered that the Genealogical Office had handed it over to John Betjamen, British Press Attache, poet and possibly spy, in 1943. He had deposited it in the chancery of Orders of Knighthood in London. The unauthorised action of the office of arms was deemed "a mistake of the first order". The Assistant Secretary to the Taoiseach, Dr. Nicholas Nolan, considered whether the Taoiseach might raise the matter on the occasion of a forthcoming conference in London in 1948. Paddy Lynch, Costello's private secretary, reported subsequently that Costello "found no opportunity of raising the matter".

Under Lloyd George, the Order of St. Patrick became embroiled in his commercial activities of selling honours to raise cash.

The Prince of Wales [The future King Edward VIII, and future Duke of Windsor] was made a Knight of the Order in June 1927.

CHAPTER 5

1932 DEFEAT

The defeat of the Cumann na nGaedheal Government in the 1932 election was a watershed for the country and had implications for all those associated with it. The defeated ministers saw their income and associated perks reduce drastically. Several had careers to return to, and did so. These included John A Costello, who returned to full-time practice at the Bar. WT Cosgrave was able to continue to derive an income from his lands at Templeogue. Richard Mulcahy alone remained solely dedicated to the party. The new Fianna Fáil government saw the IRA, with its ranks swelled by the advent of its slightly estranged former ally to power, parade openly in Dublin. The new minister for Justice Mr Ruttledge went personally to Mountjoy Jail to have the IRA leaders held released. The IRA then made a lot of the early running in party political functioning during 1932. Frank Ryan declared their attitude to Cumann na nGaedheal as, "No matter what anyone says to the contrary, while we have fists, and boots to use, and guns, if necessary, we will not allow free speech to traitors". In May 1932 WT Cosgrave was shouted down at a meeting of his election workers in Cork. Patrick Lindsay writes in his autobiography *Memories*, "If it had not been for the presence and support of the Blueshirts, pubic meetings organised by Cumann na nGaedheal and the Centre Party could not have been held in 1932 and 1933, such was the ferocity of the organised conspiracy against these meetings. The supporters of Fianna Fáil and the IRA, many of the latter just recently released from jail, some of whom had been convicted of very serious offences, set out deliberately and with malice to smash up these meetings, to howl down men like WT Cosgrave, Paddy McGilligan and Patrick Hogan who had given the best years of their lives to establishing a strong democracy in this country. deValera like the Pontius Pilate he could be, made no attempt to stop this happening"[1]

Cumann na nGaedheal people felt obliged to establish their own protective organisation to defend their supporters from the IRA harassment. TF O'Higgins, a brother of Kevin O'Higgins, became head of the Army Comrades Association, in August 1932. Cumann na nGaedheal looked to the ACA as the guardians of the people and every threat to their freedom, whether it took the form of mob-rule, Communistic tyranny, or a deValerian dictatorship. Conor Cruise O'Brien wrote from another perspective saying, "The respect for the democratic process shown by Mr. Cosgrave's government was, in the circumstances, rather remarkable. It was, indeed, too remarkable to please many members of the fallen party, and some of these set about organising a para-military movement, on the Fascist model, for the intimidation of their opponents and the recovery of power. Yeats took part in the launching of this movement and wrote songs for it"[2].

COSTELLO ELECTED TO DÁIL 1933

Amid this general mayhem, deValera called a snap election in January 1933, which Cumann na nGaedheal had confidently expected to win. Violent scenes were reported from around the country, with fierce fighting taking place in Dublin's O'Connell St. as members of the ACA tried to defend election platforms[3]. John A was nominated as a candidate for Dublin County by Cumann na nGaedheal. At a meeting in Balbriggan on 12 January he said that Mr Cosgrave's party was the only one that was really a National Party. It had within its ranks better Labour men that were ever in the ranks of any other party; better patriots than could be found in the ranks of the Fianna Fáil party or any other party and more men with a national record than any other party. He said that Mr. Cosgrave had never made a promise, which he had not fulfilled [4].

Those elected from Dublin County were, in order of votes received:

Sean MacEntee	FF	15,644.
HM Dockrell	C na G	11,710
John A Costello	C na G	10,941
Sean Brady	FF	10,622
J Good	Indep	8,961
G O'Sullivan	C naG	7,030
B O'Connor	C na G	5,816
Miss M Pearse	FF	3,876

The overall result saw Fianna Fáil returned with a clear majority.

Party	% vote	seats won
FF	50%	76
C na G	31	48
Centre	9	11
Labour	6	8
Ind.	5	9

The Garda Commissioner, Eoin O'Duffy was summarily dismissed by deValera in February 1933. The *Irish Independent* headlined "A First Class Sensation was Sprung in the Dáil Last Night" when John A Costello asserted that the Section of the 1924 Act, under which the President had stated that General O'Duffy was removed from office, had been earlier repealed. A lively discussion ensued as the Ceann Comhairle, Frank Fahy, declared that it was not his job to rule on Statute Law. deValera contributed several times but no clarity was forthcoming. Eventually Frank Fahy disallowed any further questions on the matter and went on to the next business, which was Cosgrave's challenge to President deValera to "state the reasons for the removal" and indicate whether any charges were pending. deValera replied that the dismissal was in the national interest and refused to give any further explanation, though he did clarify that no charges were to be made against O'Duffy. One of the actions O'Duffy had taken after the change of government was to have a very large volume of sensitive documents destroyed.

In March 1933 the Army Comrades Association adopted the blue shirt. In May it adopted the stiff-arm salute. On 20 July 1933, O'Duffy became leader and renamed it the National Guard. O'Duffy had a long pedigree in the national movement as a man who got things done and would be capable of confronting an enemy

The sudden change in circumstances of the Cumann na nGaedheal front bench, led to a deterioration in their attendance at the Dáil and at Parliamentary Party meetings. Cosgrave sought Mulcahy's intervention to stop the slide into oblivion, writing to him on 22 May 1933. He said, "There is a very general and growing belief that Cumann na nGaedheal is finished. This belief has been brought home to me in an intensified form over the weekend and again this morning. We have ten collectors working in Dublin City North, South and County. Their collections are much weaker than last year and the incline is downwards. The subscriber says – What's the use in subscribing; there is no effort in the party; look at the majority in the Dáil every day, forty and fifty; you are not able to beat them and evidently your Party thinks this too. At a convention in Dungarvan last Sunday, friendly criticism was, the country is watching the Dáil. They want to see Cumann na nGaedheal fighting by voice and vote and you're not[5]. Thus the party was almost irrelevant and the Army Comrades Association became the only adjunct of the organisation that appeared to have vibrancy and the will and muscle, to fight Fianna Fáil and the IRA.

In 1933 Cumann na nGaedheal amalgamated with the Centre Party, which was essentially the old Farmer's Party, and the ACA to form a United Ireland Party or Fine Gael, with O'Duffy as leader. After two general election defeats, WT Cosgrave was no longer seen as an electoral asset. Costello, Mulcahy and Blythe were nominated to the new party's national Executive by Cosgrave. Costello became a frontbencher for the party. The Fine Gael element of the new party felt that it needed a strong man to survive. However, very soon O'Duffy proved to be too attracted to strong-arm tactics for their sensibilities. There was much confrontation at political rallies and renewed talk of *coup d'etats* from either side. O'Duffy was arrested at a rally in Westport amid civil disorder.

Costello, Paddy McGilligan and Vincent Rice immediately made an application at the home of Mr. Justice Johnson for an order of *habeas corpus:* they were given permission to apply to the Supreme Court for a writ. O'Duffy was moved to Mountjoy Jail the next day. The Supreme Court case lasted two days and ordered his release, finding "no reason mentioned in the Act under Section 13/Article 2A" on which he could be shown to have transgressed[6]. Fine Gael greeted news of O'Duffy's release with elation. The bishop of Achonry sent him a telegram which read, "Congratulations on victory of justice over shameless partisanship and contemptible tyranny"[7]

Within a short time the Minister of Justice Patrick Ruttledge introduced the 'Wearing of Uniforms – (Restriction) Bill 1934'. This essentially was about banning the wearing of the blue shirt at public rallies. When this was debated in the Dáil, Costello led for Fine Gael, in an early contribution that marked him out as a formidable opponent of Fianna Fáil and as the expert lawyer that he essentially was. He claimed that for several months the police were preventing people from exercising their constitutional rights by wearing blue shirts and going to meetings or addressing meetings in blue shirts. He suggested that the police realised their actions were foolish but feared summary dismissal for any reluctance to take action. He claimed that such laws brought the law itself into disrepute. He referred to the recent debacle of the illegal arrest of O'Duffy and his release by the Supreme Court under *habeas corpus* proceedings, which found against the government action. He claimed Fianna Fáil were "blinded by their own hatred against him". He noted that the government had not sought to use the Military Tribunal or the Public Safety Act, if it was so concerned about public disorder.

Costello explained the tactical basis for wearing the blue shirt, saying, "We wear a blue shirt, or those of us who happen to be members of the League of Youth, wear a blue shirt, and the girls wear blue blouses, not for the purpose of creating disorder, as the Minister for Justice would have us believe, but for the purpose of showing their comradeship and to indicate the decent people who are present at meetings and not the rowdies who are really the cause of disturbance at public meetings. The wearing of a uniform, so far from being provocative or unlawful, is adopted by our people so that we will be able to know that we have decent people, and so that, when there are disturbances in the crowd, the people who are creating the disturbance may be distinctly seen, and no one can say that it is the Blueshirts that are causing the disturbances at meetings"

Then Costello referred to the continental experience of wearing recognisable shirts, adding comments that he would later regret. He said, "The Minister gave extracts from various laws on the Continent, but he carefully refrained from drawing attention to the fact that the Blackshirts were victorious in Italy and that the Hitler Shirts were victorious in Germany, as, assuredly, in spite of this Bill and in spite of the Public Safety Act, the Blueshirts will be victorious in the Irish Free State".

He ended his contribution by stating that, "New crimes are being created which no single individual, beyond the Front Bench of the Fianna Fáil Party, believes are crimes. The general sense of the community is being revolted by this, and it will tend to bring the law into disrepute instead of respect".

Sean Lemass acknowledged that "Deputy Costello alone attempted to frame a case against the measure, and in order to do so, he had to misrepresent its purpose, and even to misstate its terms. Deputy Costello's two reasons against this Bill were, firstly, that it was, in his opinion, a Bill brought in against a political party, and the first of its kind, and, secondly, because it was an invasion of individual rights".

Lemass then acknowledged that it was the 'wild' speeches of O'Duffy, talking of abolishing democratic government that had caused concern. He hoped that his new-found associates have instilled some sense into him, have taught him the futility of attempting to carry out any such programme in this country. But he has not said so himself".

The Bill was guillotined in the Dáil on 14 March 1934. However to the consternation of the Government, the Senate refused it a Second Reading and it thus could not become law for 18 months. In fury deValera on the very next day, introduced a Bill to abolish the Senate.

Michael McInerney, after interviewing Costello in 1967, writes of this episode, "The inconsistency of Costello's career includes his flirtation with the Blueshirts of whom he states today, were never Fascist or Nazi. Certainly Costello is no Fascist; he is the opposite, humane above all and has a genuine concern for social progress"[8]. O'Duffy as leader of Fine Gael decided that the June 1934 local elections would become the vehicle for him to lay the basis for the rout of Fianna Fáil. Unlike on previous occasions, these elections were fought vigorously and sometimes violently.

The results were;
Fianna Fáil 728 Fine Gael 596.

Another lawyer who features later in the Costello story, Cecil Lavery, won a Dáil seat in a Dublin by-election that June. The Cuman na nGaedheal element of the party was dismayed at the violence that O'Duffy created and it became apparent to him that they were not up for such radical tactics. He tendered his resignation, which after much inter-play was accepted. WT Cosgrave became the new party leader. Costello remained on the front bench. However, the old stalwarts were disappearing as economic circumstances forced them to concentrate on their own commercial realities and Fine Gael became a part-timers' political party. This stark economic reality was reflected in the Dáil when William Norton later called for retirement allowances for ministers[9]. As Cosgrave had earlier feared, his party was in steep decline and making little impression in opposition to the government. The economic war, caused by deValera's reneging on the annuities to Britain, was continuing to cause great difficulty to the livelihood of the people.

On 29 March deValera, speaking in the Dáil, expressed his disappointment that the IRA had not accepted peaceful government by majority rule. Political murders and intimidation had continued as before. In 1936 the IRA was again declared illegal and the annual march to Wolfe Tone's grave at Bodenstown was banned. In 1937 the Army Comrades Association was banned and Military Tribunals re-instated. Cosgrave must have had a strong sense of *déjà vue* as deValera took on the IRA using Military Tribunals.

Blueshirt rally, Charleville Co. Cork.

Ex General Eoin O'Duffy the centre of attention with his Blueshirt supporters.

CHAPTER 6

REPEAL OF EXTERNAL RELATIONS ACT
IN 1936

The Dáil debates which followed on the abdication of King Edward VIII, probably foreshadowed Costello's later major constitutional initiatives, and illustrate that there was a clear longitudinal logic to his thinking, which is not acknowledged even in the twenty first century. deValera informed the British Government in June 1936 that he intended to replace the 1922 constitution with one that would replace the office of the Governor General and claim jurisdiction over the 32 counties. In December a constitutional crisis arose in Britain with the abdication of Edward VIII. deValera then on 10 December had the Executive Council recognise the abdication of the King and proposed the deletion of all reference to the King and the Governor General from the Irish Constitution. He then acknowledged the new King's role relating to the Irish Free State as purely in relation to external affairs. This was intended to demonstrate that matters relating to the monarch's abdication and the precise role of his successor were properly an internal matter for the Irish Free State. The Dáil was recalled from the Christmas recess to enact both new acts. In the Dáil deValera explained that the King had no function in the internal affairs of the State but was being retained for external purposes alone "because he is recognised as the symbol of this particular cooperation with the States of the Commonwealth". The Amendment Bill, doing away with the office of the Governor General, was opposed by Fine Gael and the Independents, but supported by 5 Labour TD's and Fianna Fáil. It was guillotined and passed by 79 to 54 votes. The agreement of the Governor General was forthcoming and the measure became law that same day of 11 December.

On the following day, a Sunday, the External Relations Bill confining the King's role to external relations on the advice of the government was taken. John A Costello deemed the Bill would produce "a political monstrosity, the like of which is unknown to political legal theory"[1]. He said that he presumed that the silence from the Labour and Independent Benches was not due to shyness but rather because they could not understand the Bill. He confessed that he, with "ten years experience assisting at most of the work in connection with constitutional change wrought by the last Government and having attended three of the Imperial Conferences", had difficulty grasping what the legal and constitutional repercussions and effects of the Bill will be.

He said that the Bill produced a political monstrosity unknown in any polity in the world. He found that deValera's assertion that the two Bills would not jeopardise our position in the Commonwealth to be unfounded.

Costello said his mind was in a whirl and capsized as he listened to deValera's arguments. He could see no link between the abdication of the King and the removing of references to the King in the Bill. He thought deValera to be saying that he laid claim to the constitutional advances made up to 1931, which Costello totally rejected.

He said that the deValera governments had made no constitutional advances, rather the very fact that under the present Constitution the legal power to declare a republic, is the best testimonial to the late Kevin O'Higgins and Paddy McGilligan in 1926, 1929 and 1930. Costello claimed that the fact that the guillotined Bill meant the State would have no head of State for internal affairs but would have a foreign king for external affairs, a half head of the State acting for us sometimes and not acting for us at other times, will make us "the laughing stock of international jurists throughout the world. What sort of State is that at all?" He claimed that Michael Collins envisaged under the Treaty, that the King would become merely a symbolic head of the State, with no power internally or internationally. Costello then wearing his legal hat, said that the "recognition of our freedom, our complete and absolute independence as a sovereign State, was conceded internationally in Geneva, by the declaration of the British Foreign Minister in 1929, when Deputy McGilligan signed the optional clause of the permanent Court of the Hague". The crown was a symbol of our freedom, of our free association. These Bills now take this away. This half Crown is now to be the symbol of our cooperation in the Commonwealth. The Crown was never the symbol of our cooperation. Costello indicated how the leaders of all the Commonwealth countries including Canada, Australia, and South Africa, had backed the Free State in achieving its freedom. He said, "assuming that it is a mere trifle for us to so remove the King, whom millions of people in these Commonwealth countries had a deep attachment and loyalty to, was wrong". He said that, "we owe a slight obligation, which costs very little, to these countries which assisted us, but this measure dishonoured those slight obligations. These obligations were dishonoured by deValera today".

Costello said that he could understand being a full member of the Commonwealth or, interestingly in hindsight, he said he could understand a decent declaration of a republic. However he did not know whether we were in the Commonwealth or whether we were now a republic. General Sean MacEoin said that deValera had funked declaring a republic. He said that deValera should have put it to the British government that if they wanted us to remain in the Commonwealth then we would, but only as a republic. He said that Fianna Fáil wanted to be able to say down in the Bog of Allen that they were republicans and in Piccadilly, they wanted to say they were imperialists. This Act was the first to be signed by the Chairman of the Dáil.

❋❋❋❋

1937 CONSTITUTION

As early as April 1935 deValera had instructed the Department of External Affairs to draft the Heads of a New Constitution Bill[2]. deValera brought in a new constitution in 1937, which Costello opposed as granting the Taoiseach dictatorial powers. He felt that the leader of government should still be a Chairman rather than a Chief. One of deValera's close advisors on the constitution was his close friend, Archbishop John Charles McQuaid of Dublin. In the run-up to the Dáil debate on the proposed Draft Constitution, the *Irish Independent* carried a series of articles from prominent people on the Draft Constitution. It published a very long article by Costello on 6 May 1937, in which he was very critical of the matter. One section sounds very modern. It echoes the contemporary opposition of women, as voiced particularly in Maud Gonne MacBride's July 1937 edition of her 'Prison Bars', which was almost entirely devoted to an attack on the Draft Constitution[3]. Costello wrote that it "also comes as a surprise to find the status of women in the State affected, if not expressly, certainly by implication. We read the somewhat grandiose statement that all citizens shall be held equal before the law, but we then discover that the substance of that provision is taken away by the provision that the State may, if it likes, in its legislation declare them to be unequal. The provision that the State shall not be prevented in its enactment from having due regard to differences of capacity, physical and moral, and of social functions, allows a wide latitude in the consideration of the supposed equality of citizens before the law. That provision read in conjunction with the constitutional declaration of "the inadequate strength of women", the omission of the significant words "without distinction of sex" contained in Articles 3 and 14 of the existing Constitution, must appear curious in view of the substantially equal rights of voting and otherwise accorded to women. Under the Draft women have not, as of Constitutional right, any claim to the exercise of the franchise equally with men. The Draft as it stands. offers its Framer as a whole burnt offering to feminists and feminist associations".

Costello's main criticisms were;

1. Women have not, as of constitutional right, any claim to the exercise of the franchise equally with men. He also opposed the ban on divorce.

2. While the Draft Amendment proposed that the State should recognise the special position of the Catholic Church, no such special position is accorded to it in any practical form.

3. The King will still act for us. Our constitutional status will be judged by the fact that that our international relations are conducted through the institution of the Crown. Internationally we remain and *will* remain and will be recognised as a member of the British Commonwealth of Nations.

4. The powers and privileges proposed for the novelty of a new functionary called the President would appear to be entirely unjustifiable.

5. Under the Constitutional proposals, the Government sinks definitely into the background and the dominant personality and the person no doubt with the power is the Prime Minister.

6. The President may refer a Bill, to the Supreme Court at the public expense, in the teeth of the wish of the Prime Minister and of the Dáil.

7. If the present proposals become law, we would never have more freedom that we have under the Constitution made possible by the sacrifices of Griffith and Collins and the sacrifices and labours of O'Higgins and McGilligan.

The *Irish Press* responded the very next day in an editorial criticising Costello and the *Irish Independent*. It said, "It is unnecessary for us to animadvert at any length on the seven columns which Mr. Costello, the Attorney-General in Mr. Cosgrave's Government, devoted in the Opposition's organ yesterday. He was unable to attack the Draft Constitution on any question of substance or principle. His criticism was negative, carping, niggling and cavailing. When the Constitution is discussed in the Dáil, Mr. Costello should apply the fruits of his industry in every possible way." Costello made a contribution in the Dáil primarily on a matter we have some experience in more modern times. He spoke on an amendment by Paddy McGilligan on the matter of free speech in the Constitution. He pointed out to the members that the Constitution would most likely become an issue in the Courts where judicial interpretations would occur. He warned that judicial interpretation of the Constitution might result in something quite different from what the actual words used were intended to mean, by the framers of the document. Reference had been made that some words in the Constitution were "harmless". He declared it an elementary principle of parliamentary law that nothing could be regarded as harmless. "If you express one thing you exclude everything else". He said that if words were harmless they should not be in the Constitution. Their later interpretation could well be at total variance to what the legislators envisaged. He declared that the rights of free speech should be qualified only by the phrase "subject to public order and morality".

deValera also proposed to introduce a new vocationally oriented Senate. An all-party committee was set up to consider its composition and electoral mechanism. This committee consisted of deValera, Lemass, Costello, McGilligan and William Norton. They failed to agree and Fianna Fáil used its majority to decide the matter itself. The result was that the Senate was to be under the thumb of the government of the day[4].

The Constitution gained a relatively small majority of 56% in the referendum, being opposed vociferously by many women. deValera had also called a general election for the same day, in which Fianna Fáil lost eight seats. This resulted in its becoming a minority government again, relying on Labour for support.

The economic war ended in 1938 when the Anglo-Irish Trade Agreement was signed.

That year too saw Doughlas Hyde, on the recommendation of WT Cosgrave, become President of the country. During the 1938 general election, deValera no longer thought it necessary to break from the British Commonwealth in order to establish freedom[5].The *Irish Times* welcomed this conversion.

The war years further isolated the country. When Churchill became Prime Minister he railed against deValera over access to the Treaty ports. These had remained under the British at the Treaty, but to Churchill's horror, were handed over by Neville Chamberlain in 1938. However, most of the country backed deValera's handling of the issue in a benign neutrality. One politician who did not was James Dillon, the Deputy leader of Fine Gael. Without any advance notice to his party colleagues, he broke ranks in the Dáil on 27 July 1941, decrying Ireland's isolationist stance in dramatic terms. Cosgrave was furious and told the Dáil that his party had not debated the issue. Cosgrave said, "We are not bound to take part in a conflict of this kind. It is no part of the Christian religion or the Catholic faith to insist in our taking part in it. The duty and responsibility of everyone in public life, lies in ensuring due security and stability and integrity of this country. If that is better served by a policy of neutrality, then it is our duty to accept and adopt that policy. In times of crisis it is advisable - it is necessary - to make up your mind rapidly, to make it up correctly, and having made it up, to stick to it like a man and to do what you can towards preserving, improving and exalting the country, which it is our duty to serve"[6].

Maud Gonne MacBride
The July 1937 edition of her 'Prison Bars',
was almost entirely devoted to an attack
on the Draft Constitution.

Cumann na nGaedheal election poster of the period.

CHAPTER 7

LOSES DÁIL SEAT JUNE 1943
REGAINS IT JUNE 1944

The wartime general election of June 1943 was a most bitter affair. The economic situation was very poor and people were dissatisfied with their lot. This was exemplified by a strong campaign by the new, small and medium farmers party from the west of Ireland, Clann na Talmhan, and by Labour, representing the workers. Sean MacEntee according to Maurice Manning, "ran probably the most scurrilous and irresponsible electoral campaign in the history of the State. In a stream of frenzied vituperation which lasted until polling day"[1]. MacEntee accused Labour of being controlled by communists. He characterised Clann na Talmhan as a totalitarian party; a party of spalpeens, communistic in its outlook[2].

In Britain a national government functioned and the same idea gained some credence in Ireland. WT Cosgrave, in his last election as party leader, made national unity the theme of the Fine Gael campaign, hoping to temper civil war politics. At an election meeting in Ringsend, John A Costello raised the subject in a way that indicated that he might have had serious misgivings about any fruitful outcome from such a policy. While sticking to the party line, he also ridiculed a series of past stances of Fianna Fáil. He declared, "The policy of a National Government has loomed larger in this election. Fine Gael felt that the conditions existing during the Emergency and the problem and difficulties that would face the country after the war required the unified effort of all sections. In putting forward the idea they felt they were interpreting the earnest wishes of the great majority of the people. It was said that no matter what the result of the election might be, the Fianna Fáil party would take no part in a National Government. That party had however once declared they would never enter the Dáil: they had declared that they would never accept the international status of a member of a Commonwealth of Nations: they had said that the Oireachtas could function without a Senate and that they would abolish it: and they had said that the agricultural industry could prosper without the British markets. The only way to unite the North and the South was to unite the South first and that was what Fine Gael would do under a National Government"[3].

The results of the election were very bad for Fianna Fáil, losing ten seats, and a disaster for Fine Gael which lost thirteen seats. These included General Richard Mulcahy and John A Costello.

The first count results in Costello's constituency of Dublin Townships were:

MacEntee	FF	11,336
E Benson	FG	8,953

JA Costello	FG	7,508
E Butler	FF	6,499
J Cawley	Lab	2,205
J Browne	Lab	2,096

MacEntee was elected on the first count with both Benson and Butler being elected on the fourth count. Costello lost out by just over two hundred votes, the vote management having Backfired.

The over all result was:

FF	67
FG	32
Lab	17
Clann na Talmhan	9
Independents	13

Despite Costello's defeat, there were two Senior Counsel, eight Junior Counsel and seven solicitors in the new Dail[4].

In the new Dáil James Dillon who had left FG during the war when he defied party policy on neutrality, called for a national government involving FF, FG, Labour and Clan na Talmhan. deValera said "I do not believe in coalitions. I do not believe they will work"[5]. The tragedy for Labour was that on foot of its alleged communistic sympathies, it soon split into Labour and National Labour, with bitter personal recriminations. James Everett became leader of National Labour.

WT Cosgrave's resignation was to take effect early in 1944. In moves which would have a major repercussion on Costello's future career, Fine Gael began to look for a successor as party leader. Richard Mulcahy, who was the most senior person in Fine Gael, was without a Dáil seat. The party, through Paddy McGilligan, approached James Dillon to rejoin Fine Gael and become parliamentary leader with Mulcahy as Party President. Dillon, who remained totally committed to supporting the Allies in the war, turned down the offer, though saying that he would gladly serve in different circumstances under Dick Mulcahy's leadership[6]. The Fine Gael parliamentary party met on 18 January 1944 and Cosgrave resigned. TF O'Higgins became leader of the parliamentary party and Chairman. Maurice Manning writes that Dillon's was a costly decision for him. Manning argues that had Dillon been party leader or even deputy leader after Mulcahy returned to the front bench, it is very likely that he and not Costello would have been the compromise choice as Taoiseach, when the first Inter-Party government was being formed[7].

Luckily for Costello the eleventh Dáil had a very short life. The Government was defeated on 9 May by one vote on a technical transport issue. deValera decided that rather than call a confidence motion in the Dáil next day, he would inform President

Hyde that he was dissolving the Dáil and calling a general election for 30 May. The Labour party was split and Fine Gael was in still in transitional decline.

Costello campaigned vigorously, attacking Fianna Fáil on every election platform. He told the electorate that there would be no stable government until Fianna Fáil was defeated. He questioned whether an Executive with a large majority made for dictatorial power rather than a strong government. He claimed that in a democratic country, a strong and stable government would have to have the consent and support of the majority of the people. He believed that a one-party government, which rigidly controlled its Deputies, could "set up a dictatorial form of rule for five years, ignoring the opinions of Deputies not in the Party". He believed that Parliament should control the Executive.

On the other hand, Costello argued, that a government with a small majority, which might be composed of different groups might govern by carefully consulting all the interests before drafting legislation. If it was composed of able and respected Ministers, it must be in fact a much stronger Government. He emphasised that Fine Gael did not seek office for the fruits of office. Following the peace that they all hoped was near at hand, each nation would have to face problems of new financial systems and changed methods of international relations. The unlimited energies of all directed in harmony and unity would be required if this nation was to take its proper place in the post-war world[8].

For that election, Costello advertised his Fine Gael constituency committee rooms as located in Rathmines, Harolds Cross, Belmont Ave, Sandymount Green, Thorncastle St, Haddington Road and Ballsbridge Terrace[9].

The first count results in Dublin Townships with a quota at 9163, were:

S. MacEntee	FF	10,064
JA Costello	FG	9,528
B Butler	FF	7,894
E Benson	FG	7,059
H Good	Lab	2,192

This time Costello was ahead of his party colleague and re-elected. Joe Groome, the Fianna Fáil Director of Elections, demanded a total recount. The Returning officer, W McCracken resisted it, pointing out the time and expense involved. The recount went ahead. MacEntee and Costello were deemed elected on the first count and Butler was elected on the fourth count. deValera's opportunistic action in calling the snap election proved very successful for him, as Fianna Fáil returned with an overall majority. For the first time since 1932 Labour opposed deValera in the Dáil, but National Labour supported him, giving Fianna Fáil a clear majority of 81 to 37. The only positive note for Fine Gael was the re-election of Costello and Mulcahy to the Dáil.

The overall party result, with the 1943 results in brackets, were:

FF –	76	[67]
FG –	30	[32]
Lab	8	[17]
Nat. Lab.	4	
Clann na Talun	9	[10]
Independents	11	[12]

POST-WAR EMERGENCY LEGISLATION

At the end of the war in 1945 the Government introduced a Bill, which purported to repeal the emergency legislation introduced in 1939. It was a complicated piece of legislation and many deputies had difficulty dissecting it. James Dillon questioned deValera on precisely what powers were being retained and what powers were being dropped. deValera asserted that most of the emergency legislation would disappear. He admitted that since the end of the war the government had discovered that the IRA was continuing with its illegal activities and the government had decided not to release its leaders. Dillon was not happy with deValera's reply and said, "I hope Deputy Costello will be more illuminating". Costello said jocosely that he hoped to illuminate the darkness of Dillon's mind in a very short and simple sentence on the subject; "The residue remaining in the Act when the Bill passes into law will be everything in the 1939 Act as amended, with the sole exception of censorship. All other powers could be introduced by the Government". The Taoiseach exclaimed, "Oh, no". Costello continued saying that the Constitution would remain in abeyance. The Government could, by order, do anything they like. They could repeal Acts of Parliament. deValera interjected "If it were only correct", to which Costello retorted, "I challenge the Taoiseach or any of his legal advisors to say it is incorrect. The government, if this Bill is passed, may pass any particular legislation by Order about any matter they like, except censorship, and it cannot be questioned in the courts. That is the position we have to face here". Costello maintained that the Emergency Powers had strangled the business operations in the country. While deValera maintained that the Emergency was not over, Costello said, "I say with confidence that the emergency is over. I recognise that the country is still faced with difficulties, but they are not the type that enabled this House unanimously to grant these drastic measures to the Government in the 1939 Act". deValera asked Deputy Dillon not to base his objections on the interpretation of the former Attorney General, to which Costello retorted "Why not? They are true"[10].

＊＊＊＊

CHAPTER 8

POLITICAL MOVEMENT
IN THE LATE 1940's

In the 1945 Presidential election Patrick McCartan was an Independent candidate, supported by Clann na Talmhan, Labour and some Independents. McCartan got 19.6% of the votes cast. Sean MacEoin won 30.9% for Fine Gael with Sean T. O'Kelly of Fianna Fáil getting 49.5 %. However, it was very noteworthy for future elections that over 55% of McCartan's transfers went to MacEoin, with a mere 12.8% going to O'Kelly. Some 41.8% votes were non-transferrable. This appeared to indicate that the electorate favoured the logic of cooperation between political parties[1]. This became even more pronounced when in the three by-elections of October 1947, when Sean MacBride in Dublin County and Patrick Kinnane in Tipperary won two of the three by-elections for Clann na Poblachta, due to transfers from the other opposition parties. Over 50% of Labour transfers and 47.7% of Fine Gael transfers went to Clann na Poblachta.

DECLINE OF FINE GAEL

The continuing decline of Fine Gael was never more clearly illustrated than when it failed to contest five by-elections in 1945 because, as Richard Mulcahy stated, they could not find candidates willing to stand[2]. This was one outcome of the traditional negative attitude of Fine Gael candidates towards constituency work for local and national elections.

In some despair, TF O'Higgins, the deputy leader, wrote to the newspapers in April 1947, suggesting "some form of amalgamation or association" between Fine Gael, Clann na Talmhan, Independet Farmers and Independents. The *Irish Times* interpreted this as a call for a new party[3]. This idea was vigorously opposed by Liam Cosgrave, son of WT Cosgrave. He wrote to the party leader, Mulcahy, saying that such "a coalition or merger is extremely unlikely if not an impossibility". He was critical of the party organisation, the front bench and the absence of clear policies. He ended by writing, "I cannot any longer conscientiously ask the public to support the party as a party, and in all the circumstances I do not propose to speak at meetings outside my constituency"[4]. Mulcahy was also entirely opposed to any merger, preferring, even if Fine Gael was to go down, than bury its tradition in any kind of new party[5].

James Dillon, who was then an Independent outside Fine Gael, tried to act as a middleman in the moves towards an alliance. He found that "Blowick made decisions slowly and with difficulty"[6]. No real progress was made and of course deValera was watching such manoeuvres with an eye towards another opportunistic general election. However, in late 1947 Fine Gael appeared to make some progress as circumstances forced it to find new Dáil candidates. In this, John A Costello played an important part.

Among the new arrivals were, his son, Declan Costello, his son-in-law, Alexis Fitzgerald and TF O'Higgins, who would all play important national roles in the party for a very considerable period. The party also polled reasonably well in the November by-elections, which unnerved Fianna Fáil.

CLANN NA TALMHAN

This new party was described as "a symptom of the frustration and impotence of small farmers who felt themselves ignored and misunderstood by a remote government and bureaucracy, and exploited by big business and rapacious unions"[7]. Michael Donnellan from Dunmore Co. Galway became party leader after being elected to the Dáil in 1943. He vacated the position the following year for Joseph Blowick from South Mayo, as he believed that "honours should rotate"[8]. Those who voted for the Clann transferred a far higher percentage of votes to Fine Gael than Fianna Fáil, while taking votes from both parties in the general elections of 1944 and 1948. The Clann experimented with widening its scope by an alliance with the Farmer's Federation of Leinster. This did not work out as the interests of big and small farmers proved to be quite different. The small farmers favoured land division while the big farmers opposed it[9]. The Clann remained contentedly a small conservative party[10].

CLANN NA POBLACHTA

As I have already mentioned the austere war years brought a general feeling of increasing anger against the Fianna Fáil governments. This permeated among wide sections of the community, but deValera through clever manipulation of the political system remained unchallenged in the Dáil. However several notable events occurred, which combined, led to a sensational loss of power by Fianna Fáil in 1948. Chief among them, because it occurred in a traditional Fianna Fáil stronghold, was the emergence of Clann na Poblachta under Sean MacBride. MacBride had a pedigree in radical republicanism second to none. His father was Major John MacBride and his mother Maud Gonne. He himself had been a youth member of the IRA, advancing to Chief of Staff in 1936. He became a Senior Counsel during the war and defended IRA prisoners interned by Fianna Fáil up to 1946. At the end of censorship, the public heard for the first time the shocking conditions many of the prisoners had endured. This crystallised in the person of Sean McCaughey, a Northener who had been jailed since 1941 and who went on hunger strike to force the government to grant political status. McCaughey died on hunger and thirst strike on 11 May 1946. At the inquest Sean MacBride led a devastating questioning of the authorities, gaining the admission that they would not have kept a dog in such conditions. MacBride's Junior Counsel was Noel Hartnett. He was a member of the National Executive of Fianna Fáil and a friend of deValera. He was well known as a presenter of Radio Éireann's 'Question Time' programme. Hartnett was sacked from Radio Éireann because of his association with MacBride.

Out of their collaboration, on 6 July 1946, came a new political party named Clann na Poblachta. From the outset the party set out to be as broadly based as possible, concerning itself with social and economic problems. It highlighted the low standard of political morality in public life.

There was much dissatisfaction amid the public with a lengthy transport strike then in progress, with army lorries providing a skeleton service. A bank strike had forced the Minister for Finance, Frank Aiken, to close all the banks to prevent chaos. An austerity budget and a pegging of wages added to the public mood of gloom. The blizzard of early 1947 led to a fuel-supply crisis. Bread rationing was introduced. National teachers conducted an eight-month strike. A Tribunal of Inquiry would be set up into business matters at Locke's Distillery where allegations of corruption were made by Oliver J. Flanagan TD against deValera, Sean Lemass and Gerry Boland. On 13 October Sean Lemass had declared that if the Government were defeated in the forth-coming bye-elections, a general election would be called[11].

In June of 1947 local elections had been held, with the new party making inroads in the Fianna Fáil vote. The Electoral amendment Bill of 1947 was brought in by Sean MacEntee to bolster Fianna Fáil's chances in the next general election. Despite the fact that there was a decline in population, the number of TD's was increased from 138 to 147. The number of three seat constituencies was increased from 15 to 22. MacEntee abolished the three seven seat constituencies which tended to favour smaller parties. On 29 October three bye-elections held on the same day, with the Clann winning two of them with transfers from other parties. MacBride himself became TD for South Dublin. On 31 December in Ennis, deValera called a general election for 4 February 1948, despite the fact that one was not required for another fifteen months. He realised that the Clann was still in the process of trying to organise nationally. He decided not to give it too much more time to challenge his republican party.

DIVISIONS IN LABOUR

The Labour Party had made notable progress in the local elections of 1942 and in the general election of 1943 it achieved its best result since 1922, winning 15.7% of the vote and increasing its number of deputies from nine to seventeen. The background to this developments lay in deValera's anti-trade union stance during the social hardship of wartime. Jim Larkin who had been a figure of dissension within the labour movement, had become reconciled to it, and though refused ratification as an official Dáil candidate was nominated by a Dublin caucus and openly supported by William Norton, won a seat. The ITGWU under William O'Brien would not tolerate Larkin being admitted to the Labour Party. It disaffiliated from the Party and instructed its members in the Oireachtas to do likewise and form the National Labour Party in parliament. National Labour became the political wing of the Congress of Trade Unions[12]. To camouflage the real reason for the split, the ITGWU made allegations of a communistic infiltration against the Labour Party.

The National Labour Party challenged it to allow "the bishops or any impartial body" to investigate the matter. William Norton, Labour Party leader, set up an internal inquiry, which led to "expulsions, resignations, and recriminations". In the general election of 1944 the only Labour candidate opposed by National Labour was Jim Larkin. Relations between the two Labour Party TD's remained amicable[13]. However, the electorate was not impressed and the Labour Party vote fell to 8.8%, returning eight deputies. National Labour got 2.7% and four seats[14]. The Congress of Trade Unions pursued a process of distancing itself from traditional British based trade unions. Before the 1948 general election, the Congress held a special conference and pledged its support for the National Labour Party's campaign. The Congress circulated its policy on British based trade unions to all the other political parties. It received a favourable reply from Fianna Fáil alone for "an Irish self-contained trade union movement". After the general election a joint committee of the Congress of Trade Unions and National Labour instructed its five TD's to vote for deValera as Taoiseach. As we have seen above the National Labour TD's refused this directive, on the grounds that inter-union politics were far less important to their constituents than welfare reform.

In the general election of 1944 the only Labour candidate
opposed by National Labour was Jim Larkin.

CHAPTER 9

GENERAL ELECTION 1948

The campaign was fought in bad weather with several sitting TD's dying suddenly. Fianna Fáil tried to smear Labour and Clann na Poblachta with allegations of communism. The North did not figure in the debates. However the External Relations Act of 1936 did. Clann na Poblachta and Labour were clearly against it. Fine Gael appeared at odds on the matter with Mulcahy, the party leader, saying the party would not change the Act[1] and Tom O'Higgins attacking it. Lord Rugby, British representative in Dublin, surmised that deValera might be tempted to promise to repeal the Act to fend off attacks from the left. Despite legislation to repeal the Act having been prepared, deValera did not take up the issue.

deValera and Sean Lemass attacked the idea of any coalition. deValera said the experience elsewhere "has led to dictatorship in certain European countries"[2]. William Norton, the Labour party leader, and some Clann na Talmhan deputies were open to a coalition. The election in the Carlow-Kilkenny constituency had to be postponed to 10 February due to the death of Eamon Coogan, Fine Gael TD. This added, an air of uncertainty to the final election results.

At an election meeting in his Dublin South East constituency at Sandymount, Costello spoke using a musical metaphor, which no doubt appealed to his audience. He said: " In an effort to drown the clamour of public indignation, the instrumentalists of the Fianna Fáil band are blaring forth their themes on stable government and the spectre of communism, varied by an odd roll on the drums of war and an occasional interlude for a sorrowful solo by the leader, on the trials of proportional representation. The government sought a renewal of the confidence of the people on a sorry record of failure and futility as even its bitterest opponents had foretold. A country that has been spared the upheavals of war found its economic life disrupted and its reserves dissipated and its people disillusioned and resentful".

He said that a predominantly agricultural country with unexampled opportunities for agricultural expansion found not only that its export market was depleted but that insufficient food was being produced to satisfy the requirements of its own people. He posed the question that if as Fianna Fáil said, the years ahead are to be so critical, why did the Government not continue until the next year and a half, as the strong government it claimed to be?

Fine Gael had a policy to deal with the cost of living that was all the more effective for being unspectacular. It had a progressive agricultural policy formed by practical farmers after intense study of modern scientific advances in agricultural science.

Then Costello, who was very conscious of specific areas of need, promised that his party would help the blind by a comprehensive scheme, and the old and distressed, by the abolition of the means test.

He also appealed to most of his audience by saying that much-suffering class of the community known as the middle class, had endured too much in recent years, from the policy of the present Government[3].

A breakdown of the occupations of 349 of the 404 election candidates shows;

	FF	FG	C na Pob	Lab	Total
Lawyers	11	19	14	1	45
Medical	5	1	9	-	15
Clerical	6	-	2	2	10
Teachers	12	2	20	2	36
Farmers	43	19	15	3	80
Business Men	32	30	15	5	82
Executives	2	-	4	1	7
Engineers	2	-	1	-	3
Writers	2	2	1	1	6
Workers	2	2	6	12	22
Widows	1	1	1	1	4
Travellers	-	1	4	2	7
Army Offic. Rtd.	-	3	-	-	3
Fishermen	-	1	1	1	3
Union Officials	-	-	20	20	40
Transport	-	-	-	7	7
Students	-	-	-	1	1
Architects	-	-	-	1	1

The 17 Clann na Talmhan, 14 Farmers and 34 Independent candidates are not included in the table.

The first count result in Dublin South East was:

S. MacEntee	FF	7,371
MB Yeats	FF	2,928
JA Costello	FG	8,478
JH Douglas	FG	2,980
NC Browne	C na Pob	4,917
D. Donoghue	C na Pob	559
E. Butler	Lab	2,599

Costello MacEntee and Browne were elected. After being elected Costello said: "It is a matter of satisfaction to me to know that after 15 years of active political life, my constituents are not tired of me. The Fine Gael Party is still a resurgent force in Irish political life. The country's problems are so difficult that their solution requires the co-operation of everyone both inside and outside the Dáil"[4]. For Noel Browne it had been "an electoral risk breath-taking in its audacity" to stand in a small three-seater constituency in which two sitting members were already firmly entrenched[5].

Garret Fitzgerald and his wife participated in this election. He has written of his experience. "Under the direction of Alexis Fitzgerald, Joan and I had canvassed for Fine Gael from door to door in Mr. Costello's constituency of Dublin Townships. My understanding – for which Alexis was always to deny responsibility – was that Fine Gael supported Commonwealth membership, and Joan and I canvassed accordingly; we particularly remember reassuring the inhabitants of Waterloo Road on the point. After the election all opposition parties and independents joined together to form a coalition to replace Fianna Fáil after sixteen years of unbroken rule by that party. Not having adult memories of the sixteen years of Fianna Fáil government, I did not fully share the conviction of older people in the opposition parties that an alliance with MacBride's party was a price worth paying to provide an alternative government"[6].

The final election result,
with the number of seats from the 1944 election in brackets was:

Fianna Fáil	68	[76]
Fine Gael	31	[30]
Labour	14	[8]
Clann na Poblachta	10	[0]
Clann na Talmhan	7	[9]
National Labour	5	[4]
Independents	12	[11]

The *Irish Independent* reported on Saturday 14th February that following a meeting at Leinster House on Friday between General Richard Mulcahy, Mr. MacBride, Mr. Norton and Mr. Blowick, that it looked likely it would not be easy to find a candidate with any prospect of successfully opposing Mr de Valera on the following Wednesday. It said that the four party leaders discussed the position for over two hours but no statement was issued afterwards.

The same newspaper on Monday 16th February reported that on the previous night General Mulcahy issued a statement after a meeting of representatives of opposition parties and Independent Deputies. The newspaper said: "Responding to the unanimous request made to him by the leaders and other representatives of Fine Gael, Labour, Clann na Poblachta, Clann na Talmhan and by a group of Independent Deputies, Mr. JA Costello SC has agreed to allow himself to be nominated for the position of Taoiseach on Wednesday next. All the parties have agreed to cooperate in the formation of an Inter-Party Government".

It remained for the National Labour Party to come aboard, which it did.

*The little known Cenotaph
to Griffith, O'Higgins, and Collins, on Leinster Lawn,
facing Merrion Square Dublin.*

CHAPTER 10

THE CENOTAPH ON LEINSTER LAWN
COSTELLO'S FOLLY?

On 11 August 1923 WT Cosgrave, President of the Executive Council, amid great pomp and ceremony, officially unveiled the Cenotaph on Leinster Lawn commemorating the two dead heroes of the Irish Free State, Arthur Griffith and Michael Collins. The story of the Cenotaph offers an opportunity to take the temperature of John A Costello's political commitment to Irish nationalism.

Annual ceremonies were originally held at the Cenotaph but within a few short years those ceremonies and the monument itself fell into a sorry state with the two medallions of Collins and Griffith peeling badly. It appeared strange that the Government had lost interest in commemorating its own heroes, while at the same time donating £50,000 to the Royal British Legion's National War Memorial at Islandbridge. But practical politics dictated the latter donation. It was only after the shocking murder of the Minister of Justice Kevin O'Higgins in July 1927 that the Cumann na nGaedheal Government paid serious attention to their own monument, which was by then "an insult"[1]. It spruced it up a little, spending £170 on a ceremony there in 1928 to commemorate O'Higgins, adding a third medallion in his honour. Rebuilding the cenotaph was considered but the finance involved was felt to be prohibitive[1a].

When deValera took over in 1932 the Cenotaph was ignored and it was predicted that it would soon fall down and be forgotten. On 28 July 1939 deValera and Sean Moylan met with Desmond Fitzgerald and Michael Hayes of Fine Gael about the cenotaph. Subsequently the Office of Public Works was instructed to "design a permanent memorial including a cross"[2]. However, as Anne Dolan writes, "Gestures were made with one hand and then taken back with the other. deValera took control. Commemoration would be conceded but only without the clamour of ceremony, only if Fianna Fáil was seen to give and Fine Gael submissively and silently to receive"[3]. Then the war years intervened and nothing happened.

Towards the end of the war, a Fine Gael TD, PS Doyle of South Dublin, began to raise the matter in the Dáil through a series of parliamentary questions. Somewhat surprisingly, Doyle found his greatest ally in John A Costello. Doyle asked Mr. O'Ceallaigh on 28 June 1944 whether any plans or design had as yet been considered for the Griffith - Collins - O'Higgins Cenotaph on Leinster Lawn. O'Ceallaigh replied that a design was considered but that it would not be possible to proceed with the erection until "the end of the present emergency". Doyle again raised the matter of the crumbling Cenotaph in May 1946 and asked when it was proposed to begin work on the project. Doyle acknowledged that the matter had been under consideration for a number of years. He said that the time had come to replace the Cenotaph, "in memory of the three men who were the founders of this State"[4].

The Parliamentary Secretary at Finance, Mr. O'Grady, ignored this description of Griffith, Collins and O'Higgins, and did not answer the question asked. John A Costello put a question on 28 May 1947 on when the monument to "General Michael Collins, Arthur Griffith and Kevin O'Higgins would be replaced?" Mr O'Grady replied that the matter was "under consideration". Costello responded rather tetchily, asking " Is that the only information that can be vouchsafed after the lapse of so many years. Could the Parliamentary Secretary not give any details of what active consideration means?" The Taoiseach intervened to say, "The Deputy should ask some of his colleagues". Mr O'Grady added that Costello should take the matter up with the Chief Whip of his own Party. Costello continued in a similar vein, asking why should he take it up with his Chief Whip when he was entitled to ask the Minister for the information he wanted. Mr. O'Grady retorted that the Chief Whip and other members of Costello's Party were aware of any steps that had been taken. Costello replied that he was not aware of them and he was, as a Deputy, entitled to put the question in the House. It was clear that the Fine Gael Party was not over excited about the cenotaph.

On 15 October 1947 PS Doyle again raised the matter, asking the Minister for Finance to state the reasons for the delay and when it was intended to proceed with the erection of the "Griffith-Collins-O'Higgins Cenotaph on Leinster Lawn?"

Mr. O'Grady replied that some doubts had arisen about the entire suitability of the design under consideration for the particular location at Leinster Lawn, and an alternative design was being prepared. He said that the memorial would be erected as soon as a suitable design had been approved.

After Costello became Taoiseach, PS Doyle asked him in a Parliamentary Question, if he would state what steps it was proposed to take to have a permanent Griffith-Collins-O'Higgins Memorial erected in a suitable position on Leinster Lawn[5]. Costello replied that the memorial would be erected at the earliest possible date on the site of the former temporary cenotaph on Leinster Lawn. The original memorial had been dismantled, as it was in a dilapidated state. The medalions that adorned it were stored. He added that a design would be ready in a few weeks. It was clear that the new Taoiseach had taken personal control of the matter. He circulated a memorandum on the history of the monument, saying that he was "anxious that all members of the Government should have some knowledge of the matter". He tussled with the indolent Department of Finance, sending them stiff memos on the matter[6]. He met the Commissioners of the Office of Public Works himself and scrutinised the new design, restoring the inscriptions, which Fianna Fáil had dared to erase in its eagerness to neutralise the monument.

DOCHUN GLÓIRE DÉ AGUS ONÓRA NA h-ÉIREANN:
MICHEAL ÓCOILEAIN 1890-1922. ART Ó GRIOBHTHA 1871-1922:
CAOIMHGHIN Oh-UIGIN 1892-1927.
The design was formally agreed on 26 July 1949.

As Costello emphasised to the Office of Public Works on 27 February 1950 the monument would be "worthy of the purpose for which it is to be used"[7]. It would cost £20,000 and would consist of a 60 foot granite obelisk, capped by a gilt bronze flame, [An Claidheamh Solais] which would stand on a circular sloping base, adorned with four bronze wreaths that framed the medallions of Griffith, Collins and O'Higgins. Costello's urgency in completing the Cenotaph did not find favour with Fianna Fáil. In the Dáil they criticised him for neglecting 'their' Garden of Remembrance on Parnell Square, this despite the fact that they themselves had ignored the Garden, from 1935 to 1948. Fianna Fáil began to criticise Costello's push to complete the Cenotaph. It complained in the Dáil that the Cenotaph was raising memories of the Civil War and was a blatant attempt by Fine Gael to commemorate their own heroes, while Fianna Fáil asserted, that their Garden of Remembrance was intended to commemorate all those who died to found the Republic. Deputy Harry Colley and Sean MacEntee were to the fore in this regard. Costello decided that he had to make a major detailed statement to counter this, by outlining how the plan to erect the Cenotaph had already been agreed to, by several Fianna Fáil governments.

On 11 July 1950 Costello intervened in the estimate on the Office of Public Works debate to counter mis-statements and propaganda made inside and outside the House, which asserted that the government was trying to foment the resurrection of Civil War bitterness and quarrels. He quoted Deputy Harry Colley's earlier contribution as unfounded and untrue. He then proceeded to give a detailed account of the history of the project, demonstrating how it had become a joint enterprise with Fianna Fáil governments. A temporary cenotaph was erected in August 1923. It comprised of a central cross and two large pylons, to which medallions in plaster, of Messrs. Griffith and Collins were affixed. George Atkinson designed the cenotaph and the medallions were by Albert Power. The erection was of timber framing covered with expanded metal lathing and cement. In August 1928, a medallion of the late Kevin O'Higgins was added. The intention, at the time was that it was to be merely temporary, to be replaced in time by a permanent memorial. In 1935 cracks appeared in the structure and the OPW advised that it should be removed. The Taoiseach, Mr deValera, acting very properly after consultations with Fine Gael representatives, announced on 15 August 1939 that it was to be taken down and replaced on the same spot as soon as a suitable design was approved. The medallions were put into storage. The Government commissioned a new design, and as Costello said, "The then Taoiseach, acting perfectly correctly and with great courtesy, submitted it to the Fine Gael Party. I myself saw it with General Mulcahy on 7 July 1940".

Costello had then written to the Taoiseach;

"A Chara,
I have examined the plans for the cenotaph memorial on Leinster Lawn left with me on Wednesday last, 2nd July. They have been seen by some of my colleagues. We approve of the plan bearing date 1/5/'40, and marked that the words 'showing new scale',"

He continued his Dáil statement by stating that the Emergency intervened and no work could be completed. On 16 September 1947 the Government directed the Minister for Finance to prepare new sketch plans for a column or obelisk, including a cross and portrait plaques of Griffith, Collins and O'Higgins. It also directed that when Government approved the new design, it should be discussed with Fine Gael, who should be informed of the government's intention to erect the monument on Leinster Lawn. However on 16 September 1947 the Government decided not to proceed with the design by Mr. Leask. It asked Raymond McGrath of the OPW to prepare a new design. He submitted the new plans, but at that stage the coalition government was in power.

Costello asserted that contrary to what Deputy Colley and others had said, there was never any intention to foment old Civil War bitterness. In fact the design was according to what the last Government had stipulated. Costello also added that his government was committed to going ahead with the Garden of Remembrance.

The very next day, 12 July 1950, Deputy Kitt raised the issue of the Cenoptaph on the estimate for the Office of Public Works. Sean MacEntee recognised the historical place of "distinguished men" such as Griffith, Collins and O'Higgins and said that he did not wish to create any bitterness. However, under pressure from Con Lehane he soon reverted to form and spoke of "having beaten the Blueshirts in 1935", and not forgetting the Republican dead by commemorating them at the Garden of Remembrance at Parnell Square. There, his party wanted to see the names of the 1916 leaders inscribed, together with those of Cathal Brugha, Rory O'Connor, Liam Mellowes, Joe McKelvey, Dick Barrett and others worthy of note.

In his reply Costello decried MacEntee's "hysterical and histrionic" contribution accusing him of false sentiment. He said that he had given solemn assurances in the Dáil on the previous day, about his Government's intention to complete the Garden of Remembrance. The idea for the Garden was first suggested to the Government in 1935 by the Dublin Brigade Council of the Old IRA. The site was chosen for its historical links to the founding of the Volunteers and to the stockading overnight of the prisoners after the surrender at the General Post Office on the Saturday of Easter Week 1916. Daithi P. Hanly won the prize for the design competition in 1946. Work began in 1961 and was completed for the 1966 celebration of 1916. The bronze central sculpture of the Childen of Lir changing into human figures by Oisín Kelly, It was cast in the Marinelli Foundry in Florence.

The critical question posed at the start of this piece on the Cenotaph remains. What does the episode tell us about Costello's position on Irish nationalism?. Anne Dolan sees its completion as "bellowing the return of Fine Gael: the shout all the louder because of the indignity of coalition". She sees Costello's urgency in the project as registering his "personal claim to power and recognition, without the baggage of 1916 and reprieved executions, without the mystery or the provocation of deValera".

It is my opinion that the relatively unknown and uncontroversial Taoiseach completed the Cenotaph not out of any sense of inferiority or personal ego. Dolan goes further in deciphering what Costello was engaged upon. For her, the Cenotaph was Costello's rather grandiose link with his other great bequest to the nation, a Fine Gael Declaration of the Republic on Easter Sunday 1949. His urgency sought to knit a single garment of vindication through O'Higgins of the Commonwealth, Griffith the Dual Monarchist, Collins the soldier-warrior, to the heroes of the Easter Rising and their Republic. She concedes that her link between the Cenotaph and the Declaration of the Republic may be spurious. But it does demonstrate that John A Costello personally felt ready, able and free, to unite with Cumann na nGaedheal's heroes of yesteryear, despite his own Party's diffidence.

The fact remains that the new Cenotaph was never officially unveiled, though it was completed in October 1950. Costello, for whatever reason, decided not to proceed with any ceremonial occasion. This may be down to his understanding that to do so would cause aggravation to Sean MacBride, the IRA and to Fianna Fáil, for whom the Cenotaph might be a step too far. As we have seen Fine Gael, and even Cumann na nGaedheal, were none too energetic in commemorating these heroes. None of the Fine Gael Taoisigh, Liam Cosgrave, Garret Fitzgerald nor John Bruton, ever sought to have a ceremony at the cenotaph or even allow acess by the public to view it. The annual ceremony at Beal na Blath alone commands Fine Gael attention. There is some validity in Anne Dolan's assertion that, "In truth the Cenotaph was to be Costello's monument"[8]. Despite its elegance, it now stands as a largely unknown and unacknowledged memorial, being encroached upon by a car park for the Oireachtas. Unless someone takes an interest in it, the Cenotaph on Leinster Lawn might indeed be described as 'Costello's Folly'.

Detail of Kevin O' Higgins plaque at base of Cenotaph.

(L-R) Eamon deValera, Sean MacBride, Mrs. Costello
Col. McCormack, Mrs McCormack, John A. Costello.

Noel Browne   *Sean MacBride*

CHAPTER 11

COSTELLO AS TAOISEACH

On the day the new government was formed, the Minister for Defence Sean MacEoin called to Sean MacBride at his home, Roebuck House. He told MacBride that he had Costello's agreement to release the remaining republican prisoners from Portlaoise Jail. Liam Rice, aged 34 of Belfast and Eamon Smullen aged 24 of Dublin, were released on 26 February on health grounds. On 9 March, Tomas MacCurtain, son of the famous Lord Mayor of Cork, also called Tomas MacCurtain, whom MacBride had saved from hanging in 1941 was released together with Henry White and James Smith. MacBride was very proud of the fact that the Coalition Government was the first government since 1922 to hold no political prisoners[1]. Costello released a statement explaining the action of the Government. He said: "My colleague the Minister for Justice, after a careful examination of the facts and of the general position felt that a continuance of the detention of these three men would only result in the perpetuation of resentment and unrest and that the public interest would best be served by releasing them also. There is no truth whatever that any member of a particular party had anything to do with the decision". Costello added that he hoped it would be no longer necessary to maintain the present Special Military Tribunal[2]. Another six prisoners were later released. Brian Feeney writes that, "By September the Government had returned the bodies of executed IRA men to their families. The 1948 decision by the IRA Army Convention that there would be no military action in the Free State had also helped. Fearful of suppression after its reorganisation, the IRA was very anxious that the Government should be aware of this decision, so it was repeated in speeches at Bodenstown and regularly in Sein Féin literature"[3]. The IRA, which was very weak at that point, got an opportunity to regroup and plan a later campaign within the Six Counties[4].

In a radio broadcast to the nation on 25 February Costello said that chief of the fundamental objectives upon which the members of the government were united upon, was the determination to assert the right of the nation to complete territorial unity and to absolute freedom[5].

KEYNESIAN ECONOMICS

It was traditional that the Taoiseach was expected to get financial and economic advice from within the Department of Finance. WT Cosgrave and Eamon deValera had naturally been more concerned about fundamental constitutional affairs than economic ones. By participating in the European Recovery Programme, Ireland not only secured access to additional capital, but also opened itself to the concept of central economic planning. Patrick Lynch was at the time an assistant principal officer in the Department of Finance and was transferred to the Taoiseach's Department as an economic advisor to Costello. This was "without precedent and was further witness to the emergence of the debate about economic policy as the great political issue of the post-war years"[6]. Ronan Fanning states that this appointment "testified to Costello's conception of his own role as the mouth- piece of the Inter-Party Government on major issues which might split the coalition—a role he also assumed, for example, in the direction of the government's foreign policy. In short, the capital budget was too important a decision to be entrusted to the Department of Finance alone"[7]. Fanning writes that Costello's address to the Institute of Bankers on 19 November 1949 was the basis for the first capital budget by Patrick McGilligan. Costello said, "the government must budget primarily to allocate a certain part of the nation's finances to public purposes, but must also ensure that the resources of the nation are utilised in the way that can best advance the interests of the community. As far back as 1936, Lord Keynes declared that "the duty of ordering the current volume of investment cannot safely be left in private hands"[8].

Costello's adoption of Keynesian economics came from his discussions with James Dillon, Paddy Lynch and Alexis Fitzgerald, Costello's son-in-law and the most influential of the younger proponents of change in the Fine Gael party. When Paddy McGilligan, also a convert to expansionist thinking, came to introduce the first capital budget on 3 May 1950, it was clear that, despite contrary conservative views within his department, he had adopted the principles of Keynesian economics in line with his Taoiseach. His words indicated that he had moved radically from the traditional austerity of the Department of Finance, as he said his aim was "to promote, by an enlightened budgetary and investment policy, the continuous use of national resources in men and materials. A sound economic system is an essential condition of progress but, unfortunately, the automatic working of economic forces does not guarantee the available resources will adequately and unfailingly be employed to advance the national interest.

The modern democratic State is therefore rightly expected, not only to maintain the essential liberties of its citizens but also to take an active part in securing conditions favourable to their economic well being. This entails a continuous survey of the economic and social scene and effective intervention, not merely to protect the community against the worst effects of the periodic set-backs to which modern economies are subject, but to ensure that there is adequate capital investment to develop the national economy and to provide ample opportunities for productive employment"[9]. Of course it should be remembered that it was McGilligan who, with the backing of WT Cosgrave, and despite the conservative forces advising caution, had undertaken the Shannon Scheme as one of the first and most successful of the more ambitious experiments in public enterprises in Great Britain or Ireland.

※※※※

DEPARTMENT OF FINANCE

The new type of coalition government caused problems for those so used to single party administration. Costello was to say later that, "Civil servants, in my view, are getting too much control. The Fianna Fáil Government have landed themselves into the hands of the civil servants". Noel Browne, and of course most famously, Sean MacBride distrusted their civil servants initially. After sixteen years of Fianna Fáil rule, MacBride felt obliged to bring in his own private secretary, Louie O'Brien, to the Department of External Affairs. According to Conor Cruise O'Brien, whom MacBride appointed as Head of a new Information Section at Iveagh House, she advised MacBride on matters of personnel[10]. The Taoiseach's secretary Maurice Moynihan, was so distrusted by MacBride that he only attended the first two meetings of the new Government. Liam Cosgrave and Costello himself were in the habit of taking notes of decisions arrived at in cabinet"[11]. This possibly led to uncertainty, even in the short-term, on the minuting of certain important cabinet decisions. Continuous skirmishes occurred between the civil service and the government when Ministers flouted recognised procedures. Maurice Moynihan emphasised to Costello that Ministers had complete responsibility for memoranda going to government, and not their departments. When Noel Browne attacked the Department of Finance's reaction to his proposals for extra staff, deeming it impertinent and aggressive, he undermined the basis on which civil servants worked[12].

Sean MacBride caused great confusion in this regard by submitting proposals in areas completely outside his ministerial control. In my biography of Sean MacBride, I write, "The civil service and particularly the Department of Finance under JJ McElligott intended to get control of the Ministers as quickly as possible. Their main opponent in the early days was Sean MacBride, who bombarded the cabinet with memoranda on almost every issue before it. Although his brief was External Affairs, he got involved in all aspects of economic development"[13]. deValera asked MacBride, "Which was the driving Department charged with looking after the inter-departmental foreign trade committee as a whole?" MacBride replied, "By and large it is all centred in the Department of External Affairs, but you always have conflicting interests between the Department of Agriculture, Industry and Commerce, and very often the Department of Finance. By maintaining a policy of neutrality and by trying to provide a good service, the Department of External Affairs exercises a good deal of influence"[14]. MacBride succeeded in getting £36 million from Marshall Aid but seven-eights of it was a loan. He had looked for £120 million as a grant[15]. Ronan Fanning has written that an inspection of the Department of Finance archives reveals an explosive growth in the volume of documentation from the Department of External Affairs on MacBride's twin demands of money for re-afforestation and Health, via the Hospital Sweepstakes[16]. Noel Browne said that MacBride "would scan the cabinet agenda, and on those subjects in which he had a special interest, would submit a treatise to the Taoiseach.

In the early days, this memorandum was carefully unfolded and conscientiously read out by the Taoiseach to a politely attentive cabinet. It was treated with some respect"[17]. Conor Cruise O'Brien believed that Costello did not trust MacBride very far. However, they needed each other at that time[18].

The officials in the Department of Finance had to endure attacks from all sides of the political spectrum. Shortly after Costello came to power, Sean Lemass told him, "Beware of the Department of Finance. It has always been restrictive of development. Under Fianna Fáil it was not successful because we had our own policy and that went ahead undeterred by any impediments. With a Minister of Finance who has got the outlook of Mr. McGilligan, the Deputies opposite should beware. They will find that any plans for development which they may have in their minds coming into the Dáil will be lost and lost forever, in the dim recesses of the Department of Finance"[19]. However, Costello took a more equitable and practical attitude when he said, "not withstanding the familiar wail of the Department of Finance to which we have been accustomed to for so many years, I have the greatest admiration for the Department's officials, who have stood rock-like against the assaults of all sorts of queer characters in the shape of Ministers since 1922. They have their point of view. They have a very distinct, a very valuable function to fulfil in the machinery of government of this State. They are the watchdogs of public finance". However, he declared that their function was not to create economic policy, rather to work within the framework of a policy, economic and financial, devised by a government.

They were under an obligation to point out dangers but their function was to carry out loyally the policy of the government. His main complaint against Finance officials was that they tried to be better than the government in pointing out dangers. It was the Minister's duty to listen to them, brief the Government and for the latter to act for the public good as a whole. He advised against Deputies pretending that officials of the Department "were the enemies of the public" [20]. Ronan Fanning blames the inward looking nature of the Department of Finance officials for the very late application to join the International Monetary Fund, which began in 1947. The IMF's policy was that countries getting Marshall Aid should only get money from it, if "absolutely necessary". The Department was content to function in the Sterling area since Marshal Aid began to cover Ireland's dollar deficit. When eventually in 1957, Ken Whittaker, acting on Gerard Sweetman's instruction, approached the IMF, he found that their door was wide open for Ireland[21].

❊❊❊❊

COLLECTIVE RESPONSIBILITY

Costello, despite his high professional reputation, had little of a personal commanding presence. His authority would only be developed with time. The notion of collective responsibility established by WT Cosgrave in August 1922 disappeared with different Ministers feeling free to speak their minds in the Dáil and outside. Paddy McGilligan, in particular felt that this was no bad thing as politics was a matter of compromise. He asked, "Have we got to the stage when, on a matter which may be an important point of policy when it is decided, we cannot have freedom of speech? Have we got to the stage when men, because they join the Government circle, must all when they go out of the council chambers, speak the same language?"[22]. When Sean MacBride attacked Joseph Brennan, the Governor of the Central Bank, the latter sought assurances from Costello that MacBride did not represent government policy. Costello, without answering Brennan's question, informed him that in an inter-party government it was legitimate for a Minister in an individual or party capacity to disagree from the government view[23]. This practice understandably discommoded Fianna Fáil, which naturally hoped that each ministerial division was evidence of a split within the government. That party declared that the Constitution demanded the government take collective responsibility. The *Irish Times* later said, "The Government has been able to stand all the strains that have been put upon it precisely because it is so elastic. If Mr. Costello had attempted to discipline his Ministers, as they would have been disciplined by a party leader, he and they would have been out of office long ago"[24]. Noel Browne recounted, how on an early occasion in the Dáil, when he was being assailed on the hospital programme by Sean Lemass, Costello came to his rescue. Browne wrote, "On that occasion I was grateful to John Costello who, on the night of the debate, took on the reply to Lemass – I was certainly not up to that level of competition yet. Good lawyer that he was, he had no trouble with his brief"[24].

BATTLE OF BALTINGLAS

One Minister, James Everett, blotted the copybook of the new government when against departmental advice he decided to remove the Baltinglas Co. Wicklow Post Office, from the family that had traditionally managed it. Miss Katie Cooke wished to transfer the post office to her niece Helen Cooke. Helen had been running the post office for the previous fourteen years on behalf of her aunt. She had been brought up in Scotland and had been a nun in the Poor Clares for four years and an activist on the Republican side in the civil war, after she left the convent. Under new rules the position was advertised and Helen applied. Instead the job was given to 27-year-old Michael Farrell, the son of a former Labour councillor and friend of Everett's. The Farrells owned a public house as well as, grocery, butchers, and drapery shops. This led to local opposition which when mobilised, refused to allow the transfer to take place. A furious debate took place in the Dail[25].

One Independent TD, Patrick Cogan, who had been supporting the government, withdrew that support on the basis that Ministers should not be involved in administrative decisions. The transfer of a telephone line to the new post office was a cause for further unrest as the locals protested, and fifty Gardai had to protect the linesmen. In the Dáil the Taoiseach denied a private members motion for an inquiry and the local branch of Clann na Poblachta resigned in protest[26]. An ex-Fine Gael TD resigned from the party as a protest. The new post office was boycotted, and any local shop which did not support the boycott, was in turn boycotted. Nine days after the transfer, on 21 December the new postmaster resigned. Everett promised an independent appointments body for sub-postmasters, and Miss Cooke was appointed in late January 1951. Within a few years the Farrells settled in Rosslare. Helen Cooke retired in 1963 and went to live in Australia with her two sisters. She died in 1972[27].

The high moral ground of the new government became somewhat slippier after this debacle, and Costello's loyalty to another party leader was costly. In the middle of this debacle, most pressure was exerted on the new Taoiseach who proved quite flexible in the situation of inter-party government. He said, "I had four parties and six Independents who were looking to be represented in the Cabinet. That caused very considerable difficulties because all the interests had to be considered"[28]. It was clear that the *raison d'etre* of the government and Taoiseach was to keep Fianna Fáil out. Costello maintained that the coalition was formed on the basis of goodwill and found no great difficulty in teasing out all problems, all personal jealousies.

John A. Costello down through the years.

James Dillon regarded Costello as a bad chairman, saying that he would frequently interrupt business with digressing anecdotes, "to the extent than one would sometimes despair of doing any business. He was a good man and everyone was so devoted to him that when the chips were down no one would bring him to order". However, Maurice Manning comments that in this, Dillon may not have appreciated his Taoiseach's skill in playing for time in tricky situations[29].

Many commentators have written that Costello was ill-equipped for the task ahead. In this, I think that even at this remove they underestimate the man. Henry Patterson wrote, "Costello had few of the resources for strong leadership. His personal style was more suited to the court room than the political platform"[30]. I think that Patterson as with others are influenced by the persona of deValera, who so dominated his cabinet. There are different styles of leadership and management of people, and issues can be equally handled by a discerning *primus inter pares*, when all realise that they are together involved in a common enterprise like the first Inter-Party Government. Costello had a long parliamentary experience and a lengthy spell at the cabinet table as Attorney General. He knew what his various Ministers and their parties wanted and needed. As far as practical he tried to facilitate them.

ST. PATRICK'S COLLEGE MAYNOOTH

Henry Patterson also points out, "most significant in limiting the scope for conflict was the government's willingness to borrow to finance capital expenditure and a shared set of Catholic and nationalistic values". The Taoiseach, and four other members of cabinet were members of the Knights of St. Columbanus. The occasion of the Holy Year in 1950 saw Costello, Sean MacBride and President O'Kelly visit the Vatican. St. Patrick's College Maynooth, the Catholic national seminary, was in dire financial difficulties. In 1948 it had called in the Belfast accountants, Magee and Hillian to advise it. They advised a national collection for capital works, which was very successful. The College continued to run on a deficit and it approached the Government for an annual grant. Patrick Corish writes, "The Taoiseach John A Costello showed himself most sympathetic and got unanimous support from his colleagues. The President of the College then prepared a detailed memorandum for Costello and his Minister for Finance Patrick McGilligan". The successful bargaining point lay in the College's major role in the training of secondary teachers, which, it was argued, was an educational role rather than religious. "The Government agreed to include Maynooth in institutions sharing the university grant, and allocated £15,000 a year, with a promise to raise this to £20,000, if needed. It was raised to this level in 1957, and raised further to £27,500 in 1964"[31].

✽✽✽✽

DEATH OF A PRESIDENT

The first President of Ireland, Douglas Hyde, died in July 1949. His funeral illustrated the strictures on relations between the churches, which impinged even on State occasions. As the hearse moved slowly to St. Patrick's Cathedral, the official mourners from the nation's political and educational establishment huddled in an ally near the Cathedral, unable in an era before official ecumenism to attend the service for Hyde, that most ecumenical of men[32].

The poet Austin Clarke wrote in *Burial of a President:*

> *"Tricoloured and beflowered*
> *coffin of our President,*
> *where fifty mourners bowed,*
> *was trestled in the gloom.*
> *At the last bench*
> *two Catholics,*
> *the French Ambassador and I,*
> *knelt down outside.*
> *Professors in cap and gown*
> *Costello, his cabinet*
> *in government cars, hiding*
> *around the corner, ready,*
> *tall hat in hand"*

President Douglas Hyde

CHAPTER 12

DECLARING THE REPUBLIC

The suprising cicumstances of the announcement in Ottawa, Canada, that the Irish Government intended to repeal the External Relations Act of 1936, declare a Republic and leave the Commonwealth, have given rise to many theories as to the genesis and constitutional probity of Costello's actions. The eminent Canadian historian, Don Akenson has written, "On 7th September 1948, John Aloysius Costello, Taoiseach, made a startling announcement when on a visit to Ottawa, Canada, that Éire would become a republic. This caught everyone by surprise, although Costello's cabinet colleagues pretended that they had known all along about the idea and that it was a cabinet decision. For the succeeding months, Irish foreign policy was made with the same thoughtfulness exhibited by a downhill skier racing before an avalanche. Quick, it was: a Bill declaring Ireland to be a republic was rushed through the Oireachtas and became law on 21 December 1948, and the republic was officially proclaimed 18 April 1949"[1]. Noel Browne famously subscribed to a similar theory and as a cabinet member, is entitled to some credence. But in his autobiography Browne appears overly intent on self-justification and on settling scores with his colleagues, rather than being a disinterested witness. However, his persona as the fighting prince done down by conservative ogres has certainly won the publicity war in many areas and together with the leaking of the story by the *Sunday Independent,* has contributed to the mythology of what might really have happened during 1948. What the Sunday newspaper story actually said was that both William Norton and Sean MacBride had made speeches recently stating that the External Relations act was to go, and that Costello's recent speech in Canada had confirmed this. The speech had been approved by the cabinet long before Costello delivered it

I believe that many people do not give enough attention to the longevity of Costello's involvement in matters of State. His contribution to the Dáil debate on the introduction of the 1936 Act makes his position clear. He declared that he could understand it, if deValera declared a republic then. Of course, the Fine Gael party position on the External Relations Act and membership of the Commonwealth was confused. Mulcahy favoured the Act and the Commonwealth, while Tom O'Higgins was against. Costello, who had been his party's front bench spokesman on External Affairs for the previous fifteen years, intended to carry on deValera's tradition of being directly involved in foreign policy, despite MacBride being the Minister. Costello's position was that Ireland was not in the Commonwealth since it had ceased attending Commonwealth meetings. Sean MacBride recounts a story told him by Costello. During Costello's early political career he was outside Haddington Road church to conduct an election meeting. He heard one young man explain that a Free State meeting was "the pro-English people who want to sell out the country to Britain". According to MacBride this had a profound affect on Costello, who set out to change that impression of his party had created for itself[2].

deValera, who played his usual 'magician of political metaphysics' role in this, as in most political debates, had a draft of a Bill to drop the Act drawn up in November 1947, by the Attorney General Cearbhall O Dalaigh. That did not mention the State becoming a Republic. As has been already noted, despite Clann na Poblachta campaigning on the republican ticket, deValera did not mention the Act during the election. Shortly after the election, Lord Rugby advised the British "the annulment of the External Relations Act will not long be delayed. No party has left the door open for any other course"[3].

Much is made of the influence of Sean MacBride in the matter. Yet it would appear likely that his direct involvement was in fact minimal, despite his probable involvement in leaking the story to the Editor of the *Sunday Independent*. MacBride, due to the disappointing election result for his party acknowledged that Clann na Poblachta could not " claim that in this election we secured a mandate from the people that would enable us to repeal, or seek to repeal, the External Relations Act and other measures as are inconsistent with our status as an independent republic. These, therefore, have to remain in abeyance for the time being"[4]. However, James Dillon was not so inclined on the matter, when speaking in the Dáil that same day. MacBride answered one of his recalcitrant TD's Peadar Cowan in the Dáil in July 1948, "We are certainly not a member of the British Commonwealth of Nations". When deValera assented to this, MacBride added, "as Deputy deValera knows, well knows, we have, for external purposes, no Head of State"[5].

Costello led a strong delegation to London to negotiate a new Anglo-Irish Trade Agreement in June 1948. This agreement gave Ireland access to British markets without any reference to membership of the Commonwealth. However, Costello noted that at an official occasion at number 10 Downing St, the British Prime Minster Clement Atlee proposed a toast to "The King", thereby implying that Ireland continued to owe allegiance to the Crown and remained a member of the British Commonwealth of Nations[6]. The British Nationality Bill allowed Irish citizens who were not British subjects equal access in like manner as it has effect in relation to British subjects[7] to "any laws in force in any part of the UK and Colonies". However the relation between Britain and Ireland on constitutional status remained strained, as Sean MacBride held that Ireland's status was that of a Republic since 1937[8].

It is clear from Costello's early actions on republican prisoners and statements on a radical form of nationalism that he firmly intended to move quickly to a new and clear status in relation to the Commonwealth. This was an organic development for him from his early days as a legal official in the Free State apparatus and more recently as a front bench spokesman for Fine Gael on constitutional matters. As he said himself, "I made up my mind to repeal the External Relations Act 1936, as soon as possible. I reached this conclusion entirely on my own and never at any time did Sean MacBride try to force me on the matter.

The controversy was brought to a head in the debate on the Taoiseach's Estimate in August 1948[9]. Of course, in doing it the way he did, he outwitted Fianna Fáil and Clann na Poblachta, who thought of themselves as the republican parties.

On 28 July 1948, Peadar Cowan TD asked Costello in the Dáil exactly how Ireland had ceased to be a member of the Commonwealth. Costello replied that it was a gradual development and that, though Ireland was sovereign, independent and democratic, it was associated with the Commonwealth. He later stated, "Our association depends on the reciprocal exchange of concrete benefits in such matters as trade and citizenship rights, the principle of consultation and cooperation in matters of common concern and on many ties of blood and friendship that exist between us and these other great nations whose population includes so many of our own people". He later added that Ireland "has ceased to be formally a member but is associated with the other members". Because that association was a free one, it "can be terminated by unilateral action". William Norton said, " it would do our national self-respect good, both at home and abroad, if we were to proceed without delay to abolish the External Relations Act". deValera added "Go ahead; you will get no opposition from us"[10.] Costello was also aware that there was a possibility that Peadar Cowan or even James Dillon might introduce a Private Members Bill abolishing the Act[11].

The Government then made a unanimous decision to introduce legislation to repeal the Act when the Dáil reassembled after the summer recess. Importantly, Noel Browne appears to have been absent from this cabinet meeting. More importantly the decision was not recorded or announced. Paddy Lynch has confirmed to the taking of this decision[12]. Freddy Boland has said that the mater was discussed twice in cabinet with a consensus for repeal, but that he was not aware of a decision[13]. Costello had been very proud of the 1931 Statute of Westminster, saying it "justified all the arguments that Griffith and Collins had put forward in the Treaty debates. It received its fullest implementation in the Republic of Ireland Act, which enabled us to clear out of the Commonwealth in quite a lawful manner"[14].

Lord Rugby reported to the British government on 16/8/48 "I have no doubt that it has been decided to repeal the Act. I expect this to happen soon after the reassembly of the Dáil in November"[15].

At the last cabinet meeting of the summer, on 19 August, the Taoiseach's speech to the forthcoming meeting of the Bar Association of Canada was, unusually, read and approved in cabinet[16]. That same meeting also agreed to send an *aide memoire* to the British government recommending that the title of Irish envoys to Commonwealth countries should be 'ambassador' rather than High Commissioner. It also decided that Ireland would not be represented as a member of the Commonwealth at the proposed meeting of 'Commonwealth Prime Ministers', but postponed a decision to attend 'otherwise than as a member of the Commonwealth'.

Costello's journey to Canada was eventful from the start. As his well wishers assembled to see him off at Cobh on 24 August, bad weather prevented the tender from approaching the *Mauretania* until the following day. In New York he was received and entertained by Mayor O'Dwyer. After a two-day stay Costello's party departed New York from Grand Central Station for Montreal on the over-night train. Senator John Hackett of the Canadian Bar Association and John Hearne, Ireland's High Commissioner in Canada, met them. The status of Costello's visit to Canada and the USA was uncertain. Normally he would have stayed with the Governor General in Canada. However, he stayed instead with John Hearne. His attitude at a press conference was that, as he was a guest of the Canadian Bar Association in Montreal, he should not express views on controversial political subjects. At a garden party Costello and his wife felt snubbed by Lord Alexander, Govener General of Canada. On Wednesday 1 September, Costello delivered his speech to the Bar Association. On the Saturday 4 September, he attended a formal dinner given by Lord Alexander in Ottawa. The expected toast to the President of Ireland did not take place. A replica of the cannon 'Roaring Meg' used in the siege of Derry, was placed at Costello's table. Ian McCabe writes that some vitriolic opponents of Fine Gael accused Costello of being drunk at this dinner[17]. McCabe then adds strangely that this accusation might have put Costello on the back foot about admitting that the Government had not taken any formal decision the Act. Paddy Lynch, who was with Costello said that Alexander "seemed either anti-social or slightly hostile in his few exchanges with Costello"[18]. These incidents certainly affected Costello's mood, as he communicated to the Canadian Minister for Justice, Louis St. Laurent, and later to the Prime Minister, Mr. William MacKenzie King. It may be pertinent to note James Dillon's opinion that Costello was "a hot-tempered man"[19].

The next day's *Sunday Independent* carried a headline "External Relations Act to go". The editor Hector Legge, a close friend of James Dillon, wrote the story. Despite all that had gone on previously, the newspaper story caused a sensation then, and the identity of its inspired source since. MacBride immediately advised Costello not to comment on the story at a press conference scheduled for the Tuesday. This gave Costello plenty of time to consider his position. He received conflicting advice on the options open to him. (1). Refuse to comment. (2). Deny the story (3). Confirm the story (4). Say the Dáil would decide. Costello himself said about the leak, "This announcement caused me not merely surprise, but great worry. It posed for me a very formidable problem. I knew I would have to respond to it. As the report was true in fact and as the Government intended to repeal the Act, there was nothing in honesty and decency open to me but to admit the truth. The decision to do so was entirely my own and taken with a full sense of responsibility"[20].

At the press conference Costello confirmed the newspaper story. He also said that his High Commissioners would be called Ambassadors. He asserted "there was nothing to prevent Ireland continuing in an even closer association with the British Commonwealth"[21].

At a dinner that same evening with Mr. Mackenzie King, toasts were proposed to the King and the President of Ireland. The Canadians were bemused that such a decision was made in Ottawa. At a lengthy meeting with MacKenzie King, Costello explained the genesis of the Government's position. He wanted to take the gun out of Irish politics, and feared that Fianna Fáil might make the running on it if he did not move swiftly. He also hoped that partition could be ended and that a united Ireland strategically placed between North America and Europe could play an important role in the North Atlantic Treaty Organisation[22.]

The Irish newspapers naturally gave banner headlines to Costello's announcement that the Act was to be "scrapped". The die was cast irrespective of whether it had been a formal decision of cabinet or not. The fact that there was no consultation with the British could have been strategic, but as Manning put it, "traditional courtesies had been discarded"[23].

The *Irish Times* reported on 8 September 1948 that the Taoiseach had announced the previous night in Ottawa that Éire was preparing to scrap the External Relations Act of 1936. It said that the cabinet had already decided to sever the last constitutional link with the British Crown. deValera had indicated that the Opposition would not vote against such a measure which would strip the 1921 Treaty of its provisions. The paper also stated that the cabinet had also decided that Éire would not join a defence pact with the Western European countries unless partition was ended. Costello had also reiterated that Éire would continue in association with Britain, but not as a formal member of the Commonwealth. Éire's representatives in Commonwealth countries would henceforth be called Ambassadors rather than High Commissioners. He was certain that Éire could persuade many of its former citizens to return home, noting that the population of the country had dropped from 8 million in 1800 to less than 3 million.

Costello told a Canadian parliamentary committee that the greatest need of the country at present was American dollars. He hoped to negotiate a loan from the USA under the European Recovery Programme for about $121 millons, which would be used to revitalise the agricultural industry and to buy capital goods for its industries. It was also planning a scheme against tuberculosis. Costello was asked whether Éire had any difficulty with communists. He replied, "None whatever, because we are a Catholic country". "So is Italy" said a correspondent, to which Costello replied, "Well, we are more Catholic".

At the Department of External Affairs in Dublin, Sean MacBride, like the staff, appeared to be aghast with the *Sunday Independent* leak. When I was researching my book on Sean MacBride in 1992, Louie O'Brien, who had been his private secretary at the Department, was one of my sources. I interviewed her twice at length. She told me, "We suffered from the same shock as Costello was suffering over there in Canada. The wires between Canada and Ireland lit up that night, as Costello sought advice from Dublin".

I later exchanged correspondence with Louie. She wrote:

"Garden Flat
51 Pembroke
Dublin 4

Dear Tony,

I feel I have to explain about the MacBride – Noel Browne conversation in the Russell Hotel. If I gave you the impression I was there [in Hotel] I was wrong. I was there [in Iveagh House] when Sean came back from that meeting and I took down a detailed note from Sean of Browne's comments.

As to Sean's having sent a memorandum to Costello in Canada: one has to remember that we did not know that it was Sean who had leaked the information to Legge. We were all disgusted that it could have happened – Sean joining in! It was a long time afterwards that I learned the truth – from the Newspaper man that Sean had chosen to leak the misinformation to Legge. Afterwards I was able to believe that it was Sean who had set out Costello's options.

It was the first glimpse I got of the feet of clay!

So many dishonest and dishonourable acts followed with the years that I became totally disillusioned.

Don't hesitate to contact me if I can help in any way.

Yours sincerely
Louie O'B.

I asked Louie subsequently why she had not challenged MacBride on the matter. She replied on 5 March 1992: "I was wondering what the explanation was for not telling S. Mac B. that I knew it was he who had leaked the scoop to Legge, of course I did not know for many years afterwards that it was MacB. who had done the leaking".

As Louie O'Brien has been a source for many writers on this episode, including myself, it is worth recording that she had become very antagonistic towards MacBride in later years over personal matters.

MacBride's own account of the reaction in his Department was,

"There was complete consternation when they realised that we were going to repeal the External Relations Act, because it was exposing Fianna Fáil policy. This could have been done at any time but we were doing it and showing that it could be done without any repercussion. Most officials in the Department were strongly Fianna Fáil"[24.]. Patrick Keating writes that MacBride's views on the Act could not be ignored and found support within cabinet. Keating continues, "Under these circumstances, there could be no return to positive membership of the Commonwealth, and Mr. Costello abandoned this traditional aim of his own party and declared the Republic, retaining some semblance of independence by publicly announcing the policy, without prior notice and when outside the country"[25]. Garret Fitzgerald blamed the influence of MacBride for the announcement. He writes, " After the election MacBride became Minister of External Affairs. I still recall my disillusionment at this development. His later conversion to constitutionalism had seemed to me ambivalent. My unhappiness was intensified when the Taoiseach announced the Government intended to declare a Republic. At that time, this clearly meant leaving the Commonwealth, for the evolution of which into a body of sovereign independent States John Costello, as Attorney General, with people like my father, Paddy McGilligan and Kevin O'Higgins, had worked so successfully in the years before 1932. Moreover in the months that followed that announcement the Government also decided not to join NATO. I attributed the dynamic of this decision to MacBride also"[26]. Dr. Fitzgerald appears to 'forget' that the Government was led by a Fine Gael Taoiseach, and that Costello, after de Valera, took a firm grip on external relations, despite MacBride, being the Minister. Richard Mulcahy commented "Costello must have been drinking some heady wine in Canada"[27].

Costello wrote to Bill Norton shortly after the announcement, on 11/9/48, admitting that, "As you well know, I very nearly, if not actually 'declared' the Republic – in Ottawa above all places. I will explain when I return why I decided to state publicly that we intended to repeal the External Relations Act. It was really the article in the *Sunday Independent* that decided me"[28].

This is the truth of the matter. Hector Legge maintained in later years, in correspondence in the *Irish Times* with Noel Browne, that his story was "written from journalistic intuition". Browne's forthright response was understandable as he replied to Legge, "Only a political imbecile or an accomplice in the deceit would have swallowed the story without taking the cub-reporter's precaution of 'checking it out'"[29]. MacBride's direct or indirect involvement, ironically worked against him on a personal level, as it only reinforced Costello's determination to personally handle the already agreed policy of declaring a Republic. Thus MacBride lost out on the historic possibility of taking such legislation through the Oireachtas. A meeting of the cabinet took place in Dublin on 9 September. It considered a memo from MacBride, which accompanied a draft of a Bill to repeal the Act. Section 4 (2) sought leave to describe the State as the 'Republic of Ireland' in any instrument concluded before the passing of the Act. The memo contained a certificate for immediate action on the Bill, due to 'recent developments have made it imperative that a decision should be arrived at immediately'. Thus the formality of what had already been agreed was put into emergency mode as approval was given for the drafting of a Bill repealing the Act[30].

❋❋❋❋

A meeting of some cabinet ministers occurred at Costello's home on 7 October where Noel Browne claims Costello offered his resignation in the knowledge that he had acted unconstitutionally. Several Ministers deny this[31]. A formal meeting of the cabinet on 11 October approved "the action by the Taoiseach during his visit to Canada and the United States"[32].

The British response contained a warning that repeal of the Act could affect the most favoured nation treatment enjoyed by Ireland. A meeting was called and the Irish sought the involvement of the Commonwealth leaders. The Commonwealth Prime Minister Conference was then in session at Chequers. An invitation to Costello and other Ministers was issued to come to Chequers. MacBride and McGilligan went and met the leaders of Britain, Canada, Australia, New Zealand, and the Commonwealth and British cabinet secretaries. The British wanted a firm line with the Irish if they left the Commonwealth. However, to the annoyance of the British, these other leaders proved very favourable to their common ties with Ireland. The Irish cabinet later reciprocated saying that while Ireland was not in the Commonwealth, ties of blood and kinship, tradition and economic links, had long established rights and privileges with the countries of the Commonwealth[33].

The *Irish Times,* was appalled by the move out of the Commonwealth and held that Clann na Poblachta was calling the shots. Costello refuted this, saying, the Coalition partners were at one on the matter[34]. The Archbishop of Dublin, John Charles McQuaid, who favoured a close connection with the Commonwealth, told Sir John Maffey that he could not imagine that the Costello Government would commit the folly of repealing the External Relations Act[35]. Maffey was the British representative in Ireland at the time of McQuaid's ordination as Archbishop. Lord Rugby reported, "Mr Costello has conducted this business in a slapdash and amateur fashion, one by one loose individual pronouncements have started an unexpected, unnecessary and unfortunate drift, which has certainly not increased general confidence in the Government and the man at the wheel"[36].

Deirdre MacMahon writes that "If as Costello was wont to claim in later years, the decision had been agreed in cabinet, this reflects even more unfavourably on his government, since the archives do not reveal that there was any preparation for such a momentous step, which was bound to have serious implications for Irish trade and for the thousands of Irish people living in Britain"[37]. Conor Cruise O'Brien writes that quite early on in the life of the new Government "the conduct of Ireland's international affairs became a more serious matter and propaganda concerning it also began, to a great extent, to be taken out of MacBride's hands and therefore out of mine. MacBride induced the new government to pass the Republic of Ireland Act". Dr. O'Brien adds that this changed nothing, as the 1937 Constitution remained in full force after 1950, as before[38].

On 12 November as the Bill was in its final drafting, the British prepared an *aide memoire* claiming that repeal of the Act would make Ireland a foreign country as regards trade and citizens rights. However, the Commonwealth leaders in Paris were shown the note and objections were made. Another more conciliatory note was drafted and sent the following day calling for a postponement of the Bill. Again Commonwealth leaders undercut the British and MacBride sought a meeting with them. An Irish delegation went to Paris on 15 November. There a proposal emerged that citizens of Ireland and Commonwealth countries would have reciprocal rights due to the fact of a special relationship. The British were forced to accept this formula by the attitude of the Commonwealth leaders[39] .

It would have been correct protocol for the Minister for External Affairs to pilot the Bill - the Republic of Ireland Bill - through the Dáil. However, significantly the Taoiseach himself introduced the Bill in the Dáil on 17 November. Noel Browne has written, somewhat tongue-in-cheek, "It was surely both ill-mannered and ungracious of Fine Gael and Mr. Costello to deprive Sean MacBride of his right as the relevant Minister, to introduce the Bill. Mr. Costello choose to introduce the Bill himself[40].

On the second reading of the Bill on 24 November Costello made a major speech on the matter. He began by expressing his pride at the privilege of sponsoring the Bill. At the same time, he acknowledged that there were members on both sides of the Dáil who had merited such a privilege more than he. The Bill would end the country's long and tragic association with the British Crown and make it an independent republic. There was no hostility meant to the British people or their Crown. The Bill was intended to be an instrument of domestic peace, of national unity, and of international concord and goodwill. He acknowledged that there had been much arid, futile and unending discussions on the constitutional and international relations over the previous 25 years. The Bill did not burn any bridges to closer friendship with Britain. He said the Treaty did put order on Anglo-Irish relations, and those who undertook the task of honouring it, had walked the *via dolorosa* for ten bitter years and achieved international recognition. After 1932, the new governments carried out a different policy but accomplished a close relationship with Britain. The removal of the Oath and the 1937 Constitution all played a part. He acknowledged that over the last 25 years Ireland had a close relationship with the nations of the Commonwealth, many of which saw Ireland as a mother country. He also acknowledged the close ties with Great Britain in trade, commerce, religion through our missionaries, and movement of peoples. He said that the Bill removed all obstacles to a close relationship with Britain, apart from partition. He mentioned Canada in several ways and thanked particularly Mr. Mackenzie King in recent times, but also Mr. St. Laurent and Mr Pearson. He named Dr. Evatt of Australia and Peter Frazer of New Zealand. Costello spoke particularly about Ireland's relation with South Africa mentioning that, "we looked with admiration and respect and gave whatever support we could to the efforts of the South Africans to achieve their independence nearly 50 years ago. That admiration was increased by the fact that some

Irishmen, headed by the father of the present Minister for External Affairs, [Major John MacBride] fought and helped the Boers in their struggle during that period, and all the time we were working at these Imperial Conferences, the representatives of South Africa came step by step with us in our efforts to achieve the constitutional victories which we ultimately achieved".

He said that his reason for dwelling on the help received from all these countries was to make it known that it would have been unthinkable to jeopardise our relations with these great nations. He acknowledged that the press in England had written malicious and poisonous propaganda recently about Ireland.

Addressing English people, he said that the Irish were a race, with a distinctive nationality, a distinctive language, an ancient culture all its own. When attempts made to attain freedom were regarded as treason to the British Crown, its ministers and officials acted against Irish patriots. The other countries in the Commonwealth did not have such a history with the Crown. Those who signed the Treaty felt obliged to honour it, including the oath to the King. However when the 1937 Constitution was introduced and accepted by the other party to the Treaty without demur, those who objected were released from their obligation. Costello then quoted what he had said during the debate on the 1936 Act, indicating that he thought it a constitutional nonsense. He quoted James Dillon asking, "Are we a republic or are we not, for nobody seems to know?" deValera replied " This is a republic. We are associated with the Commonwealth". Costello recalled his own statement that he would have no problem if a republic were then declared. He said that the reason he accepted his role as Taoiseach was "to take the gun out of Irish politics and bring about unity and domestic concord in our lives". That is the reason for this Bill. He acknowledged "that while partition remained we could not claim that Emmets' epitaph was in place", but he claimed that the Bill assisted in that process.

deValera supported the Bill only regretting that he was not the Taoiseach to introduce it. The *Irish Times* again was not impressed with Costello's speech writing that, " Nothing that the Taoiseach said yesterday can justify what appears to have been a flagrant breach of political faith" by Fine Gael as the Commonwealth party[41]. The Bill became law on 21 December. It came into effect on the symbolic day of Easter Monday, 18 April 1949, amid great official celebration. However, Fianna Fáil refused to participate and Sean MacBride himself was abroad on the occasion. Noel Browne wrote, "MacBride, in a pitiable protest, did not appear at the Easter Sunday march. In his absence I acted as Minister for External Affairs at the circus"[42]. Messages of congratulation came from the Pope, President Truman, King George VI, Atlee and the Prime Ministers of the Commonwealth.

Representations from the Northern Ireland Government led to the Ireland Bill 1949, being passed in Britain which said that "in no event will Northern Ireland or any part thereof cease to be part of His Majesty's dominions and of the United Kingdom without the consent of the Parliament of Northern Ireland".

Public meetings in the South vigorously opposed this. In the Dáil, a unanimous motion was passed condemning the Bill. Costello spoke on 10 May. He declared that the British Government, which had introduced the Bill, had learned nothing from the last 169 years nor the last 35 years of the consequences of their actions to the Irish people. Apparently the British Government, whether it be Tory or Labour would learn nothing from a friendly or peaceful Ireland, declaring it a matter that "makes one almost despair". He bemoaned the fact that the Bill had secured that hundreds of thousands of Irish men and women, in the territories of Tyrone, Fermanagh, Derry, South Armagh and South Down, had to remain under the North Eastern Parliament against their will, by the creation of an artificial entity created by the British Act of Parliament 1920. He finished in some anger saying, "that part of our country has been taken from us and is being annexed. We wanted to get the unity of our country on the basis of friendliness with the North and with Great Britain. We no longer need to play the role of the wounded Samson. We can hit the British Government in their prestige and in their pride and in their pocket"[42].

deValera reiterated all that the Taoiseach had said. He was amazed that the British 'would introduce such a measure purporting to confirm the partition of our country'. It appeared to him that it had been inspired to give our people "a slap in the face". He speculated that it might be due to the Irish people deciding that they wanted a republican form of government. He said, "I myself had declared that position in 1945". He asserted the right of the Irish people to claim the whole of the national territory. He agreed with the Taoiseach that some British ministers did not know the facts.

The new British representative in Dublin, Gilbert Laithwaite reporting to London criticised Costello's " petulance, his refusal to see the argument for the other side, his readiness to appeal to prejudice. Mr Costello fails to recognise the difference between the tactics and phrases that can properly be adopted by an advocate anxious to move the feelings of a jury, and those arguments appropriate to a Prime Minister"[43].

Attlee in admitting that the Ireland Bill copper fastened partition, said that he had so warned the Irish at Chequers. He then claimed to have assumed that for the Irish, leaving the Commonwealth was more important than ending partition. Thus the Irish paid this heavy price for the declaration of the republic.

ANTI-PARTITION CAMPAIGN

deValera had already been waging his own politically motivated anti-partition campaign since losing office. He travelled to the USA, Australia and Britain. He received a great welcome in America, including being received at the White House by President Truman.[44]. As Conor Cruise O'Brien has put it, "This put pressure on his successors, the Inter-Party Government, to show at least as much sense of urgency about the problem as Mr. deValera was doing in Opposition[45]

Costello had no option but to join in the campaign. He had broadcast to the USA on St Patrick's Day 1948, telling his listeners that the government intended to "bend our energies to the restoration of the territorial integrity of our native land".

He then, rather unwisely, claimed that Irish people in America and other countries "could not be expected to be fully directed towards the task of helping European recovery. While partition persists, the defences of western civilisation are weakened. The world cannot afford to let the unnatural partition of our country distract the generous sympathies of the Irish race" He hoped that by next year "Mother Ireland will be able to walk through four of her beautiful green fields, and that she will walk with the walk of a queen"[46]. In July 1948 Costello told the Dáil that, For the first time since 1922, this cabinet will give some hope of bringing back to this country the six north eastern counties"[47]. This was in reference to a holiday visit to Ireland by Attlee, in the course of which, MacBride entertained vain hopes of persuading him of the inequity of partition[48].

In May 1949 the Irish government set up an Irish News Agency to promote anti-partition around the world. A snap general election called in the North by Sir Basil Brooke, saw Costello invite the political parties to an All-Party Anti-Partition Conference in the Mansion House. It considered how they might help anti-partition candidates in the North. Some £20,000 was collected outside church gates. This figure soon doubled. This action prompted a greater number of Unionists to vote than usual and they won a resounding victory. The British Ambassador reported to his Government, " Mr. Costello continues to hold his Government together. Personally very friendly and approachable, he appears to feel bound from time to time to make speeches, particularly on the partition issue, which are uncalled for and unhelpful"[49]. One result of Costello's speeches was that Fine Gael virtually outmanoeuvred MacBride, to the extent that Costello's voice came to be recognised as being at least as authentically emotional on the evils of partition as Clann na Poblachta.

The Mansion House Committee, consisting of deValera, MacBride, Norton and Frank Aiken met and decided that in the light of their negative experience in the Northern elections, it would not intervene in the forthcoming British Election.

Some elected Northern nationalist began to seek permission to occupy seats in the Dáil. MacBride favoured this. deValera in line with an earlier decision by WT Cosgrave opposed it saying,"it would be a demonstration without any value, and would have a lot of evil consequences"[50.]. However, after much debate and despite pressure from Clann na Poblachta, Costello turned down the request.

NATO

Costello was extremely anti-communist and pro-American. He told the Dáil in 1946 that "it should above all be clear that, whether or not we were neutral in the last war, there can never be any question again of this country being neutral in any future war" [51.] Sean MacBride was an assiduous attendee at international meetings. He raised the question of partition on every occasion possible at the Council of Europe, the OEEC.

The USA was keen that Ireland would join NATO, the new post-war defence association. MacBride saw this as an opportunity for striking a bargain on the ending of partition. However, the American State Department insisted that partition was a matter for the Irish and British governments solely. Despite meeting Dean Acheson in Washington in March 1951, MacBride could not convince the Americans to view Ireland in any way except through British eyes. MacBride, in an address to the National Press Club castigated Britain and Russia from stopping Ireland from playing a role in international affairs. He said that Britain was responsible for keeping us out of NATO and that Russia had vetoed Ireland's membership of the United Nations. He then said that there was no difference between Russia and Britain, as far as "orderly democracy" was concerned. Liam Cosgrave described this as an extravagant statement and said it did not represent the views of the people of Ireland[52]. MacBride complained to Costello saying that American papers interpreted that Cosgrave was speaking with Costello's authority. As MacBride was soon to meet President Truman, he asked Costello to correct that impression[53]. Though Cosgrave had spoken entirely on his own initiative, Costello did not respond to MacBride's request. This incident may be indicative of the reality that MacBride's standing within the government diminished as it went on. It appears that in its later stages, the Cabinet Estimates Committee, which did not include MacBride, Joseph Blowick or James Everett, took many important cabinet decisions. The fact that MacBride was so often abroad on State matters may also have been a factor. The other party leaders would have also been conscious of the deteriorating nature of Clann na Poblachta[54].

The fact that America already had military bases in Northern Ireland undermined The Republic of Ireland as a strategic location for NATO. When the actual invitation came to join NATO, MacBride, who was himself committed to Europe, replied, "In these circumstances, any military alliance with the State that is responsible for the unnatural division of Ireland, which occupies a portion of our country with its armed forces would be entirely repugnant and unacceptable to the Irish people"[55]. Costello was a reluctant party to this government decision. Russia had vetoed Ireland's application to join the United Nations in September 1949.

ECONOMIC POLICY

The economic policy of the Inter Party Government was initially conservative. On 3 March 1948 Costello wrote to each minister stressing the importance of a tight fiscal policy and called for a revision of estimates. He wrote, "It is not too much to say that the fate of our government depends on the success or failure of the economy drive by individual ministers". This advice was not heeded as Costello wrote again in June expressing disappointment, saying "it is incumbent on each of us to do all in his power to ensure that further substantial economies are made with the minimum of delay"[56]. Noel Browne claimed that Costello had virtually no understanding of fiscal policy and that he was shocked to notice that the 1950 Budget, taken all together, required more than £100 million. Browne went on: "His response was characteristically simple minded and of doubtful morality. He issued an appeal to all of us to send in falsified figures on the assurances that after the Budget was passed, we would be permitted 'all the money we needed to run our departments'. This money would be made available in subsequent supplementary estimates. To my surprise all my Cabinet colleagues appeared to have agreed to these proposals. I refused to accede to this request. Appeals were made to me to change my mind repeatedly but I declined to do so"[57].

Paddy McGilligan, the Finance Minister, felt obliged in 1948 to announce a National Loan for £12 million and in the following year one for £15 million, taking the total of National loans to £65 million. Money coming from the post war reconstruction Marshall Plan was also being used for state capital investment. This was partly due to the influence of Keynesian economics in the person of Patrick Lynch, special economic advisor to Costello, and to Costello himself who was open to new ideas. Ken Whitaker in the Department of Finance was also pushing new economic theories. Eithne MacDermott has written that " the astonishing conversion of McGilligan, Costello and Mulcahy to the delights if Keynesian economics, together with the conviction with which they were to express their complete conversion to economic planning and development on the part of the state, is one of the major mutations undergone by a political elite since the foundation of the state"[58]. This led to the foundation of the Industrial Development Authority in February 1949. It remains one of the jewels in the crown in the continuing economic advance of modern Ireland. The IDA was opposed by the Department of Finance, which argued for it to have to submit all proposals to cabinet, "insofar as Cabinet is protection against foolish or corrupt ministers"[59]. As Joe Lee has written, "The IDA had a difficult birth. However, though it made only an initial modest impact, it survived the troubled early years to become later a virtually independent republic in the formulation of industrial policy[60.]. This of course did not find favour at the Central Bank either, where Joseph Brennan advised against. In November 1949 Costello said radically that one of the government's roles was, "to abate poverty and reduce unemployment" and accepted this "as a criterion for our success or failure".

A lack of hospitals and housing was a far worse evil than the temporary disequilibrium in the balance of payments. The price of food and drink, which had been increased in deValera's crisis budget of 14 October 1947, were reduced, as was taxation on commodities. However, Costello cautioned that, "A new Jerusalem cannot be built overnight. It would be useful if this policy of capital investment for productive and social purposes by means of repatriating part of the sterling assets were clearly indicated to the public by making a distinction between the annual revenue budget, or the national housekeeping budget as it may be called, and the capital budget"[61]. This policy, including the availability of Marshal Aid money, led to a massive investment, particularly in housing, where from 1,118 houses[62] built in 1947, the annual figures rose to 8,117 in 1950 and to 11,305 in 1951. This was a ten-fold increase from 1947.

The number of telephones installed rose from an annual average of 2,300 to 6,600. MacBride's favourite scheme of forestation saw over 30,000 acres planted during 1949-1951.Unemployment fell from 9.35% in 1947 to 7.3% in 1951. The Trade Agreement with Britain gave agriculture production a huge boost with increased exports to England. James Dillon promised to 'drown England in eggs". A massive Land Rehabilitation Project was undertaken with the Marshall Aid money. The Department of Finance was against accepting this money, as it believed the politicians would squander it. The scourge of tuberculosis was tackled by the expansion of hospital services.

When the British decided to devalue sterling in September 1949 the Inter Party Government was split on its reaction. Lengthy meetings of the cabinet took place before it was decided that " the course of least disadvantage" was to follow the British course. The Irish pound was devalued from $4.03 to $2.80. This led to MacBride campaigning for a break with the sterling link and the repatriation of investments in London, as he predicted, "a further and more substantial fall in the purchasing power of the pound may be expected"[63].

Most of Ireland's exports, mainly agricultural products, went to Britain, whose economy was performing poorly and which also had a cheap food policy. This was a bad economic situation for Ireland. When the Marshall Aid ended, Ireland had no access to other capital funds. The Korean War and the devaluation of sterling added to the difficulties as the cost of living began to rise again.

Noel Browne

He later wrote of the cabinets rejection
of his mother and child scheme,
"I reflected that one Judas was bad enough,
but twelve of them must be some kind of record,
even in Ireland"

1948 - 1951 Government
Seated (L to R.) Gen. R. Mulcahy, John A. Costello, Sean T. O'Kelly, William Norton.
Standing (L to R.) Noel Browne, Sean MacBride, J. Blowick, T.J. Murphy, Sean McEoin,
J. Everett, J.Dillon, P. McGilligan, Dr. T. F. O'Higgins.

CHAPTER 13

MOTHER AND CHILD CONTROVERSY

One of the great success stories of the First Inter-Party government was the eradication of tuberculosis. The death rate had been halved by 1951. This was in part due to MacBride's insistence that money be provided from the Hospitals Trust and the energetic action of the Minister of Health, Dr. Noel Browne.

By mid-1950 Browne felt that action was well in hand and he decided to deal with the 1947 Health Act, which was to provide for free medical treatment for expectant mothers and of all children up to 16 years. Dr. James Ryan, Fianna Fáil Minister of Health in the previous government, had introduced a new public health scheme into the Dáil in June 1947. Ryan was a conciliatory figure and accepted several amendments from the Opposition. One section of the Bill, concerning compulsory medical services to mothers and children, proved somewhat controversial. James Dillon objected vociferously to this aspect of the Bill, and asked the President to consult the Council of State before signing the Bill into law. The President did so and received a positive response. This did not satisfy Dillon who wanted the constitutionality of the Bill tested in the Supreme Court. He issued a summons on 3 December 1947 against Ryan seeking a declaration that the Section of the Bill on Mothers and Children was repugnant to the Constitution. Dillon retained the formidable legal trio of John A Costello, Cecil Lavery and Paddy McGilligan. Dillon was not aware that the Catholic hierarchy had already voiced their objections to the Fianna Fáil Government on the same issues. However, as the matter was then 'before the courts', the Fianna Fáil Government was able to play for time in its response to the Catholic bishops. Crucially the new Inter-Party Government and Noel Browne did not know of the bishops stated concerns. Browne got cabinet approval in 1948 to proceed with the redrafting of the Bill. This was not completed until mid 1950.

IMA OPPOSITION

Opposition came immediately from the doctors who feared a diminution of income from their private practice, if a means test was not part of the scheme. They were against the State interfering in the doctor/patient relationship, dubbing it State medicine. The president of the IMA said, "We fear a general extension of State medicine which would make us civil servants, subservient to a soulless and oppressive bureaucracy"[1]. Browne retorted that it was "unworthy of members of the medical profession to try to confuse the simple matter of pounds, shillings and pence with questions of high principle and morality"[2].

At a later meeting with the IMA Browne unwisely confirmed that his personal preferment was for a fully-salaried medical profession[3]. When the IMA announced a ballot on the scheme Browne said, "This is a final decision of the Government, taken on behalf of the people, which the Medical Association or profession has no power to alter"[4]. The IMA ballot rejected the Scheme by a huge majority. Costello and Norton then met the doctors to try and sort out the problem. On 6 March Browne published details of the Scheme, which would provide free medical care for mothers during and after pregnancy. Free medical care would also apply to under 16-year olds, with a choice of doctor. There would be no compulsion, means test or fee[5]. Attempts continued to be made between the parties, to try to get reconciliation. Costello had a very high opinion of the medical profession and accepted that, as professional people, they should get a fair fee for their work, just like his own profession. Tom O'Higgins had close contacts with the IMA. Costello's son-in-law, Alexis Fitzgerald, who was a close advisor of the Taoiseach, had two brothers who were doctors and friends of Costello. Joe Lee has commented that while the doctors campaigned against 'socialised medicine', "some unkind observers suspected that their real opposition was less to 'state medicine' than to 'cheap medicine'"[6].

Sean MacEntee later commented that while oppositon to the Scheme focussed on the means test, no such opposition had come when the childrens' allowance was paid to all comers. He said, "The only difference between the two forms of benefit would seem to be that while Dr. Browne's scheme affected the income of the medical profession, the children's allowance did not"[7].

BISHOP'S OPPOSITION

Dr John Charles McQuaid, a doctor's son from Cavan and President of the Holy Ghost Blackrock College in Dublin, was the surprise appointment as Archbishop of Dublin in 1940. John A Costello reported that news of this 'outsiders' nomination was received poorly by the local diocesan clergy.[8] The careers of the Archbishop and future Taoiseach were to be closely intertwined in the 'Mother and Child' controversy. Archbishop McQuaid, together with Bishop Browne of Galway, and Staunton of Achonry, met Noel Browne in October 1950. They expressed their dis-satisfaction with his Bill, and said they had written a letter accordingly to the Taoiseach, which McQuaid then read out to Dr Browne. Despite this, Dr. Browne still believed that the answers and undertakings, "he had given had satisfied the bishops". McQuaid informed Costello to the contrary, adding that Browne had "terminated the interview and walked out". The letter to Costello, under the name of Staunton, secretary to the Hierarchy, said, "the powers taken by the State in the proposed Mother and Child health service are in direct opposition to the rights of the family and of the individual and are liable to very great abuse"[9]. Costello then met Browne and intimated that he wanted to sort things out with the bishops.

In November 1950 Noel Browne quarrelled with his party leader Sean MacBride. He intimated that he intended to break up Clann na Poblachta and bring down the Government. The Clann had already been enduring party dissatisfaction, with defections and disillusionment among some radical members at its role in government.

These divisons, which included attitudes to the Mother and Child Scheme got increasingly bitter and personal[10].

The Taoiseach, like many of the cabinet were pious Catholics and were conditioned to defer to the hierarchy. On taking office Costello had sent a message to Pope Pius XII saying, " On the occasion of our assumption of office and our first cabinet meeting, my colleagues and I desire to repose at the feet of Your Holiness the assurance of filial loyalty and devotion, as well as our firm resolve to be guided in all our work by the teachings of Christ and to strive for the attainment of a social order in Ireland based on Christian principles"[11].

Up to Browne publishing his Bill in March 1951, Costello had played a conciliatory role. However, he later intervened directly and wrote formally to Browne, "My withholding of approval of the scheme is due to the objections set forth in the letter from the Secretary of the Hierarchy written on behalf of the Hierarchy, and to the reiteration of their objections by His Grace the Archbishop of Dublin"[12]. Costello also realised that the only decision of the Government on the matter was that of June 1948, which allowed Browne to redraft the Fianna Fáil Health Bill. MacBride was then in America and Costello asked him to return immediately[13]. McQuaid came to Government Buildings on 5 April for a lengthy meeting with Costello to clarify his position. The hierarchy had the previous day decided that the Scheme was against Catholic social teaching. According to McQuaid "The Taoiseach at once and fully accepted our decision, as one would expect"[14].

The cabinet met the next day and considered the hierarchy's letter. Browne has written, "Costello took up the letter. Clearly for him, it was holy writ. Slowly and solemnly he read out the Archbishop's letter... Grudgingly Costello allowed my request that I ask every one of the cabinet, 'Do you accept?'[15.] Each in turn refused to back Browne's scheme. He then left the meetings asking for time to consider his position. Browne wrote, "The medical profession heard from Dr. Tom O'Higgins of the dramatic dissolution of my support on all sides in the cabinet. In turn, Mr. Costello informed the hierarchy.[16]. Browne later wrote spitefully, "I reflected that one Judas was bad enough, but twelve of them must be some kind of record, even in Ireland"[17]. The details of what was occurring were of course not in the public domain, though there were hints available. Browne consulted with the Irish Congress of Trade Unions and let it be known that at their request he was reconsidering his resignation. This was too much for his colleagues. MacBride got a mandate from the Ard Chomhairle of Clann na Poblachta to take whatever action he deemed necessary. MacBride then decided to take direct action himself and demanded Browne's resignation from the government. Browne complied and wrote on 11 April to Costello telling him "as demanded by Mr. MacBride, I hereby send you my resignation from the Government, to take effect tomorrow". Though Browne refused Costello's request that he accompany him to Áras an Uachtáráin to inform the President, Costello, playing an adroit hand, replied in a friendly manner,

"I myself and the other members of the Government who have been your colleagues during the past three years appreciate the work which you have done in the Department of Health, and regret that circumstances should have arisen that have made your resignation unavoidable"[18]. Later that night Michael Mulvihill, Browne's private secretary, on Browne's instructions, undertook a devastating public relations coup, by delivering all the correspondence between Browne, Costello, MacBride and the bishops to the three national daily newspapers. The newspapers duly published the material and created a major sensation, with the *Irish Times* editorialising that "The Roman Catholic church would seem to be the effective government of the country".

Costello later maintained that he had hoped that "a satisfactory settlement could be achieved" and he believed that had Browne not resigned, they could have reached a settlement with the hierarchy[19]. The release of the correspondence put huge pressure on MacBride and Costello to defend their respective roles.

That same day of 12 April Noel Browne made a personal statement to the Dáil on his resignation. He said that he had mistakenly thought that his exclusion of a means test in the Health Scheme had the full support of his colleagues. He however, did not accept the way his cabinet colleagues had handled the matter. The Hierarchy had declared the Scheme as against Catholic social teaching. He said, "This decision I, as a Catholic, immediately accepted without hesitation". He outlined the events, which led to the debacle, making the point that when the Taoiseach did not forward his document of 11 October to the Archbishop of Dublin, he "told the Taoiseach orally that his failure to forward that reply had placed me in a very embarrassing position and might easily give Their Lordships the impression that I had omitted to give any consideration to their objections". He went on, "I was surprised also to learn from the Taoiseach that he had been in constant communication with His Grace, the Archbishop of Dublin, on this matter since the receipt of the letter of the 10 October from the hierarchy, so presumably he was fully aware that Their Lordships' objections were still unresolved. He offered no explanation as to why, in the light of his knowledge, he had failed to keep me informed of the position; had allowed me continuously to refer in public speeches to the scheme as decided and unchanged Government policy".

Costello immediately asked for an adjournment so that he could have an opportunity of replying to a statement "in which there were so many - let me say it as charitably as possible inaccuracies, mis-statements and mis-representations"

COSTELLO'S DÁIL REPLY TO BROWNE

Costello replied to Browne's statement. He said that over the past long and agonising months he and three or four of his colleagues had tried to act as peacemakers to get the Minister out of difficulties created by his own obstinacy. "He has made reckless and untrue charges against me and my friends and colleagues in Government". Costello then gave a detailed outline of the Health Bill from its introduction by James Ryan, Dillon's objections and his own involvement as a Senior Counsel in 1947.

He acknowledged that he was not in the habit of making notes or memoranda and so was unsure of dates. He stated that he only became aware on the 7 October 1947 of the bishops' objection to the Health Bill in a private capacity. He said deValera only replied to the bishops' letter on 16 February 1948, saying that Dillon's legal action had put the matter on hold. Costello gave the copy of that bishops' letter to Browne after 10 October 1950, to enable him to answer the bishops, stated objections. Costello regarded the existence of that 1947 letter as proof against Browne's assertion that Costello and the Government had "roped in the Hierarchy to get us out of a scheme we did not like".

Costello asserted that on 25 June 1948 the Government approved a Bill repealing the offending sections dealing with the Mother and Child scheme. The actual scheme, which Browne produced and circulated to the medical profession, never came before the Government for consideration or approval. Costello only saw Browne's correspondence to the doctors when a friend showed him a copy.

On 12 October 1950 Costello went to meet Dr McQuaid to be appraised of the Hierarchy's position. Dr. McQuaid and two other bishops had had a meeting with Noel Browne on the previous day, which the former described as "incredible". Though Noel Browne had reported that he felt he had satisfied the bishops, Costelllo said this was not so and repeated how Browne had terminated the meeting and walked out on the bishops. Costello said that while Browne in his Dáil statement now acknowledged his erroneous opinion, but still maintained that Costello had confirmed that opinion as correct, after his own meeting with the three bishops on the succeeding day. "In other words, he accuses me of deliberate lying". Costello then stated that according to one Irish newspaper that day, Browne accused him of keeping the bishop's letter in reply from him, for a month. He apologised to the Irish people for calling it an 'Irish' newspaper. Costello said that in fact McQuaid had read the letter to Dr. Browne at his meeting with the bishops on the previous day. Costello believed that it was at that point that he gave Browne the bishops' 1947 letter. He also told Browne that he was not proposing to answer the bishops' current letter. He told Browne that the bishops were only motivated by Catholic faith and morals. He asserted that the Tánaiste Mr. Dillon, Dr. O'Higgins and himself, had done everything possible to settle the matter, "until the Wednesday of Holy Week, the 21 March, when I was obliged to take a firm stand".

When Dr. Browne returned both the Bishop's letters to Costello, he made no comment on them. However, Costello found a memorandum from Browne within the envelope. Browne had asserted in the Dáil that this should have been sent to the Bishops. Costello did not do so, and said that it was something that could not be sent. Costello and the Tánaiste got Browne's agreement that they would meet the IMA. Browne later accused them of selling him out to the doctors, and said "we were not to continue any longer the negotiations with the medical profession". Costello said that the doctors have been maligned and slandered and libelled in every dishonourable way",

He declared that "They acted the part which you would expect a noble profession to act in regard to this matter and the only thanks they got is vilification".

Costello told the Dáil how he had briefed Mr MacBride who had then had reiterated to his colleague the "necessity for satisfying the objections of the Hierarchy"

When, in 6 March 1951 Browne issued a pamphlet outlining the Scheme, he sent a copy with an accompanying letter to McQuaid. Costello received an urgent letter from McQuaid expressing his surprise. He also included a copy of a letter he had sent to Browne. It said, "I regret that I may not approve of the Mother and Child health service, as it is proposed by you to implement the scheme". Costello then said that if, as Browne claimed, he believed that he had already satisfied the bishops on 11 October, why did he not write immediately seeking an explanation? Instead the letter dated 8 March went unacknowledged and Browne did not consult Costello about it. Costello showed his copy of the letter to his colleagues. On 12 March the Tánaiste asked Browne what he was going to do about the letter from the Archbishop. Browne replied that he was going to do nothing about it. "There is nothing in the Archbishop's allegation". The Tánaiste reported this to Costello, which gave him "rather some food for thought". On 14 March Dr. Browne sought an interview with Costello. He sought a cabinet meeting that night to approve £30,000, which he claimed would allow him to "kill the doctors". Costello asked him about the Archbishop's letter. Browne replied "There is nothing in that. I am assured on the advice of theologians"[20].

Costello then "took my stand". He said "Whatever about fighting the doctors I am not going to fight the bishops and whatever about fighting the bishops, I am not going to fight the doctors and the bishops". He told Browne "it may come to a point where either you or I will leave the Cabinet on this, unless we can settle the matter with the bishops". Browne asked for a Cabinet meeting and Costello said he would organise one for the morning if possible. Browne rang again that night. Costello continued, telling the Dáil that newspaper reporters were immediately able to report their conversation, commenting "there is someone of sinister and evil influence who informed the journalists of the conversation".

The next day 15 March Costello wrote formally to Browne about the matter. He quoted McQuaid's judgement on the Health Scheme, and noted that the letter had not been answered and that Browne had continued to publicise the Scheme. Costello asked Browne to consult the bishops so as to remove any grounds for objections. He promised whatever financial resources were necessary to manage a Health Scheme. Browne replied on 19 March and asked extraordinarily, if Costello was under the impression that the Hierarchy was opposed to the Mother and Child scheme? Browne said that a member of the Hierarchy has assured him that as far as he knew, the Hierarchy had no objection to the scheme "on the grounds of faith and morals". It also became evident that Bishop Dignam of Clonfert was a supporter of Browne's, though Dignam did not carry much weight in Episcopal circles. [It has been claimed that his ordination as a bishop was a payback by Monsignor Luzio, Papal Legate, who had come to Ireland in

1923 to seek to end the civil war. He was received badly by the bishops. Returning to Rome he said that while in Ireland he had encountered "26 Popes"[21]. In almost complete disbelief Costello replied on 21 March pointing out the letters of condemnation on record from the Hierarchy on the matter. On 22 March, Holy Thursday, Dr. Browne went to see the Archbishop. He subsequently rang Costello saying that he had agreed with the Archbishop that the entire Hierarchy would adjudicate on the Scheme "as a matter of Faith and Morals". Browne assured the Archbishop that he would abide by that ruling. Browne submitted an 8-page document for consideration. He asked Costello to send it to the Hierarchy, which Costello did while on a visit to the Archbishop. On 5 April. Dr. McQuaid delivered the unanimous findings of the Hierarchy that the scheme was against "Catholic social teaching" to Costello at Government Buildings. According to Costello he was informed authoritatively the verdict carried the same weight as "Catholic moral teaching". Noel Browne had refused to tell the cabinet that he would accept the bishops ruling. Costello then told the Dáil how Sean MacBride took charge of the situation with the Minister. MacBride had brought Browne into the government and he would undertake to remove him too. Costello said MacBride's action was "entirely in accordance with the Constitution" Costello said that, "I regret my view is that Dr. Browne is temperamentally unfitted for the post of a cabinet minister".

Costello concluded that since Browne had put the correspondence into the newspapers, it was inevitable that the government action would be seen as due to the intervention of the Church in State affairs. He added, "I am not in the least bit afraid of the *Irish Times* or any other newspaper. I, as a Catholic, obey my church authorities and will continue to do so, in spite of the *Irish Times* or anything else, in spite of the fact that they may take votes from my Party, or me, or anything else of that kind.

I regret that this should be done. I regret that it may be misrepresented in the North but I wanted to make it clear that there was no intention of the Hierarchy interfering in any way in politics or with the activities of my Government or the activities of the State. They confine themselves strictly to faith and morals. The public ought never to have become aware of the matter. It was because the then Minister for Health took the unusual course of saying " I want a special, authoritative decision from the Hierarchy in general meeting and an immediate decision" that this matter took the form it did. It is now a matter of public controversy, due entirely to the fact that he published all these documents, for his own purposes and his own motives, in the newspapers this morning".

At the end of the debate, which followed his resignation, Noel Browne spoke briefly. In his reply to the Dáil debate on his resignation, Browne referred to the Taoiseach's stating that he had helped Browne "when I had got into trouble with the Hierarchy". Browne challenged Costello's intention to convey the impression that there was " no unsavoury implications whatsoever" involved. He said that in fact he wanted hospitals run by local authorities to be staffed entirely by nurses, and furnished with the opportunity to "reach the top". He again reiterated that the Taoiseach did not send Browne's document of 11 November to the hierarchy.

He also claimed that the Taoiseach had said to him at the last cabinet meeting, "you may publish what you like, Dr. Browne". Joe Lee writes "Browne was probably his own worst enemy, despite the competition from Costello, MacBride and McQuaid". Despite without acknowledging Browne's obvious political deficiencies, Lee adds that due to the publication of his detailed memoirs, "No one can ever ever look at the first Costello cabinet again without seeing it at least partly through Browne's jaundiced but piercing eyes"[22]. Sean Lemass surmised that the whole matter might have been a conspiracy to unload an impossible Noel Browne from the cabinet. James Dillon coined the phrase, "My Bleeding Heart" as an apt nickname for Browne[23].

Costello always claimed that the government acted correctly in accepting the ruling of the bishops. He described it as "the correct attitude for any Catholic government to take. I would do the same again and I know the government would have to do it"[24]. At the same time there is little doubt that Costello genuinely tried to assist Noel Browne introduce a Health Scheme, which would be a huge advance socially. However, due to Costello's own admiration for the doctors and his allegiance to the bishops, and in no small way to Browne's own difficult character and the internal politics of Clann na Poblachta, the matter blew up in the Taoiseach's face. The later introduction of a similar scheme by the next government demonstrated that, had Browne been a practical politician, he could have introduced a modified Health Scheme. He won the publicity battle with his release of the correspondence, and has continued to be viewed by liberals as a victim of medical, episcopal and conservatives forces. Sean MacBride, by seeking Browne's resignation, succeeded in removing much of the resulting opprobrium from the Taoiseach on to himself. Joe Lee says, "Costello played an adroit hand. MacBride did not. The strength of Costello's position was that while his piety was genuine, it also happened to coincide with the material advantage of the position he represented"[25]. Conor Cruise O'Brien rather astutely said that the episode was "atypical, in its blatancy. Issues were aired which were, and are, normally discussed behind closed doors. To outsiders it looked like a case of the church dictating to the State. It actually was a case of a politician asking for a *public* intervention by the Church, for political reasons, and spectacularly bungling the whole business"[26].

POSTCRIPT

When Fianna Fáil returned to office in 1951, negotiations between the new government and the hierarchy took place on the Health Scheme. Noel Browne summarises the end result. "In May 1953 the Episcopal committee which dealt with health matters met Eamon de Valera and Dr. Ryan in Cashel, Co. Tipperary. The detailed notes of this fascinating meeting are at last available. deValera and Ryan outlined the new amendment demanded by the bishops and already accepted, but the hierarchy now reconsidered the earlier amendment. Once again re-shaped to their joint requirements, they were in turn accepted meekly by deValera. All pretence at being independent members of the Cabinet of a sovereign parliament had been abandoned". The Bill finally became law in October 1953[27].

The stability of the Inter-Party Government majority in the Dáil was always problematic, depending as it did on placating so many parties and individuals. It was defeated on some votes. As early as 1949, Clann na Poblachta began to splinter, losing Peadar Cowan TD. Fine Gael lost Sir John Esmonde. William Sheldon, an Independent who represented the Protestant population in Donegal, withdrew his support due to the constitutional changes and the refusal to join NATO[28]. Other TD's continued the drift away leaving the government with a majority of just four. The loss of Browne and of his colleague Jack McQuillan TD made the government majority susceptible to lots of variations.

The price of milk became an issue between James Dillon and the farmers in late April 1951. The government offered an increase of one penny a gallon. This brought more defections from rural deputies. It was obvious that the government could not continue for long. As the Government struggled to win votes in early May, Costello, who had considered dates for a general election, dissolved the Dáil.

In his summary of The Inter-Party Government, David McCullagh says that "No other Taoiseach had to undertake as delicate a balancing act as that facing John A Costello – trying to satisfy five parties and a mixed bag of Independents, some of them eccentric to say the least, was a task of monumental difficulty. Most observers expected it to last a year, the fact that it survived as long as it did is a tribute to Costello's skills as a chairman. Costello took upon himself the role of mediator between ministers, interceding to try to reach a compromise which would ensure the government's survival"[29]. The government did not 'fall'; its dissolution was due to the disintegration of Clann na Poblachta. Costello himself described what happened, "The stability of the Government had recently been endangered by the efforts of a few independent deputies who have irresponsibly sought to embarrass the Government by exploiting sectional grievances"[30].

Speaking at a function in his constituency on the occasion of his retirement as party leader in 1959, Costello said of his first Government: "history will judge that the inter-party government of 1948 was the enterprise that finally proved that Irish democracy would efficiently work. Then, despite differences in party, despite indeed the historical antagonisms which decided some elements, in recognition of the undoubted desire of the people for a change of government, public men came together and gave the people the Government they desired.

The Inter Party Government did one thing even more important. It inaugurated the trend of events which has led to the present situation in which men are prepared to forget, and are forgetting, the civil war, when the relationships of public men are governed by many considerations other than the position they once occupied *viz a viz* that lamentable conflict"[31].

When John Charles McQuaid died in 1972, Taoiseach Jack Lynch and John A Costello contributed to his memory. Costello used the occasion to bolster his own actions during the Mother and Child episode. He said that he attended McQuaid's Consecration some thirty years previously. He felt sure that his achievements as a "great Ecclesiastic, a fearless and uncompromising exponent and defender of his Faith and a very saintly priest, were appreciated. Costello acknowledged that Dr. McQuaid's appointment was received "coldly, if not resentfully". He said that McQuaid's endured, "constant criticism, irritating misrepresentation and misunderstanding", but that he remained serene and unwavering, providing schools, hospitals, convents and churches, as well as providing for the poor, the sick, and disabled. He inculcated the principles of Catholic social teaching into the work of the archdiocese.

Costello recalled that McQuaid always insisted that the annual mass for the new Law Term was a Latin High Mass, because the legal profession was the last of the learned professions.

Arising out of the controversy over the Mother and Child Scheme, Costello said that McQuaid was subjected to "unmerited, even malicious criticism and comment". Right reason and the moral law were his guidelines. They did not require that account should be taken of ephemeral public opinion or passing popularity. No abuse or harsh words fell from his lips or his pen. "When I greeted him and asked how he was, he invariably replied, 'As well as my enemies permit me to be'. But he said it with a smile. His outstanding characteristic was his utter calmness. "I was with him on some difficult and trying occasions. He remained always calm, steady and unruffled in the face of difficulties. It was the strength of deep waters flowing powerfully and strongly but without turbulence or disturbance"[32].

Old newspaper photograph of Archbishop John Charles McQuaid
with President Sean T O'Kelly (centre) and the Spanish Ambassador.

CHAPTER 14

GENERAL ELECTION 1951

The election of 1951 was fought on purely economic issues, with the coalition parties seeking support for each other. Costello declared that he would prefer to lead a coalition government rather than a purely Fine Gael one. In a major speech on the dissolution, he defended the Government's record. On the Declaration of the Republic he said; "I offer no apology to anyone. On the contrary I feel that events have more than justified the reasons that induced me, and the Government, to take the action. We rejoice in that as a result, our friendship with Canada, Australia, New Zealand, South Africa and India have been strengthened and the way cleared for better relations with Great Britain". Costello rejected deValera's criticisms of the impossibility of effective coalition government over one party government. He said that "There was as much if not more harmony in the inter-party government as in the single party governments that I experienced", adding, "The only one party government which could do that job on its own terms, is to be found far away from here in Moscow"[1].

While speaking in Tullamore on 13 May, a heckler shouted out to Costello, "What about Dr. Browne?" Costello responded in some detail before adding, "We have always respected family responsibility. I have never been able to understand why anybody should stand over a scheme which involved the old age pensioner in Connemara and the agricultural labourer in Laois-Offaly paying for the rich lady in Foxrock, when she was having her children. That was a free for all"[2].

Costello answered criticism of the Government's economic programme at a meeting in his own constituency at Rathmines on 15 May.

He said that there were three options open to the government.

It could continue borrowing Irish money for suitable capital development in Ireland.

It could slow down capital development. This would affect housing, hospitals, telephones, and land reclamation.

It could increase taxation.

Sean MacEntee was, together with the now Independent Noel Browne, Costello's constituency colleague. MacEntee often made savage attacks on the opponents of Fianna Fáil during election campaigns. One of his usual tactics was to associate them with communism seeking to raise a 'red scare'. Speaking in Arklow on 16 May he succeeded in attacking both the Tánaiste, William Norton, and the Taoiseach in this fashion. His thesis was that there had been an agreement between both men to exchange posts after the next election, making Norton the dangerous left-winger, Taoiseach. He said, "Mr. Costello happened to be Taoiseach at the moment. Everybody knows that he had been drafted in for the job. The slip-shod manner in which he had led the Government, the ineptitude in which he had handled the problems of External Affairs, the social welfare scheme, and the mother and child proposals indicated that he had little liking for the task". MacEntee then declared that a labour parliamentary secretary, Brendan Corish, had intimated that Norton would be the next Taoiseach, following the agreement with Costello. MacEntee added, "Everyone knew that the height of Mr. Costello's private aspiration was represented by a seat in the Supreme Court". He explained that Costello really could not resign from being Taoiseach to take a seat on the Supreme Court, but as Tánaiste it would be much easier to do so[3]. During the campaign Costello covered 2,100 miles attending 27 meetings[4].

The voters in Dublin South East returned its three outgoing T.D.'s. The first preference votes cast were;

Costello JA	FG	9,222
Browne N	Ind	8,673
MacEntee S	FF	8,334

When the election results were complete the *Irish Times* headlined;

"ALL OTHERS OUTNUMBER FIANNA FÁIL BY NINE"
POSITION VIRTUALLY UNCHANGED

Clann na Poblachta had disintegrated, with only MacBride and John Tully of Cavan winning seats. MacBride dropped from 8,648 first preferences votes in 1948 to 2,853 in 1951, and was only elected on the eleventh count. He wrote to Costello saying that in the circumstances, "I do not consider that my services in the Government are of any particular value to the country and therefore, I feel entitled to be released from future duty in Government"[5]. Costello replied, complimenting MacBride on the discharge of his ministerial duties, "exhausting yourself to the extent of often causing me anxiety for your health". He acknowledged that MacBride, due to his work, ability and personal qualities, had ensured that Ireland had been able to take such a prominent and nationally beneficial part in the activities of the OEEC.

The overall results, with the 1948 result in brackets, were:

FF	69	(68)
FG	40	(29)
Lab	16	(20)
C na P	2	(6)
C na T	6	(5)
Ind	14	(17)

This was a remarkable result for Fine Gael. deValera claimed that as his party had a majority of five over the combined Inter-Party grouping, Fianna Fáil alone could form a stable government. The Inter-party group felt it could rely on seven of the Independents to vote for Costello as Taoiseach. This brought their total to 72 votes for

Costello. The outcome depended on the remaining six Independent TD's. The cabinet continued to meet and felt that they would be remaining in office as all sides completed negotiations.

When the Dáil met on 13 June it was evident that four of the six Independent TD's would vote for deValera. These were Noel Browne, Peadar Cowan, John Flynn and Michael ffrench O'Carroll. The first business was to elect a Ceann Comhairle, which in itself could have been crucial to the outcome of electing a Taoiseach. Patrick Hogan of Labour was elected, thereby cutting one vote from the Inter Party group. Costello was first proposed as Taoiseach. He was defeated by 72 votes for to 74 against. As Manning has written, "The change of Ceann Comhairle had made the difference"[6] deValera was then proposed and was elected by 74 to 69. Browne, Cogan, Cowan, Flynn and ffrench O'Carroll voted for deValera and against Costello[7]. Clann na Poblachta had all but disintegrated, and its collapse brought Fianna Fáil back into office.

Costello later claimed that the coalition had won the election but several TD's who had supported it, went over to Fianna Fail[8].

PART-TIME POLITICIAN AGAIN 1951-1954

Costello lost little time in renewing his practice at the Bar, thus reverting to the Fine Gael tradition of being a part-time politician. The years 1951-54 were a difficult time to be in government. deValera's sight was becoming a major problem during this period as Taoiseach, and he did not assume the Ministry of External Affairs. After rivalry with Sean Lemass on policy, Sean MacEntee won out and became Minister for Finance. He took a very conservative stance with austerity budgets. There was a deficit of £55 million that year and one of £62 million the next year. MacEntee argued that these had to be eliminated to ensure confidence in the currency. Fianna Fáil decided that if corrective measures were required, it was better to do it early when they could blame Costello's outgoing government for the poor economic state. The Independents, on whom they depended to stay in office, would not want to face a snap election. MacEntee therefore introduced a deflationary budget in 1951 and repeated this in 1952. He increased income tax by one shilling in the pound and increased prices on bread, sugar, tea, alcohol and petrol.

Speaking on 2 April 1952, Sean MacBride launched an attack on MacEntee's budget, saying it was somewhat sinister to have the Minister for Finance introduce a budget, which was practically drafted for him by the Central Bank. He said the deflationary policy could only lead to unemployment and the restriction in credit, increases in bank charges and further unemployment. He asked who ruled the country? Several of the independent TD's came under pressure on the charge of keeping Fianna Fáil in power, especially as they had not indicated to their electorates, that they would do so. Realignment gradually took place within the Independents in the Dáil.

Costello remained leader of Fine Gael in the Dáil with General Mulcahy as party leader. He soon invited the leading Independent TD James Dillon to rejoin Fine Gael, which he did. Another, Oliver J. Flanagan, followed him only a week later. Noel Browne, Patrick Cogan and ffrench O'Carroll joined Fianna Fáil. Eight by-elections occurred during those years in which Fine Gael did well. So much so that by October 1953 the combined Inter-Party group, equalled Fianna Fáil's sixty-nine seats. On 1 November 1953, TF O'Higgins TD, father of Tom O'Higgins, died suddenly. James Coburn a Fine Gael TD from Louth had also died at this time. Fianna Fáil had good majorities in both constituencies. Fine Gael headed the poll in both, winning the by-elections handsomely, with an 80% transfer of votes from Labour. This was a shattering blow for Fianna Fáil.

deValera then declared that he could not continue in government without a fresh mandate. The electoral die was cast. On 21 April Fianna Fáil introduced a very mild budget. It proposed to free up to 40,000 people from the tax net. It lowered stamp duty to 1% on houses up to £1,000 and a maximum of 3% on houses up to £32,500. It reduced the price of bread and flour. It stabilised the price of a box of matches at one and a halfpenny and cut the tax on entertainment. In the Dáil Costello objected to an outgoing government bringing in a budget saying, "many of the provisions, due to statutory provision fáil to have any real effect and could hamper an incoming government and its policy and operation of the plan". Three days later the Dáil was dissolved.

This time the Inter-Party group was composed of three parties and ran as a block with a ten-point plan. Clann na Poblachta was offered one ministerial post in cabinet. It was in such disarray that it did not join the government, but gave it general support. The Clann's national executive had opposed going back into government, though it is probable that MacBride might have wished to do so. For the first time the *Irish Times* favoured Fianna Fáil, complaining that under pressure, Fine Gael had reneged on its principles as the party of the Commonwealth and could not be trusted not to do so again. The campaign was regarded as the 'dullest campaign in recent years'[9]

At the final rally at the GPO on 17 May Costello identified the issues as:

1. Policy of expansion or policy of austerity
2. Policy of freedom or that of control.
3. Policy of low taxes and cheap food.
4. Policy of high taxation.

The result in Dublin South East was:

Costello	FG	11,305
MacEntee	FF	5,971
Browne	FF	5,489
O'Donovan J.	FG	2,598
MacDowell V.	Lab	1,455

Costello's surplus brought in his Fine Gael colleague John O'Donovan but Noel Browne lost his seat, though he came close to unseating his party colleague, Sean MacEntee. Costello's son Declan headed the poll in Dublin North West.

The national result was:

Fianna Fáil	65
Fine Gael	50
Labour	19
Clann na Talmhan	5
Clann na Poblachta	3
Independents	5

However, before we move on to Costello's second term as Taoiseach, it is appropriate to consider one particular court case he was involved in during the earlier part of 1954. It was the famous or, as some people would term it, infamous libel case, of Patrick Kavanagh versus *The Leader*. It may tell us more about the person and character of Costello, than many of his political manoeuvrings.

L. to R. Liam Cosgrave, A. Chester Beatty, John A. Costello,
Thomas McGreevy and Thomas Bodkin, 1950.

Patrick Kavanagh
He was always quite confident in his own merit as a poet,
and railed against the fact that he could not find a position,
which would be commensurate with his literary prowess.

CHAPTER 15

PATRICK KAVANAGH'S LIBEL CASE

Patrick Kavanagh was a famous poet from Monaghan who had made Dublin his home, leading a precarious and impecunious existence in the city. He was well known man-about-town and particularly well known in a variety of public houses. He was quite confident in his own merit as a poet, and railed against the fact that he could not find a position, which would be commensurate with his literary prowess. Like other artists in the city at the time, he was continually on high alert for contact with those who might be in a position to further his ambitions in this regard. He had no compunction in pressurising and even pestering those whom he felt could and should help him. By a strange coincidence one of his targets turned out to be the ex-Taoiseach and soon to be again Taoiseach, John A Costello. This episode, which went on for several years, tells us quite a bit about Costello the man.

The *Leader* was a literary magazine, which carried profiles of notable persons, written anonymously. A 'warts and all' profile of Kavanagh was published on 11 October 1952. It dealt with his pub life, where he was described as a freeloader. It also described his provincial fantasy of urban literary life projected on to a London, for which he longed, rather than the Dublin where he lived, and of his contempt for the rural barbarity of Inniskeen, from which he had escaped. It forgave all his ills, due to his poetry. It praised his *Great Hunger* as the best poem written in Ireland since Goldsmith's *Deserted Village*. It condemned his shoddy treatment by various editors and by the establishment.

Kavanagh was outraged by the profile, as were many of his friends. He decided to sue for libel, hoping for a few hundred pounds in compensation. He did not think that the case would ever come to court and he was so advised by his legal team of Sir John Esmonde SC, Thomas Connolly SC, Thomas Doyle and Niall McCarthy. As the date of trial approached, and there was no sign of a settlement, Kavanagh began to panic. He feared that he might face a cross-examination that could inquire into every aspect of his life.

The case opened in the High Court before Judge Teevan, hearing his first case, on 3 February 1954. John A Costello led for *The Leader*. The fact that he was an ex-Taoiseach only added to the notoriety of the proceedings. The courtroom was packed to overflowing each day, with queues of people outside. Kavanagh went into the witness box on the second day to be examined by his own counsel. Then Costello began his cross-examination. This examination has gone down in legal and literary history as a brilliant tour de force by Costello against a formidable opponent. Kavanagh held his own fairly well in portraying himself as a serious writer, until he made a fatal mistake.

Sir John Esmonde had outlined the case for Kavanagh going through the profile in the *Leader* in detail. During this examination he came to a sentence which contained the word 'Gurrier', and after pronouncing it said, "I take it that is the proper way to pronouncing that word. It is the first time I have seen it". Costello intervened immediately saying, "It is in Mr. Kavanagh's writings". Esmonde retorted, " I know that the *Leader* is burning to get going, but there will be plenty of opportunity later". Costello apologised saying, "I am sorry; I could not resist it".

The newspapers gave extensive coverage to the proceedings, with the *Irish Times* giving it a full page overflowing on to another page each day. During Thomas Connolly's examination of Kavanagh, Costello objected on several occasions. As Connolly read a series of laudatory descriptions of Kavanagh's poem *the Great Hunger* as having "the mark of genius", Costello intervened to say, "I suppose I could bring forty people in to say Mr. Kavanagh is not a good poet". At another point Costello objected, saying that he could not hear Mr. Kavanagh's replies, suggesting that he did not want the jury to hear that his voice "sounds like gravel sliding down the side of a quarry", as stated in the *Leader*.

Costello had obviously immersed himself in Kavanagh's writings in preparation for the trial. He began his forensic cross-examination of the witness on the afternoon of the second day. There were regular bursts of laughter from the overflowing courtroom, as repeatedly the judge demanded silence. Kavanagh gave brief and succinct answers. He had described his philosophy to his own counsel thus;

"My argument has been that literature is not the activity of wild bohemianism; that it is part of a religious mind: that, in fact it is religious. A wild life is anathema to me"[1]. Costello asked:

"I suppose it was because of your religious attitude that your book was banned by the censor for three days?"
"I don't know".
"And portion of the Great Hunger was banned because of obscenity?"

Costello then changed tack saying,
"Before we have our little encounter I would like you to define for His Lordship and the jury, certain expressions, what is a gurrier?"
"It is a euphemism for 'gutter'.
"Its part of your verbal currency?"
"It is not".

As the interplay continued Costello remarked:
"May the Lord preserve us from your explanations!"
At that the Judge intervened, objecting to Costello's remark.

They then examined the words 'wan' 'buck leap', and 'forbolgs', as contained in Kavanagh's writings.

Costello changed tack again saying,

"There would be many among the intelligentsia surprised when they heard Kavanagh described "as a quiet unassuming, early-to-bed man, who only wanted to be considered as a good writer".

He continued returning to *The Great Hunger* again:

"You have had a book suppressed for indecency?"

"Portions".

"Was not portion of The Great Hunger suppressed for indecency?"

"I have no knowledge of it"

"Nonsense" rapped the leading counsel.

"Excuse me for one moment. I changed it on the grounds of Art, not on morals. I still stand by what I did. All the obscene bits are still there"

This provoked general laughter with Kavanagh himself joining in. Costello then questioned him about a police visit under the Obscene Publications Act 1857.

"They visited me under the old puritanical Victorian Act. They talked amiably for twenty minutes. We parted in a haze of goodwill".

At that stage, the judge asked Costello when he would be finished with the witness, to which Costello replied;

"I have only just begun. I am only skirmishing".

During the following day's cross-examination, Costello raised the question of a Fianna Fáil Minister refusing to allow the Arts Council pay the expenses for a visit to the USA by Kavanagh. After some time Costello declared:

"I only want the fact for the jury".

"I want what is more important than fact. I want the truth", Kavanagh retorted.

Costello declared that Mr. Kavanagh was cleverer than he. He then went on to consider Kavanagh's own criticism of the other writers, which drew the response:

"I set Olympian standards. It was not destructive, provided it was true".

He declared that he judged himself likewise.

They discussed Kavanagh's criticism of the writers, Robert Farren and Austin Clarke, and their employment by Radio Éireann. According to Antoinette Quinn, Kavanagh's biographer, despite some artful dodging and parrying on Kavanagh's part, Costello's cross-examination demonstrated, "the far more vicious and personal streak in the poet's own criticism". Kavanagh explained:

"I believe that only the man who has earned the right, has the right to be wrong. However if you have no rights, you must be definitely on the side of truth. I know that the only person in whom error is tolerated is a great genius".

"I have not the remotest idea what you mean by that", Costello replied.

When asked what was amiss with the profile in the *The Leader*, Kavanagh replied;

"It is a perfect portrait of a pervert; some atrocious person. It is ridiculous".

Kavanagh agreed that he frequented pubs because they were the only places where he could come into contact with anyone who could give him work. He admitted that he liked a pint of stout or a glass of whiskey as much as anyone. Judge Teevan asked Costello if he was passing on to something else in his cross-examination.
Costello replied; *" I am passing out"*.
"Are you not finished with the witness?"
"Oh, not at all. I am passing out myself with fatigue".
The judge then called an adjournment at four o'clock for the day.

On the next morning Costello began an examination about a paper called *Kavanagh's Weekly* in which the witness wrote extensively. He examined the meaning of the word 'yous' and Kavanagh's attitude to women in pubs. In a discussion on *Soul for Sale* and an article Kavanagh wrote on Rome, they entered the field of religion.
At one point Kavanagh said:
"I hope we all have something of Christ in us",
to which Costello replied; *"I believe we all have"*.
As Costello examined him about his article on Rome, Kavanagh explained:
"I am speaking mystically of God, of the city without walls. It does not mean any mortal city. It means an immortal city".
Costello declared that he did not know the meaning of the word 'mystical'. He then moved to consider contemporary artists. Kavanagh described John Betjamen as a "good poet", but declared WH Auden as, "one of the greatest living poets". When Costello mentioned the name of Brendan Behan, Kavanagh became agitated for the first time, and made derogatory comments about Behan. Costello asked; "Why are you so hot under the collar about it?" During the following days cross-examination Costello had acquired his trump card from a person, who had been annoyed with what the witness had said about Behan on the previous day. He returned immediately to the person of Brendan Behan. Costello had acquired *Tarry Flynn*, a book by Kavanagh and inscribed by him, in very friendly terms to Brendan Behan.
Costello asked Kavanagh if the writing was his.
"That is my handwriting surely. I have been weak on many occasions, and have given my books and written my name".
The inscription read;" For Brendan, poet and painter, on the day he decorated my flat. Sunday 12th 1950". Kavanagh then went on a diatribe about Behan saying that he was no friend of his. Costello pressed home his advantage as Kavanagh lost his composure, after thirteen hours in the witness box.
Towards the end of this, speaking of Radio Éireann he said:
"There is at the moment a small pernicious minority…" and then he referred directly to Costello indicting him; *"as the representative of that small pernicious minority"*.
However he paused immediately, realising just what he had said.
He went on to retract it:
"I am sorry to say that. I am very sorry"
"Ah, Mr. Kavanagh, I don't mind. I didn't take offence from it"

Costello had apparently demonstrated that Kavanagh had been economical with the truth about his friendship with Behan. Antoinette Quinn states starkly, "the jury could recognise what appeared to be a palpable lie on his part as to his relations with Behan". Despite his efforts to explain away his action in signing the book for Behan, the jury agreed with Costello's interpretation, and on the seventh day of the trial returned a verdict of not guilty, after a short consideration of one and a quarter hours. The story newspapers headlined, "Dublin Journalist Loses Action".

Patrick Kavanagh had summoned his brother Peter, from London to be with him for the duration of the Trial. They were extremely close, with Peter highly conscious of his brother's unacknowledged genius. Peter has written several books about his brother. In his *Patrick Kananagh A Life Chronicle*, he wrote that he had often been asked was there not among the three or four million Irish people some outsider, some wealthy person, who helped his poverty stricken brother. One of the two people he named was, "Prime Minister John A Costello who late in life got him a sinecure – conscience money – of four hundred pounds a year from University College Dublin, after he had first degraded and demeaned him when he was opposing counsel in a law suit"[1a]. He adds that by that time, his brother was an invalid suffering from cancer. Antoinette Quinn writes that after the law case "Kavanagh sensed that Costello, as victor, would feel some sympathy for the vanquished poet. He was right. The new Taoiseach was eager to make amends. He secured another powerful patron and would call on his services in the near future"[2].

Peter Kavanagh has written of the trial, that Costello's "defence was based on Edward Carson's defence in the first trial of Oscar Wilde. His tactic was to attack Patrick as if he were the defendant. Costello used every courtroom trick while Patrick's lawyers were not alert enough to forestall his trickery. It was a shameless performance by Costello, a performance afterwards denounced by his peers in a private review"[3]. Two months later, the Dáil was dissolved, and in May, Costello was re-elected as Taoiseach. Patrick Kavanagh lived in Costello's constituency and was a Fine Gael supporter. As he was coming out from the polling booth on 18 May Kavanagh "ran into Costello"[4]. Costello shook hands with him and said, "I hope that you hold no grudge against me". Patrick assured him that he did not and informed him that he had just voted for him. Peter Kavanagh writes that Costello was a man who loved the limelight of a court case, especially one involving literature. Peter acknowledged that there was still a matter of ethics, as technically, Costello still represented the opposition. He adds rather judgementally of Costello that, "Oddly he had a conscience of sorts, unusual in a politician"[5].

It is difficult nowadays to understand the poverty-stricken fashion in which the poet existed. He was continually on the lookout for a job. In October 1954 the post of curator of the Municipal Gallery was advertised. The salary at £12 per week was poor, but Kavanagh's interest was taken by the availability of the free accommodation attached. He made contact with the Taoiseach to assist his application, which was unsuccessful[6].

Kavanagh fell seriously ill between the trial and the appeal. He was admitted to Rialto Hospital. Brendan Lynch writes that, "the poet's physical reserve came to the rescue and he gradually improved. To his delight he was no longer an ordinary patient. Visits by Mr. Costello, Professor Tierney and Archbishop McQuaid had greatly boosted his status among staff and fellow patients alike"[7]. During one visit at the end of 1954, Dr. McQuaid promised Kavanagh that if he ever again required hospital treatment, he would organise a private room for him in the Mater Hospital, all expenses paid[8].

By June 1954, Antoinette. Quinn says that Kavanagh was "hounding" Costello for employment[9]. Peter Kavanagh terms these contacts as, "a series of quiet communications between both of them"[10]. At Christmas, Patrick sent Costello an as yet unpublished poem, *"From a Prelude"* as a Christmas present. Costello replied assuring Kavanagh that he had not forgotten his promise of help.
He wrote;

> *Dear Patrick Kavanagh,*
> *I wish I could acknowledge more gracefully and more substantially the grace and substance of "From a Prelude".*

Quinn terms Kavanagh's actions "part of a strategy of coaxing or coercing Costello into providing the writer with a livelihood"[11]. On 16 December Costello wrote: "You may be assured that though you have not heard from me, I have not forgotten you. I warned you that it probably would take time and not be too restive if you didn't hear from me. I have been inquiring and will continue my searches". When nothing happened Patrick wrote again saying that his economic position had reached, "the impossible" and that he was considering emigrating. He was turning to, "the man who of all people in Ireland probably knew him most intimately". He appreciated that it was probably not easy for Costello to identify and execute matters on his behalf. He suggested three possibilities, which the Taoiseach himself had already mentioned. A grant from the Arts Council would be useful. He might secure employment as a journalist on the news staff in Radio Éireann or on the staff of Aer Lingus in the publicity department.

Costello replied by hand to this letter in a sympathetic manner, marked 'Personal and Confidential' from the Department of the Taoiseach on 17 February 1955:

> *Dear Mr. Kavanagh,*
> *I have received your letter of yesterday's date and am sorry that things are bad. I have not forgotten you. Last week I had a conversation with the President of UCD and we discussed the possibility of using your services as a lecturer on Poetry - giving lectures around the country. I said that if he could arrange that, I would see if I could get the Arts Council to contribute something to the expenses involved. I would be glad if you would regard this as strictly confidential and mention it to no one. If that does not come off - and I have good hopes that it will - I will try something else. You can rely on me to appreciate your news.*

> *Sincerely yours, John A Costello.*

In his earlier book, Peter Kavanagh continued the story, saying "Costello finally came through with a sinecure as promised". From that date Patrick would get a salary of £400 annually. Later that year Patrick visited his brother in London. Peter saw that Patrick's health had improved and that he would be able to "live somewhat above the poverty line".

In *Patrick Kavanagh, Sacred Keeper, a Biography*, published in 1980, Peter Kavanagh had written "Costello was a generous fellow despite his tactics in the courtroom – he had a conscience, had a sense of shame, qualities unknown in many people. In the court, his sense of fairness had to be cast aside – he was an advocate and his obligation was to win. What matter that his client was a scoundrel and that he was an advocate for the lowest elements in Irish society"[12].

However in his later book, Peter added with some bitterness, "In retrospect it was a miserable amount, about $1,000 a year, to give a man of his genius, when compared with the salaries of Michael Tierney or John Costello, which must have been twenty times or more that amount, men who are not likely to be remembered beyond this page"[13].

In later years Parson's bookshop at Baggot St Bridge became a meeting venue where Kavanagh received and left messages. Among the people who sometimes called there offering their services was the ex-Taoiseach[14].

When Kavanagh died in 1967 and was buried from the nearby Haddington Road Church, John A Costello was among the mourners[15].

*Patrick Kavanagh statue
alongside the Grand Canal Dublin.*

Liam Cosgrave

Tom O'Higgins

CHAPTER 16

SECOND INTER-PARTY GOVERNMENT
1954-1957

In proposing Costello as Taoiseach in May 1954, Richard Mulcahy spoke of him as following in the tradition of Pearse and Griffith. He recalled how in 1948 Costello had to make up his mind within 24 hours to leave all that life meant to him by way of profession and the ordinary course of life that he had been used to. Mulcahy continued, "He had been with us here, and he had stood before British courts-martial to demand the rights and liberties that were those of Irishmen. He had stood for the civic rights of our people in difficult political circumstances here, and he knew something of the political world, but he could hardly have imagined that some day or other he would be asked to leave the quiet of personal family circumstances, and in 24 hours he did it". Each of the other Inter-party leaders supported Costello's nomination and he was elected by 79 votes to 66. deValera's nomination was defeated by 66 votes to 78. Frank Fahy of Fianna Fáil had earlier been re-elected as Ceann Comhairle.

Costello's apparently rather casual nomination of his Minister of Health had occurred earlier that morning at the Four Courts. Tom O'Higgins had spent the morning in court and had ensured that he would be free in the afternoon to attend the new Dáil session at Leinster House. As he was leaving the Law Library he happened to meet the Taoiseach-in-waiting, who was attired in court dress and about to change into civilian dress enroute to the Dáil. Costello stopped O'Higgins and said "Tom, I want you to join the government". O'Higgins was rather stunned and felt sure that he must have looked astonished, as Costello then asked him, "do you want to?" O'Higgins just about managed to respond affirmatively and asked, "what post?" He records that at that point Costello became quite formal, replying, "I want you to become Minister for Health in my government, and furthermore, I want you to take health out of politics". O'Higgins was elated and thought immediately of how proud his late father would have been. The matter was thus finalised and as O'Higgins records, "that was that"[1.] When Costello returned to the Dáil after visiting the President, he nominated his Ministers:

William Norton, Labour, Tánaiste and Industry and Commerce:
Richard Mulcahy, Fine Gael, Education:
Joseph Blowick, Clann na Talmhan, Lands:
James Everett, Labour, Justice:
James Dillon, Fine Gael, Agriculture:
Sean MacEoin, Fine Gael, Defence:
Michael Keyes, Posts and Telegraphs:
Liam Cosgrave, Fine Gael, External Affairs:
Brendan Corish, Labour, Social Welfare:

Gerard Sweetman, Fine Gael, Finance:
Patrick O'Donnell, Fine Gael, Local Government:
Thomas Francis O'Higgins, Fine Gael, Health:
Patrick McGilligan, Fine Gael, Attorney General:

The newcomers were Liam Cosgrave, Gerard Sweetman, Pa. O'Donnell, Brendan Corish and Tom O'Higgins. Dan Morrissey, a Minister in the first Inter-Party government, had chosen to stay on the backbenches[2]. Young Jim Larkin refused the offer to become a Minister[3].

Clann na Poblachta had been returned to the Dáil with only three seats. MacBride at first had proposed a national government with John A Costello as Taoiseach. He said, "I feel certain that the President or His Eminence Cardinal d'Alton, would willingly assist in the resolution of conflicting views. To dispel any ungenerous criticism that may be made of this initiative, let me state, as I did in 1951, that by reason of the small representation of my Party in the Dáil, I would not expect representation in such a national government"[4]. Costello had indeed offered MacBride a post in cabinet, which he declined, saying, " With all the goodwill in the world, on the part of all concerned, I would ultimately find myself in the position of a lodger who was not paying for his keep"[5]. He told Costello that he had no difference with the government's proposed policy. On the proposal of Costello as Taoiseach in the Dáil, MacBride said, "He is a man of integrity, honour and ability". The National Executive of Clann na Poblachta had forbidden its elected TD's to participate in government, though it offered its support from without. At that stage MacBride had lost much control within his own Party.

deValera used the occasion in the Dáil to express his view that coalition governments were bad for the country. He said that large political parties have quite different objectives and he would prefer to see a Labour Party Government or a Fine Gael Party Government.

It was a matter of great personal pleasure for Costello when his life-long friend, Arthur Cox, took his place in the Seanad on 22 July 1954 as one of the Taoiseach's nominees. Cox's law firm had been closely associated with the development of major state enterprises, including the Shannon Scheme, Bord na Mona, and the Irish Life Assurance Company.

GERARD SWEETMAN

Paddy McGilligan's decision not to take Finance again turned out to be of fundamental importance. He was sixty-five and in moderate health. The new Finance Minister, Gerard Sweetman was a son of James M Sweetman, a member of the Banking Commission, 1934-38, and a member of the Currency Commission, before his death in 1939. Gerard Sweetman turned out to be in the mould of Sean MacEntee, believing that financial probity had to take precedence over political strategy. He had a strong personality. Manning describes him as "Charming or ruthless as the occasion demanded but always vigorous in expressing his deeply-rooted conservative beliefs. His conservatism was to a great extent doctrinaire, and differed in its depth of intellectual conviction from the instinctive conservatism of so many of his colleagues. He was not a man to make easy concessions and his style of debate left little room for compromise"[7]. Sweetman, born in 1908, was a Dubliner from an Anglo-Irish family, educated at Downside Public School in England and Trinity College Dublin. He became a senior partner in the legal firm of Fottrel & Sons. He failed to be elected to the Dáil in 1932 and 1943, for Carlow Kilkenny. During the intervening years he did not seek office due to ill health. He became a Senator in 1943 and a TD in 1948.

Tom O'Higgins reports how Costello had antagonised Sweetman on the occasion he appointed him Minister of Finance in 1954. He wrote, "Mr. Costello, in a bantering fashion had said in his presence to a number of us that Sweetman would always have available the advice and help of Paddy McGilligan, the former Minister of Finance, and of John O'Donovan, the well-known economist, who was secretary of the Government. That was a profound mistake. Sweetman was extremely annoyed. He was determined to be his own man and did not feel the need for help from anyone else, and he certainly never sought it"[8]. The fact that relations between Sweetman and McGilligan were distrustful did not help. A character like Sweetman's had the potential to disrupt the relative *laissez faire* operation of Costello's cabinet.

Patrick Lindsay wrote that Sweetman and himself had a "sort of love-hate relationship which was based on mutual respect. He was a great worker who would not ask anybody to do something he would not do himself. He was a man of great courage and had an integrity that was often mistaken for ruthlessness"[9].

Sweetman wasted little time in telling the Dáil that MacEntee had "scraped the bottom of the barrel" leaving no financial reserves[10]. He sent a memorandum to his cabinet colleagues saying that, "Current outgoings should be met from current revenue; exchequer borrowing requirements are excessive and there is an urgent need for swingeing cuts in public expenditure, the overall objective should be to secure a substantial easement of the tax burden"[11].

It was politically necessary for the new Government to demonstrate that it would reduce some food prices. It reduced a pound of butter by six pence, costing £2 million annually. Some public pay increases refused by Fianna Fáil were sanctioned at a cost of £1 million per year. The important Estimates Committee was composed of Costello, Norton, Dillon and Sweetman. Initially Dillon backed Sweetman's policies but neither Norton nor Costello ever did. Discontent within the Labour movement was particularly obvious and Norton was placed under considerable pressure. The first year and a half of the new government went well. Bye-elections were, of course, of enormous importance in a tight parliamentary situation. During 1956 Clann na Poblachta retained its seat in Kerry due to transfers from Inter-Party voters, as did the son of Alfie Byrne retained his father's Independent seat in Dublin defeating Charles Haughey of Fianna Fáil by 4,000 votes.

COSTELLO'S FOREIGN POLICY
1954-57

Sean Macbride had departed External Affairs and with him went the 'surrealist interlude' of the first Inter-Party Government's foreign policy. Freddy Boland spoke of the "surrealist simplicities" of Costello's first government and commented that it had about as much a notion of diplomacy as I have of astrology"[12]. Of course as Joseph Morrison Skelly writes, "small nations have their own national interests which they "assiduously protect in the international system by bilateral relationships, overlapping alliances, neutrality, non-alignment, economic agreements, trade pacts and so on.". Skelly adds that " the utility of ethics or principles in the formulation and execution of foreign policies have a part to play – and it is very significant. But relative to interests their place recedes into the background"[13].

In Costello's second term as Taoiseach, he returned his government to his earlier principles espoused at the League of Nations. Ronan Fanning wrote "No longer encumbered by the unreconstructed republicanism of MacBride, Costello had joined the realist camp[14]. He outlined this in a memorandum to the cabinet delineating foreign policy guidelines, shortly after returning from a visit to America in early 1956. Its central thesis was that "while we cannot muster big battalions, our moral influence is, or could be, considerable. Accordingly it was vital to wield this authority within the wider world so as to strengthen the Christian civilisation of which Ireland is a part"[15]. The new Minister for Foreign Affairs, Liam Cosgrave, described by Ronan Fanning as, "then a relatively junior party colleague of Costello" emphasised that Ireland "belonged to the great community of states, made up of The United States of America, Canada and Western Europe" and it was in Ireland's national interest that this group of states should remain strong and united"[16].

The Taoiseach outlined the new policy in more detail in the Dáil, when speaking on External Affairs. He said that the maintenance of world peace was vital to all small nations. He added that it was his conviction that Ireland should also promote the acceptance of Christian principles in international relations.

He quoted from a speech he had given to the National Press Club in Washington, in which he had said that his foreign policy sought to promote the spirit of justice, Christian charity and goodwill. "We seek our own survival, the welfare of our people and the preservation of peace and of the rule of law in international relations". For himself, he sought the "restoration of the territorial unity of Ireland". The next policy point was opposition to atheistic Communism, which confronted the established order of society. He emphasised that he had no quarrel with Russia or the Russian people, but the spread of imperialistic communism must be repelled no matter how well it may be camouflaged. Ireland should do nothing, by which subtracting from the power of the USA or Great Britain, would relatively strengthen the power of Russia.

He acknowledged that he had been criticised for not being consistent on Partition in statements made in America. However, he declared that "Ireland can never pursue adventurous policies and the risk of war which would therefore hazard the nation's survival". Ireland's foremost policy on partition and its inability to join military alliances were understood. He reiterated again that Ireland would raise Partition at the United Nations, but at an appropriate time and on the proper occasion. It was not going to become a sore thumb there. He said that anyone who had experience of " attending international organisations saw how particular countries and particular individuals, who are constantly putting forward their own interests and their own particular grievances to the exclusion of all other interests, lost all influence and came to be regarded as nothing but a mere nuisance". He regretted that having been excluded from the United Nations for nine years, Ireland had lost valuable experience in the mechanisms of diplomacy at that body.

Costello held that it was necessary for Ireland to have friends. Partition could not be solved without the help of friends and friends could not be obtained by pursuing an entirely selfish course. It was a question of timing, a question of discretion, a question of making friends, a question of doing good turns for other nations so that they would do good turns in return. Trade was obtained through international contacts and friendship. It was along those general lines that he felt Ireland should operate on partition. He stated, quite bluntly that "the American State Department's official policy is that America will not interfere between us and Great Britain on the question of Partition". He acknowledged that Ireland had other powerful allies in America, who together with allies gained by Ireland's activities at the United Nations would be the best way forward.

Costello paid tribute to the officers of the Department of External Affairs, who if anything, were underpaid. He said that he was often pressed to extend our representation abroad, especially when there were so many Irish missionaries in Africa and the East.

He ended his speech by thanking the President of the USA, the Government and official America for their recent extraordinary welcome for him as head of the Irish Government, at a time when they carried the greatest weight of international responsibility[17].

The previous Minister of External Affairs, Sean MacBride, would not have been amused when Costello spoke about how Ireland would be more circumspect about raising partition at international *fora,* and be intent on avoiding becoming a sore thumb in the eyes of their allies. This was clearly a reference to MacBride's *modus operandi.* MacBride never forgave those who crossed him, and he would bide his time to seek revenge on Jack Costello[18].

※ ※ ※ ※

When Liam Cosgrave spoke at the United Nations, he outlined the principles, which would guide Ireland's position. It would be faithful to the UN Charter, be independent, and work for the preservation of Christian civilisation, the defence of the free world and would resist the spread of Communism. When Frank Aiken became Minister in 1957, this realistic policy changed for a period, until Sean Lemass became Taoiseach and reaffirmed the realist tradition. When Aiken voted for a discussion on the admission of China to the United Nations, and caused such angst to the Americans, Costello challenged him in the Dáil to state whether his action represented Government policy. Aiken refused to give a direct answer[19].

The establishment of diplomatic relations with Israel had to be considered in 1955, when Professor Leonard Abrahamson wrote to Costello saying, "I am writing because I understood from Sean MacBride, when we had the pleasure of your company and his, that in his term of office, the matter had not been concluded simply because of neglect and not for any special reason. As there would, I believe, be economic advantages in full diplomatic relations between the two countries, I now venture to raise the matter with you"[20]. However, not surprisingly, it was not until December 1974 that full diplomatic relations were established[21].

1954 - 1957 Coalition Government
Seated (L. to R.) S. MacEoin, B. Corish, W. Norton, J.A. Costello, R. Mulcahy,
J. Blowick, M. Keyes, J. Dillon.
Back standing (L. to R.) G. Sweetman, L. Cosgrave, T.F. O'Higgins, P.A. O'Donnell.

CHAPTER 17

COSTELLO REBUKES CATHOLIC HIERARCHY
AGRICULTURAL INSTITUTE CLONLARA INSIDENT

While it is often argued that the '*Mother and Child*' controversy was an example of the State 'capitulating' to the Church, little attention has been given to examples when the State, under John A Costello, confronted the Church and as WT Cosgrave had done in 1922-3, effectively told the Church that civil matters were properly within the sphere of the State and would be so conducted. This happened in the cases of the Agricultural Institute and the Clonlara incident in County Clare. Of course, as I also show below, the Church did not cease from making challenging representations the State, with varying results The controversy between the bishops and Costello over the Agricultural Institute exemplified his position of an inclusive Ireland composed of Catholics and Protestants. It focussed on the institution that was Trinity College Dublin and as in the 'Mother and Child Controversy, other 'external' vested interests, specifically the universities and farming organisations were also heavily involved.

An attempt to set up an Agricultural Institute during the life of this Government became a matter of great controversy. James Dillon, Minister of Agriculture, was very conscious of the absence of any major scientific research in agricultural or veterinary matters. University College Dublin had a large faculty of agriculture; Trinity College had a small one; University College Cork had a faculty of Dairy Science; University College Galway was agitating for an agricultural faculty; with the Department of Agriculture having some offices around the country. Dillon's idea was that agricultural students would attend the universities for the first two years of their studies, and spend the next two at a new Agricultural Institute for fundamental scientific education[1]. He hoped to establish this independent institute, which might attract Marshall Aid or other American finance. He had received conditional approval from Costello and the cabinet in 1950. Very soon vested interests from the veterinary profession in UCC, UCD the National Universities of Ireland, began to oppose the idea. The change of government allowed the Department of Finance, which disapproved of the expenditure involved, to delay any great progress from 1951 to 1954, despite deValera's backing for the scheme.

That period saw a new initiative propose that the new Agricultural Institute would incorporate UCC's Dairy Science Department, UCD's Albert College, the Veterinary College, and affiliate to both NUI and Trinity College. It would have as much autonomy as the universities, which together with the farming organisations would nominate a majority of the governing body. The fact that Trinity College was to be included with the same status as the NUI colleges did not please the Catholic bishops. No central campus was envisaged. Though this plan was agreed in principle, the opposition continued apace with the involvement of Bishop Lucey of Cork on a delegation to see deValera from UCC. At that stage the universities at Cork, Galway and Trinity College began looking for an increase in their own agricultural faculties. When the government changed in 1954, Dillon maintained previous policy. The Catholic Hierarchy requested a meeting with Costello in 1955. He agreed to meet Bishop Browne of Galway and Bishop Lucey of Cork[2]. They were not as subtle as John Charles McQuaid and told Costello that their NUI 'must not be impaired', and that Trinity College must not have a say in the teaching of agriculture in the new Institute'. Costello was easy meat for the bishops where Catholic teaching was involved. But he felt that there were no such issues involved here. He was very firm with them saying that the Institute was already agreed in principle and "that the association of Trinity with the Institute was already agreed in principle, and was now an accomplished fact". He told them that he had been assured by deValera that Fianna Fáil were fully behind it. He noted that when Bishop Lucey had earlier met deValera as part of the UCC delegation, there was no objection made to TCD being an integral part of the new Institute. He assured them that the government "would not do anything which would give material for unfriendly persons to make charges against us of intolerance or unfairness towards the Protestant minority".

At a Christus Rex Congress in April 1955 Bishop Lucey said, "The church was not just one group among the many groups making up the State, but had a firmer and broader base than any of them. Thus it was that when the bishops in this country took a stand not so long ago on the Health Bill, they were not acting as a mere pressure group: they were not exercising the democratic right they undoubtedly had as citizens to make representations directly to the Government. They intervened on the higher ground that the Church is the divinely appointed guardian and interpreter of the moral law. In a word their position was that they were the final arbiters of right and wrong, even in political matters. In other spheres the State might for its own good reason ignore the advice of the experts, but in faith and morals it might not"[3].

Intensive lobbying of the Taoiseach took place by other vested interests also. Letters and memoranda came from Professor Tierney of UCD, Mayor Russell of Limerick, Senator Roger McHugh, Bishops Browne of Galway and Lucey of Cork, and Cardinal d'Alton. The National Farmers Association was also heavily involved, with other more specialised farming interests also to the fore.

During this time, the Government was also in negotiation with the American Foreign Service for finance for the new Institute. In the middle of 1955 Costello received a letter from WH Taft III on the matter. One sentence, which indicated that Taft appreciated what was afoot, said, "It must be very difficult to reconcile so many parties' interests in the Institute of Agriculture". In August the Government announced that there was an account in the Central Bank, established by the Minister of Finance called the 'American Grant Counterpart Special Account'. There was £6,142,00 in the account, which had been given by the American Government under the Marshal Aid Plan. In 1954 the American and Irish Governments had reached general agreement to use this money to establish the Agriculture Institute[4].

The bishops were not giving up easily. On receipt of a memorandum outlining the structure of the Institute, Bishop Browne wrote to Costello on 30 July in an aggressive manner saying;
"I thank you for your memorandum on the Agriculture Institute. There is a legal - maxim, *Quod ab initio nhil fit, non formatur tractu temporis*. As the proposed Institute violates the University settlement of 1908, not even the agreement of yourself and Mr. deValera could heal its fundamental defect"[5]. James Dillon received government approval for a Bill on the Institute on 29 August.

Bishop Lucey launched a public attack on the Institute at a Confirmation ceremony in September. He said that the scheme was "socialism of a gradual, hidden and underhand type". He described Trinity College as an institution "if not wholly Protestant, is free thinking or indifferent as regards religion". He argued that it should not therefore have a position of equality with the NUI Colleges. Only Archbishop Walsh of Tuam within the hierarchy supported the Institute [6], though he said at a meeting in Galway that he had "no confidence in any institute established in Dublin to direct agricultural activities in Ireland"[7].

On 19 September 1955 the Taoiseach had met the Archbishop of Dublin, Dr. McQuaid. That same day he wrote to the Archbishop, "With reference to our conversation, I enclose the following documentation relating to the Agricultural Institute". The letter listed the eight lengthy documents which the Taoiseach had sent to the Archbishop. The Bishops formally wrote to the Taoiseach on 18 October 1955. A covering letter from Bishop James Fergus, secretary to the hierarchy, said that the bishops had considered the Agricultural Institute at their recent meeting at Maynooth. He continued:

"As their Lordships do not wish to cause any embarrassment to the Government, they are not issuing their views for publication, but I have been instructed to forward them directly to you". The bishops' long memorandum attacked the Institute as "another incursion of the State into the sphere of higher education. We are particularly concerned at the grave injury which the Institute, as proposed, would inflict on the National University of Ireland. It would transfer Catholic students to a purely secular institute and it was a serious setback to the historical efforts of the Catholic people to secure higher education". The real agenda of the bishops was sectarian and they did not mince their words, writing, "The Catholic bishops have never denied to their Protestant fellow citizens their just rights and due proportion of State endowment, in accordance to their numbers. We regard with serious misgivings the trend in recent years to allocate to Trinity College, a state subsidy out of proportion to the number of Protestants in the State even though Trinity had an extensive endowment originating from the confiscation of State property. It is a serious matter for the Catholic taxpayer to be asked to endow an institution which is prohibited to Catholics as intrinsically dangerous and it raises issues of serious importance as to who are charged with the defence of the Catholic faith"[8].

At the risk of complicating the matter, I feel the need to refer back to an event relating to Trinity College, that occurred during the latter days of the first Inter-Party government, which I believe may have influenced Costello's handling of the present matter. At that time students attending Trinity College comprised 34% from the Republic, 30% from Britain and 18% each from Northern Ireland and overseas[9]. The College was in desperate need of extra finance and had approached the Government for extra assistance in 1947. It received a grant of £35,000. The College then put on a series of lectures as a gesture towards the State "in Irish on Mathematics and on Irish archaeology" for a brief period. In 1949 Trinity sought an annual grant of £88,000 and a capital grant of £250,00. However, the new government did not see the universities as a priority, and both Trinity and University College Dublin saw their grants unchanged for three successive years. In the spring of 1951 UCD's total grant increased to £233,000 per annum, while TCD's increased to £60,000. Trinity College felt that it was being discriminated against due to the Minister of Finance's close association with UCD. Paddy McGilligan still retained the part-time post of Professor of Law at UCD.

The Provost of TCD, Dr. Alton and the Registrar, AJ McConnell met McGilligan and Costello on 19 March 1951 to discuss the matter. McGilligan spoke for the government and told the Trinity men that there was no valid comparison between their College and UCD. Trinity was a private institution catering for a small minority. Many of its courses were offensive to Catholics, and such Catholics as attended it did so, only because they did not want to learn Irish or because they were put off by the higher intellectual standards of UCD. There could be no question of parity of treatment. UCD was part of what was justly called the National University. When Costello was asked directly if he agreed with McGilligan's views, he "shifted uneasily in his chair and made a non-commital reply". In a letter written after the meeting, Alton regretted that he could not have talked to Costello alone, as whenever he spoke McGilligan interrupted him. It appears that the meeting developed into "an argument before two impotent spectators, between a Ballymena Presbyterian and a Derry Catholic – a confrontation that was unlikely to end in détente". The Trinity representatives were soon advised that the attitude of the government might be linked to a desire to appease the Catholic Archbishop of Dublin. They were also appraised of the pending crisis in government between Dr. Noel Browne, a Trinity College graduate, and the rest of his cabinet colleagues. The Provost later wrote to Costello thanking him for the "sympathy which he had shown"[10]. I believe that Costello's action and attitude in 1955 towards Trinity College may have been influenced by this particular episode, with which he was so distinctly uncomfortable

❋❋❋❋

The letter from the bishops on the Agricultural Institute was acknowledged on 21 October 1955. Costello's response, as Maurice Manning has written, "was angry and spirited, and backed by the entire government"[11]. Costello's reply on 4 November rejected the bishops' charges and inaccuracies, particularly their assertion that this was "another state incursion". He outlined the correct facts involved. He did not accept that having representatives of Trinity College on the Board of the Institute was " an injection of external and hostile elements". He continued;

"The proposal of representation to Trinity College is not a question which can be decided on the basis of the number of Protestants in the 26 counties. Broad conditions of the national interest could not close their eyes to the fact that Protestants amount to 24% of the population of Ireland as a whole, and that the ending of partition is a primary aim of national policy". He ended his letter saying that the government would try to meet the views of the bishops and all other interested parties "to the utmost extent that may appear compatible with the general interest of the country as a whole" [12]. The bishops were most displeased with Costello's total and unexpected rebuke.

In a reply dated 19 January 1956, Bishop Fergus said "that the Hierarchy expresses its deep regret at the tone and contents of the document which the Government thought fit to address to it. The Standing Committee is satisfied that none of the main objections put forward by the Bishops have been answered".

A note in the Taoiseach's file, dated 25 January 1956 says: "At a meeting of the Government held on 24th January the Taoiseach brought to the notice of his colleagues the letter dated 19th instant, addressed to him by the bishop of Achonry". It was clear that Costello's anger with the bishops was unabated, as the note merely records: "The view was taken that the letter does not call for any reply"[13].

The Government realised that to implement its basic idea of agricultural research it had to compromise. It needed the agreement of the farmers and the universities. It decided to set up the Agricultural Institute independent of the universities, with its own staff and authority to carry out or co-ordinate research. The idea of it being a teaching institute was dropped. The farmers agreed with this plan and the Agricultural Institute Bill was finalised by November 1956. On 2 November Costello wrote a confidential letter to Mr deValera outlining how the Agricultural Institute Draft Bill was being revised. He added, "As you know the proposals met with a considerable amount of criticism, on various grounds, from the interests concerned".

On 7 November 1956 Mr. deValera asked the Taoiseach, in the Dáil, when the Bill embodying the Government's proposals for the establishment of the Agricultural Institute would be introduced. Costello replied that the general scheme had been approved by the government as a basis for further discussions between the Minister for Agriculture and the interests concerned, including the United States authorities, the universities and farm organisations The existing Agricultural Faculties will remain with the Universities for the granting of degrees in Agriculture, Veterinary and Dairy Science.

Under the proposed legislation, the Institute will be empowered to grant a higher degree, to engage in research and to assist in the extension and development of research in existing institutions. Whether there would be any teaching at the Institute will be a matter for the Institute".

On 12 November a note in the Taoiseach's file says: "The Taoiseach sent under cover of a personal letter to His Grace the Archbishop of Dublin, Dr. McQuaid a copy of the general scheme of the Agricultural Institute Bill in the form approved by the Government. He received an acknowledgement from His Grace"[14].

When Fianna Fáil came to power the Hierarchy again made almost identical representations to deValera. This included that they "would feel it their duty to oppose any determination against the interests of the University (NUI) which Catholics after a long struggle obtained as some measure of their rights, there is serious danger that Catholic students may be forced or drawn to attend Trinity College"[15]. It fell to Fianna Fáil to actually set up the Agricultural Institute in 1958. While this controversy was not directly a clash between Church and State, it indicated clearly that the Catholic bishops still felt that they could call the shots with Government. The bishops and their allies challenged the government's clear intentions on the Institute, but Costello and his Government do come out of the episode well for the way they responded to the hierarchy's sectarian involvement.

One of the best explanations of Archbishop McQuaid's persona and attitude is to be found in the book by the two Trinity College Professors already referred to. They write "He was a man of great energy, ability and (as far as personal contact was concerned) suavity and charm. The force of his personality was enough to transfer the primacy, if not *de jure then de facto*, from Armagh to Dublin. He had been Headmaster of Blackrock College, and preserved as Archbishop a headmaster's interest in detail and a determination that his wishes should be carried out without question and without compromise. And the most prominent of his aims was to make the Catholic Church the unchallenged arbiter of all questions in which it could reasonably claim to have an interest. Protestants and infidels were entitled to their civil rights and to the direction of their private institutions, but they need not expect any share in the direction of public education, welfare, medicine or even famine relief. Ireland was to be in as full a sense as possible a Catholic country. This attitude was not enunciated with any arrogance, or even very explicitly, but it was implemented by continuous hints, directives and pressures, and more than one mixed committee for charitable work had to be dissolved and reconstituted on sectarian lines. McQuaid was able to carry out his policy all the more effectively because he was obviously a devout, and indeed a holy man, and was not primarily in pursuit of personal power". The authors add that his ban on Catholics attending Trinity made him a bogeyman for Protestants and liberal Catholics. They add, "The reaction was natural enough, but it was to some extent needless, for McQuaid's inflexibility on paper contrasted strangely with his accommodating attitude in personal interview; and neither from the diocese of Dublin nor from Ireland as a whole did the number of Catholics decline"[16].

SOCCER MATCH VERSUS YUGOSLAVIA
OCTOBER 1955

An international soccer match against Communist Yugoslavia was scheduled for Dalymount Park in October 1955. The Department of Justice contacted the Football Association of Ireland shortly before the match to say that the visiting team needed permission to enter the country. The Department required the names of the visitors and an assurance that the FAI would meet the expenses if any of them sought refugee status in Ireland. This was the first time such assurances were sought. Some days later the FAI received a message from Fr John O'Regan on behalf of the Archbishop. He was unhappy about the visitors too. McQuaid had consulted the Taoiseach on the matter and got his agreement that the visit was unfortunate. The Government had already given permission for the President O'Kelly to welcome the visitors and attend the match. However, Costello advised the Archbishop that he would countermand that permission. O'Kelly saw Costello and, on hearing of the Archbishop's attitude, did not press the matter. The Tánaiste William Norton also cancelled his attendance at the match.

CLONLARA INCIDENT

Members of the Jehovah Witnesses were operating in County Clare in the mid-1950's, visiting houses trying to interest people in the bible. In the village of Clonlara locals attacked two of their number and burned their bibles. The parish curate was party to this action. A court case ensued where the judge used the Probation Act in relation to the charges against the perpetrators. He bound over to the peace the two Jehovah Witnesses on bonds of £200 each, finding that they had committed blasphemy. The bishop of Killaloe, Joseph Rodgers, attended the trial. He subsequently wrote to the Taoiseach complaining angrily about the prosecution of local Catholics.
He wrote:

> *Westbourne*
> *Ennis*
> *Co. Clare*
> *27th July, 1956.*

To,

An Taoiseach, Mr. John A. Costello T.D.

My Dear Mr. Costello,

> *I have just returned home from a sitting of the Limerick District Court where the case of the Attorney-General V. Patrick Ryan C.C., Clonlara [diocese of Killaloe] and Others, was heard before District Justice Gordon Hurley, acting for District Justice D. F.*

Gleeson. The case, as you already may be aware, arose out of a complaint lodged by the 'Jehovah Witnesses' in the persons of a Mr. Millar and a Mr. Bond [a lapsed Catholic] for alleged assault, and seizure and destruction of 'Jehovah Witnesses' "literature" at Clonlara, Co. Clare, on 13th May 1956.

I would suggest that you get the full transcript of the Court proceedings, and study it carefully. I am not easily shocked, yet I freely admit that I was thoroughly shocked and disgusted by what I heard in the Limerick District Court today from Mr. Millar, the "minister" of the Jehovah Witnesses. Blasphemy is but a mild term to use for his smug denial of (a) the doctrine of the Blessed Trinity, (b) the Divinity of Jesus Christ, (c) the Divine Motherhood of Our Blessed Lady, and his repeated assertions, under oath, that all religions and all forms of civil government originate from Satan. Mr. Millar, in open court, blandly claimed parity and equal authority with Jesus Christ Himself. I will not give any more of his disgusting statements – you will find them all in the transcript of the Court proceedings.

I find it hard to credit that the Attorney-General, had he been fully aware of the pernicious and blasphemous literature distributed and sold in my diocese by these self styled 'Jehovah Witnesses', would have proceeded against one of my priests for upholding and defending the fundamental truths of our treasured Catholic Faith. I also find it passing strange that, despite the fact that the preamble to our Constitution invokes and honours the Blessed Trinity, your Attorney-General should arraign in Court an excellent priest of my diocese and the other loyal Catholics of Clonlara Parish, for their defence of the doctrine of the Blessed Trinity, a doctrine so nobly enshrined in our Constitution.

Are we to have legal protection in future against such vile and pernicious attacks on our faith? We censor obscene literature: your Attorney General prosecutes one of my priests for doing what I, and all good Catholics here, regard as his bounden duty and right. The matter cannot rest.

Yours very sincerely
Joseph Rodgers
Bishop of Killaloe.

The Taoiseach replied to the bishop of Killaloe thus;

14 August 1956.

My dear Lord Bishop,

I received Your Lordship's letter of the 27ᵗʰ July on the subject of proceedings recently taken in the District Court against Reverend Patrick Ryan, C.C. Truagh, and certain laymen, and I have made inquiries into the circumstances of the case.

I am informed that Fr. Ryan and the laymen concerned were charged with common assault and malicious damage and that the charges were brought in consequence of a complaint made to the Gárda Síochana by Mr. Stephen G. Miller, following incidents which occurred at Clonlara on the 13th July. It appears that it was alleged, and was not denied, that Mr. Miller was assaulted by one of the laymen who accompanied Father Ryan on the occasion referred to, that Father Ryan and others seized certain books and papers and other property found by them in possession of Mr. Miller and his companion and that a quantity of the books and papers were subsequently destroyed.

I fully appreciate the just indignation aroused among the clergy and the people by the activities of the "Jehovah Witnesses" and by the character of the matter, which, I understand, they disseminate orally and in writing. It is essential, however, to bear in mind that the law provides means of dealing with persons whose conduct is calculated to lead to a breach of the peace or who utter blasphemy or whose utterances constitutes the offence of blasphemy. The evidence to sustain such a charge would not be satisfied by admissions made in other court proceedings.

There is, therefore, a lawful, orderly and effective method of dealing with matters of this kind; and it would be incompatible with the duty of those who are responsible for the maintenance of peace and order to acquiesce in the adoption of other methods, such as assault and the seizure or destruction of property. When any person, whether priest or layman, has reason to believe that blasphemy is being or has been uttered, or that conduct calculated to lead to a breach of the peace is occurring or has occurred, or is likely to occur, his proper course is to make a complaint to the Gárda Síochana and to leave to the Gárda the responsibility for dealing with the situation in accordance with the law. Instead of adopting this course, however, a different course was chosen by those who took part in the Clonlara incident.

The action, which they took, was prima facie contrary to law and, when Mr. Miller complained to the Gárda Síochana – as he did on the very day of the incident - the authorities concerned had no choice but to allow the machinery of the law to take its course.

I do not need to remind Your lordship of the grave evils that would ensue if it came to be accepted that persons who are roused to indignation by the conduct of others – however just that idignation might be – were entitled to take the law into their own hands and to give expression to their feelings and to enforce their views by violent means. If such a situation were to arise, not only would the public peace be threatened but the true interests of religion and morality would inevitably suffer.

I am

My dear Lord Bishop
Sincerely yours,
John A Costello.

Costello also conferred with Dr. McQuaid on the matter and sent him a copy of his reply to Dr. Rodgers. McQuaid replied saying that he had spoken with Dr. Rodgers and was able to assure Costello that the incident would not be repeated[18].

Hugh Lane Gallery, Parnell Square, Dublin.

CHAPTER 18

THE ARTS COUNCIL
RECOVERY OF THE LANE PICTURES

Costello had a longtime personal and political interest in the Arts. In April 1935 he ridiculed the government for the paucity of the remuneration for the Director of the National Gallery. As a part-time post it drew £200 and as a full-time post it was to rise to £500[1]. He described the National Gallery as "an asset of the most tremendous value to the State". He said that no person of competence or capacity ought ever have been offered such a paltry sum. He said that the outstanding art in the gallery focussed attention on the country. He praised Dr. Thomas Bodkin for the outstanding work he had done at the Gallery and criticised the Minister for not uttering "a single word in appreciation of his services. The attractions of the Gallery to visitors abroad have never been properly promulgated…the magnificent collection of priceless pictures acquired by Dr. Bodkin should have seen him paid twenty times that amount. The services which Dr. Bodkin gave to this country would have been passed over if attention had not been directed to them from this side of the House".

As Taoiseach, Costello commissioned Thomas Bodkin to write a report on the Arts in Ireland from which the Arts Council was established. Costello was to use the latter as a vehicle to campaign for the Lane Pictures at a non-political level. Bodkin was to report on the National Museum, the National Gallery and on facilities available for teaching art in schools, universities, and the National College of Art. He was also to report on the links between the arts and industry. He completed his report in 1949.

Costello was then proud to have introduced the Bill establishing the Arts Council in April 1951. He regarded it as an attempt to stimulate public interest in and to promote knowledge and appreciation and practice in the arts. By arts he meant painting, sculpture, architecture, music, drama, literature, design in industry, the fine arts and applied arts generally. He said the Bill was a modest if not meagre contribution to the intention and desire of the Government, announced in 1949, to promote the arts. Costello paid tribute to Bodkin's work and acknowledged that the Deputies surely had had enough time to study the report by then. Costello saw the Bill as a beginning. He acknowledged that there might indeed have been a deliberate policy to obstruct anybody who sought to further the arts in Ireland or the application of art to industry. He quoted Cardinal Newman as saying, "The fine arts are to be encouraged, if only because of their strong tendency to divert mankind from the pursuit of more brutish pleasures". He said that unfortunately, private individuals were often not in a financial position to assist the arts. He thanked Mr. Chester Beatty for donating his pictures to the National Gallery. State support was small compared to other countries, representing about one and a half penny per person. He hoped that the Arts Council would carry out work, which would be a spiritual enrichment but also bring material advancement.

While the Taoiseach hoped that this financial contribution was only a beginning, he acknowledged that that would probably come as a great shock to the officials of the Department of Finance. He hoped that good advice would be available which would not allow the "present atrocity on top of Nelson's Pillar, an atrocity which completely destroys the line and beauty of that monument", to recur. He also looked forward to the Arts Council "carrying on the fight for the recovery of the Lane pictures"[2].

It fell to Costello to make the first appointment to the Chair of the Arts Council in 1956. He offered the post to the most eminent writer of his generation, Sean Ó Faoláin, at a meeting in Government Buildings. Ó'Faoláin was flattered to be asked and accepted the post. He told Costello that it was the first honour his country had ever given him. The post was part-time at a salary of £1,000. The proposed appointment did not find favour with the Archbishop of Dublin who made representations to the Taoiseach, "to prevent this man being appointed". As usual, Costello tried to placate McQuaid and approached Dr. Thomas Bodkin of the National Gallery to accept the post instead of Ó'Faoláin. Bodkin was very surprised as he had been present when Costello had offered the post to Ó'Faoláin some days previously. He refused Costello's shameful request. McQuaid himself then approached Dr. Bodkin, who would not budge from his principled stand[3]. When the appointment of Ó'Faoláin was confirmed, Costello wrote to McQuaid asking for his prayers, if not his blessing. Ó'Faoláin's biographer, Maurice Harmon, writes that McQuaid's opposition to Ó'Faoláin was "understandable. Not only was he a banned writer and an outspoken anticlerical, but as President of the Irish Association of Civil Liberty he had drawn particular attention to censorship"[4].

RECOVERY OF THE LANE PICTURES

When John A Costello was asked, in 1967, to list the achievements of his time in government, he included the recovery of the Hugh Lane Paintings. His involvement in that cause was long and varied and, like much of his legal work, was mostly behind the scenes. The controversy over the French pictures collected by Sir Hugh Lane, which he intended to donate to the people of Dublin, had arisen when the codicil to his will was not witnessed. His subsequent death in the sinking of the Lusitania in 1915 meant that in strictly legal terms the pictures were still owned by the National Gallery in London, to whom he had earlier willed them. Lane was a nephew of Lady Gregory and a collector and connoisseur of paintings. In the Senate on 9 May 1923, WB Yeats described it as "an old question". While Lane had made the Dublin Municipal Gallery the most important collection of French paintings outside Luxembourg, he was somewhat discourteously treated by some of the Dublin newspapers and certain persons, and an acrimonious controversy arose. In 1913 Lane decided, in response to the controversy, to leave the French pictures to the National Gallery in London, where he felt they would be better valued. In his will he left all his property to the National Gallery of Ireland, except for those French paintings.

When he was going to America in 1915 he realised the danger of the journey and added a codicil in ink to his will and signed it on each page, directing the English National Gallery return his French pictures to Dublin. Though he mentioned the codicil to several people, it was not witnessed. Among the people who swore an affidavit about Lane's intention was his sister, Ruth Shine. The codicil would have been legal in Scotland. An Act of Parliament in England was necessary to make the codicil legal there. Speaking in the Senate, WB Yeats pointed out that while the paintings were very valuable, they would never come on the market again. He added that some English critics wanted the paintings to remain in London as they conferred great prestige on the their National Gallery.

In 1925 the Commissioners of the City of Dublin prepared to build a Gallery in Parnell Square to house the Lane Pictures.

Various prominent Irish people became involved. Sir James Craig supported the Irish claim. Lord Carson introduced a Bill in the House of Lords " to enable the Trustees of the National Gallery to transfer the Lane pictures to the National Gallery in Ireland"[5]. He wrote to the Irish High Commissioner in London, James MacNeill, fearing that his Bill may do more harm than good. In 1926 concerted representations were made to the Irish government to take action on the recovery of the Lane Pictures by a variety of individuals and organisations. These included, the the Royal Irish Academy, the Town Clerk of Dublin Corporation, the Water Colour Association, the Architectural Association, Waterford Corporation, the National Gallery, and particularly Hugh Lane's aunt, Lady Augusta Gregory.

As this was a legal matter, in due course the then Attorney General John A Costello was consulted on the matter. He delivered his advice to the President of the Executive Council of the Irish Free State, WT Cosgrave, on 8 June 1926.

He wrote that:
1. No person was specifically named as donee in the clause of Hugh Lane's will bequeathing pictures to the British National Gallery
2. The pictures are bequeathed " To found a Collection of Modern Art in London".
3. The bequest is a charity bequest.
4. The law does not allow "charitable" intentions of the testator to be defeated.
5. Therefore the English Court of Chancery should settle a scheme to execute the Trust as per the will.
6. The Trustees of the British National Gallery would be declared entitled to the pictures within Section 3 of the National Gallery Act 1856 and was probably so ordered by the High Court ruling on 25th May 1917.

Costello had not yet been able to verify the last point. The summary of his advice then was; "This only serves to emphasise the international character of the question and to take the entire case outside the sphere of a dispute between two picture galleries"[6].

The Trustees of the British National Gallery would have preferred an agreement at governmental level. However it was pointed out that governments are not corporate bodies and do not enter into agreements of that nature[7.].

President Cosgrave wrote to WJ Thompson, Colonial Secretary, pressing for the return of the Lane paintings[8]. The British government had set up a committee to investigate the matter. The Wilson Committee reported to the British Government in June 1926. It advised the government that it would be improper to modify Sir Hugh Lane's will by legislation. It said that an agreement between the British and Irish National Galleries on some form of a loan arrangement of the paintings from time to time was the best way forward. LS Amery Secretary of State for the Dominions communicated this to President Cosgrave on 24 June 1926. Cosgrave replied, "We are unable to agree to the proposed agreement for the loan from time to time of a number of the pictures to Dublin as fulfilling Sir Hugh Lane's last wishes as expressed in the codicil to his will on 3 February 1915"[10.].

In 1929 both Lady Gregory and Lady Lavery continued the campaign on the paintings. Lady Lavery, who was in discussions with the Prime Minister's son about the pictures, exchanged letters with WT Cosgrave[11.]. Ramsay MacDonald let it be known privately that if he could he would send the paintings back to Ireland, though he noted that a parliamentary question on the matter would be unhelpful[12].

A major international exhibition of Italian paintings took place in London in 1929/30. Several paintings from Ireland were among those exhibited. In the reviews of the Exhibition no mention was made of this Irish contribution. Thomas Bodkin wrote to President Cosgrave on the matter on 2 January 1930. The letter gives an insight into the politics involved in the arts world. It said;

"On making inquiries through the invaluable Lady Lavery, I found, as expected, reason to believe that Sir Robert Witt, a Trustee of the National Gallery and Chairman of the National Collection Fund and Dr. DS McColl, late Keeper of the Tate and Wallace Collections, both skilled intriguers, both determined enemies of Ireland and both bitter opponents of our claim to the Lane Pictures, had carefully arranged the whole business"[13].

The Irish Free State Government commissioned Thomas Bodkin, a barrister and secretary to the Commissioners for Charitable Bequests and a future Director of the National Gallery in Dublin, to write a definitive work on the Lane Pictures themselves and Ireland's case for their return. WT Cosgrave wrote an introduction to the publication, which contained large plates of all the French paintings, in which he stated that in the codicil Hugh Lane had written "My friend Tom Bodkin should be asked to help". This volume, which cost 83,640 French francs to produce, was sent under President Cosgrave's name to a wide variety of national and international institutions and well placed individuals especially in Britain[14]. Ironically by the time acknowledgements were being sent, the Irish government had changed, and replies were made to Eamon deValera. One such came from Cardinal Pacelli on behalf of the Pope[15].

Ireland's case was made again but a lot of impetus was lost when Lady Gregory died in 1932[16]. Years passed without any likelihood of an outcome favourable to Ireland. John A Costello continued to pursue the matter on a political front as well as through Thomas Bodkin, who served as Director of the National Gallery from 1927-1935. Bodkin then became Director of the Barber Fine Arts Institute in Birmingham until 1952. Costello claimed that Fianna Fáil had done nothing about the pictures from 1932 to 1948, adding, "But then of course Fianna Fáil never had much interest in the humanities. It was left to the Inter-Party Government also to set up the Arts Council"[17].

On the periphery of the Anglo-Irish Trade talks in 1948, Costello raised the matter with Clement Atlee. Costello found the Prime Minister, " a difficult man to get to know. He was very reserved and laconic but after ranging over many aspects of the Irish problem we came to that of the Lane Pictures". Costello put the case strongly for Ireland's ownership, while acknowledging that Britain had the legal right, he said that Ireland had the moral right. He told Atlee that he should at least make a gesture to Ireland on that basis "or even make a present of the pictures to us"[18]. Attlee prevaricated.

In 1949 Costello as Taoiseach made an address to the Friends of the National Gallery Collection in which he said that the artistic conscience of the British was becoming uneasy at the retention of the pictures. He was asked in the Dáil on 7 April 1949 whether that statement was his own opinion or whether it was based on negotiations that had taken place and whether the Government had made recent representations on the return of the Lane Collection and if so with what result. Costello replied that his statement reflected his own opinion. He added that representations of an informal character had in fact been made to the British Government urging the return of the paintings, but that so far these representations had not led to any tangible result.

The British politician who most impressed Costello at that time was Aneurin Bevan. He surprised Costello by his extraordinary knowledge of Irish history, including James Connolly, Jim Larkin, the Anglo-Irish War and the Civil War. Costello had known Bevan previously, "as I had to cross-examine him in a case between two trade unions". A "young Harold Wilson" also impressed him[19].

A Bill was introduced in the House of Commons in October 1954 seeking to legalise Lane's codicil. The Bill received backing from all the members from Northern Ireland, Unionist, Nationalist and Labour. Hartford, Montgomery Hyde and Cahir Healy, spoke. No solution emerged.

During his second government Costello again got deeply involved in the matter at several levels. On 14 July 1955, speaking on an estimate for the Arts Council, Costello informed the Dáil that the Arts Council was fortunate in securing the services of Dr. Thomas Bodkin as a consultant. He also noted that a remit of the Arts Council was to make every effort to secure the Hugh Lane paintings for Ireland. In that connection he was glad to tell the House that Dr. Bodkin had recently given a broadcast on the Lane Pictures. Furthermore Bodkin had secured the agreement of Sir Alec Martin, Managing

Director of Christies and an associate of the Wallace Galleries to broadcast a similar lecture. Martin had become a recent convert to the Irish view on the pictures. Costello instructed the Arts Council to commission and publish a new edition of Bodkin's earlier work, "Hugh Lane and his Pictures". This came out in 1956. Bodkin's summary of the situation remained the same as in 1932. He wrote in the Preface to the second edition "So the Arts Council at the suggestion of the Taoiseach Mr. Costello, decided to ask me to prepare a new edition in order that the history of the controversy over the final destination of Sir Hugh Lane's paintings, which has persisted during the past forty years, shall be clear". He added, "The Irish recognise that the Hugh Lane Pictures are in law the absolute property of the British people. They also believe that the Irishman who collected them wished that after his death, they should belong to his own countrymen, and did his best to ensure that they should"[20]. Costello used this book, as WT Cosgrave had done in 1932, as a vehicle to influence British public opinion. He despatched copies to British parliamentarians, and, those of influence in the arts world there.

Costello's recent initiatives were paying off as long time supporters in Britain took heart that a settlement might be possible. Lord Moyne[Bryan Guinness] had already spoken in the House of Lords on the matter in late 1953 on the possibility of dividing the collection on a permanent basis between Britain and Ireland. This was firmly opposed by the Government speaker, the Earl of Selkirk[21]. Three hundred Members of Parliament signed an expression of their opinion that Ireland should have the paintings one year later. The Duke of Wellington became involved and suggested a formula that was taken up by Lords Moyne and Pakenham as a basis for a solution. Costello understood that the hands of the Trustees of the National Gallery in London were tied legally, and, even if they were favourable to the Irish 'demand/request', they were hamstrung by their legal obligations as Trustees. A series of tense meetings took place with the Trustees over quite a long period.

Harold MacMillan, the Prime Minister, sought a report on the paintings. This report said that a settlement of the issue would assist relations with Ireland. But it also said, "It is questionable whether a compromise would ever satisfy the Irish, feeling as strongly as they do. Is it not better to leave the pictures where they belong and where they are valued, and to leave the Irish with their grievance, which they enjoy?"[22]. MacMillan did not accept that advice and negotiations continued officially at one remove from government. The individuals on the Irish side were Lords Moyne and Pakenham, and Dr. Thomas Bodkin. Every detail was filtered through the Irish Government, which was essentially negotiating the deal. Costello, though out of government in 1957, was being kept abreast of matters as Ambassador Hugh McCann duly informed the secretary to the government, Maurice Moynihan, on 23 October 1958. Bodkin was advising Costello that in his opinion direct governmental negotiations remained desirable[23].

As negotiations were possibly drawing to some finality, Taoiseach de Valera was astute enough, politically and legally, to keep Costello abreast of the situation and to seek and act on his advice. On 4 March 1959, he sent voluminous material to Costello writing:

"I enclose Draft Agreement relating to the Lane Pictures, together with some explanatory notes, prepared by the Attorney General. This material has not yet been shown to the Commissioners of Public Works and is therefore subject to any desire they may offer. I also include:

Lord Pakenham's Draft Statement of 7 July 1958 to the National Gallery sub-committee.

Letter of 11 July 1958 from Dr. Bodkin to Lord Pakenham

Lord Pakenham's note on the position on 11 July 1958

Professor Robbin's letter to Lord Pakenham

The British Trustees are anxious that the Government would undertake to refrain from instigating or supporting, and would disassociate itself from any campaign to overthrow the Agreement. Each Government would associate itself with the Agreement.

I should be glad to have any comments or suggestions you may wish to offer".

Costello replied on 25 March in a letter that clearly demonstrated his discomfort and annoyance, but his pragmatism won out, as he wrote;

Dear Taoiseach,

I have read and considered all the documents and have delayed, perhaps overmuch, in replying to your letter because of my desire to take as calm a view as possible of the proposals...In general the proposals and the approach to a settlement of the matter by the Trustees of the National Gallery, do not appear to me to be either generous or gracious. However, in all the circumstances I fear nothing can be achieved by maintaining a recalcitrant attitude, and the substance of the Agreement may be regarded as some advance, provided that the Irish claims are not prejudiced, as they certainly might be if the suggested revision of Lord Pakenham's draft statement were accepted. The first part of these revisions stated that the Agreement had been reached "which should settle the question of the disposition of the Lane Pictures". The phrase, slipped in rather casually, is a fundamental alteration of Lord Pakenham's draft, which suggested the phrase " which should settle for a considerable period the question of the disposition of the Lane Pictures".
You will notice that the Trustees' Draft omitted the significant words "for a considerable period".

I appreciate your courtesy in keeping me informed of the progress on these events.

Sincerely yours

John A Costello

deValera wrote again to Costello on 3 April and 8 April keeping him updated on proceedings. Costello replied on 8 April saying;

Dear Taoiseach,

I am much obliged for your letters with reference to the draft Agreement. I think the Draft as finally devised is quite satisfactory.

John A Costello

The newspapers heard of the proposed Agreement that same month and reported it in a positive way as a great breakthrough, though definite details were scarce.

The Taoiseach wrote again to Costello with the final Agreement. He replied on 13 May saying:

"I have read the document and I am sure it comprises the best that could be done in all the circumstances".

Within the Government there was a dissenting view being expressed by the Attorney General, Aindrias Ó Caoimh. A Minute from the Office of the Attorney General in the Department of the Taoiseach's file says:

"The Agreement has now taken the shape of an arrangement for a Loan by the Trustees under statutory powers, under onerous conditions. It is hardly likely that an Agreement on the lines of the present draft would be well received in Ireland": The Minute then suggests breaking off the present negotiations and opening negotiations with the British government. It continues: "It is most unfortunate that Lord Pakenham and Lord Moyne and Professor Bodkin took part in these discussions. I suggested to the Taoiseach that the Ambassador should now 'come into the picture'. The whole matter has got to a stage where private negotiators would be better left out. I should of course stress that I am concerned mainly with securing an Agreement worded in a way likely to be acceptable here. Questions of principle are not my concern. The wording of the revised draft would not be acceptable to me". It was initialled A.Ó'C and dated 18 May 1959.

In the meantime Eamon deValera was elected President and Sean Lemass became Taoiseach. An Agreement was finally signed in London on 6 November 1959 between the Commissioners of Public Works in Ireland and the Trustees of the National Gallery. The Irish Ambassador, Hugh McCann, was present.

On 12 November 1959 simultaneous announcements of the Agreement were made in the Dáil and the House of Commons. The Taoiseach, Sean Lemass announced in the Dáil that the Commissioners of Public Works and the Trustees of the National Gallery in London had concluded an Agreement on the Lane pictures. In entering the Agreement, the Commissioners were acting as agents for the Government. The Agreement provided that the 39 Lane pictures would be divided into two groups, to be lent, in turn, for public exhibition in Dublin for successive periods of five years, over a total period of twenty years.

The Government would not initiate or support any alternative arrangement during the currency of the Agreement. Mr Lemass then said that he felt obliged to pay tribute to those whose untiring efforts have helped so greatly to secure the Agreement. " In the first place" he said, " it gives me special pleasure to express the Government's sincere appreciation of the active interest displayed by Deputy John A Costello in this matter, both during his periods of office as Taoiseach and when in Opposition. As Taoiseach he availed himself of every opportunity to renew, in a vigorous manner, the representations of previous governments for the return of the pictures to Ireland, his advice and co-operation have been generously given and have been of inestimable value in the course of the discussions that led to the present Agreement. The Taoiseach also thanked Thomas Bodkin for a lifetime's service in the cause, and in more recent years, Lord Pakenham and Lord Moyne. He also thanked the many friends of Ireland in Britain who had assisted.

In response, Costello said that it was a great privilege and pleasure to join with the Taoiseach's expressions of gratification at the end of a long road, which had to a considerable extent secured the wishes of Hugh Lane. He described the Agreement as "an honourable compromise in a prolonged and difficult controversy". He acknowledged that the Trustees of the National Gallery had gone to the fullest limits of their authority in making the Agreement. He joined with the Taoiseach in thanking the many people in Ireland and Great Britain who had assisted. In particular he thanked Lord Pakenhan and Lord Moyne. He said his own work in the matter had been inspired and directed by the unflagging energy and unfaltering hope of Dr. Thomas Bodkin. He added, " For forty four years he has borne practically the entire burden that Hugh Lane placed upon him in his codicil. The Irish people should guard these treasures as their own. Generations to come will derive that cultural and spiritual advantage from the study of the beauty of the pictures, which Sir Hugh Lane had intended to bequeath to the people of Dublin as an inestimable gift".

In the House of Commons Harold MacMillan, whom Thomas Bodkin believed was in favour of returning the paintings to Ireland, welcomed the Agreement. He said that the British Government had not been involved in the negotiations. The two Houses of the British Parliament welcomed the Agreement.

Both the *Irish Times* and the *Irish Independent* quoted Costello in their editorials, describing the Agreement as an honourable compromise. *The Irish Times* made the point that "A few short years ago it appeared Ireland would not have accepted this Agreement and the pictures would remain in London. Happily, wiser counsels prevailed". The Agreement was to some extent the same as suggested by DS McColl, the English art critic, as far back as 1917, but rejected by Lady Gregory. WT Cosgrave had felt obliged to take a similar stance in solidarity with Lady Gregory, who had been the main stay of the struggle to vindicate her nephew's wishes. *The Irish Independent* reported that the pictures were valued at £847, 500.

While the Agreement was generally welcomed, there was some opposition. The *Irish Times* reported the artist Sean Keating as saying, "It is all a washout. I understood we were going to get all the paintings on a definite loan. This half baked business is all baloney". The complexity of succeeding Agreements gave some credence to Keating's reaction.

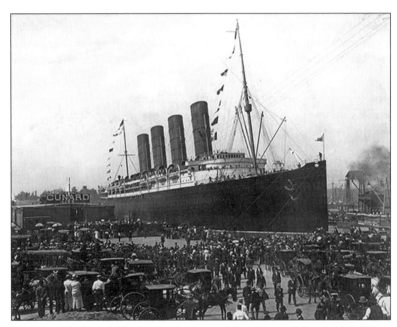

The Liner S.S. Lusitania which was sunk by a German U-Boat in 1915.
Among the passengers who perished was Sir Hugh Lane.

CHAPTER 19

STATE VISIT
TO UNITED STATES OF AMERICA

The Taoiseach made an eleven-day state visit to the United States in March 1956. He flew to New York and travelled that same day to Washington where Vice President Richard Nixon met him. He was taken immediately to the White House to be greeted by President Eisenhower. John Hearne, Irish Ambassador to the USA, and Joseph Brennan Counsellor at the Washington Embassy, Charles Murray and Alexis Fitzgerald, accompanied Costello. After the White House meeting they went to Blair House, where they were to reside for their four-day visit in the capital. That afternoon they met Herbert Hoover at the State Department. Over the next few days Costello was received at a National Press Club luncheon, the House of Representatives and the Senate. He made major speeches at all three venues. At the Press Club he re-emphasised that Ireland could not join NATO while partition lasted. At the House of Representatives, Acting Speaker John McCormack introduced him. The proceedings there were broadcast by radio and television. At the Senate, Costello said that he brought them greetings of a very old nation. He spoke of both countries common outlook and common ideals, based on a Christian democratic and free, way of life. He talked of Ireland's spiritual empire of many millions of Irish birth in every corner of the globe. He presented the Library of Congress with five letters written by Richard Fitzpatrick, an Irishman in the British army during the American War of Independence.

JACQUELINE BOUVIER KENNEDY

The Department of the Taoiseach had planned minutely the visit of Costello to the USA. Many letters had come from America inviting him to visit specific places and people. Among those was one from Wilmarth Sheldon Lewis of Farmington Connecticut, proposing a visit to Yale University. Lewis wrote on 11 November 1955, "It would be a great honour to Yale to have you. And how pleased Fr. Leonard would be! Annie Burr adds her hopes that you will come". A follow up letter from the same source, on 8 December 1955 said, "Annie Burr joins me in sending you and Mrs Costello our warmest seasons greetings and we are very happy indeed that we are to have you here again so soon"[1].

The Taoiseach stayed at Yale University for a few days during his trip. He lectured to law students on Irish foreign policy and presented a copy of the Book of Kells to the University. He was taken on a tour of the Atomic Centre at Brookhaven. He made a major speech as guest of honour at the annual dinner of the Knights of St. Patrick of New Haven at Yale. He spoke of the many links between Yale and Ireland. He mentioned that George Berkeley was a benefactor, that the Wagner Collection of Irish Economic and Historical tracts, as well as the Boswell Papers, were held at Yale.

He said that the current distinguished United States Ambassador to Ireland, William Taft, was a Yale alumnus. He also referred to a particular friend of his own, a Trustee of Yale, Wilmarth Sheldon Lewis, who had forged a friendship with an Irish Vincentian priest named Joseph Leonard of All Hallows College in Dublin. Lewis had met Fr. Leonard at Strawberry Hill in London, the former home of Horace Walpole. Lewis was a collector and connoisseur of the Arts. He was the editor of the Horace Walpole Letters. He and Leonard had exchanged visits in Yale and Dublin.

Lewis was also an uncle of Jacqueline Bouvier [Kennedy] She had also become closely acquainted with Fr. Leonard, and indeed John A Costello, through her uncle. She had left the USA on an extended visit to Europe in 1948, remaining away over a year. She and her stepbrother, Hugh Auchincloss, came to Dublin for the Horse Show with Fr. Leonard's name as a contact. Unfortunately he was away on the day they arrived and they had difficulty getting accommodation. However, Fr. Leonard appeared on the following day and everything fell into place for the visitors. He wined and dined them at Jammet's famous restaurant, and the American Ambassador entertained them at his embassy. Fr. Leonard also brought them to meet the Taoiseach, who, like Fr. Leonard, corresponded with Jacqueline Bouvier [Kennedy] for many years. Costello gave her several signed books about Ireland. Fr. Leonard was a well-known author of spiritual books. After attending the Abbey Theatre the Americans toured Limerick, Killarney and Cork before returning to Paris[2]. Fr. Leonard continued to correspond with Jacqueline on spiritual matters. Costello remarked that while Leonard was a deeply spiritual man, he had little time for the "dangerously devout". Jacqueline and her husband Jack Kennedy visited Dublin in late September 1955, where Fr. Leonard gave them a book inscribed, "To Jack and Jacqueline, With love and admiration Joseph Leonard 29 September – October 2 1955". Costello was then ending a ten-day visit to Rome with his wife. According to Costello, Jacqueline invited Fr. Leonard to come to Washington to baptise her son in 1960, but ill health prevented him from making the trip. He died in 1964.

In New York, Costello stayed at the Waldorf Astoria. He had a private lunch with the Secretary of the United Nations, Dag Hammarskjhold, at his residence. On Palm Sunday Costello attended Mass at St. Patrick's Cathedral, celebrated by Cardinal Spellman. He dined with Henry Cabot Lodge, American Ambassador to the United Nations. Mayor Robert Wagner hosted a luncheon for the Taoiseach. In his address, Costello hailed the USA as the arbiter of the world's destiny. He said, "We in Ireland hope to contribute what we can, as a small nation, and act as the interpreter of Europe to America and of the USA to Europe. Among the guests at the mayoral lunch was Denis Larkin, Lord Mayor of Dublin.

The Taoiseach received several honorary degrees on his visit. One was from Iona College in New Rochelle, run by Christian Brothers. At the ceremony Costello said,

"The pre-eminence of the Christian Brothers in the field of education in Ireland is proven by the fact that 40% of all Irish boys who receive secondary education in Ireland are attending Christian Brothers schools".

Costello attended a luncheon at the United Nations in his honour, at which he made an important speech on Irish foreign policy, to which I have already referred. He declared that, "Ireland will take a militantly anti-Communistic stand at the U.N. Ireland will never allow herself to be used as a tool to serve communistic imperial interests". He said that Ireland would raise partition at the UN "if we get a favourable opportunity to do so, but they would reject Soviet support on the question. We are not going to be a sore thumb on partition. We are not going to raise it at every opportunity".

The last part of his return journey to Dublin was via Shannon, in a seven-seat aeroplane, accompanied by his son Declan and Liam Cosgrave, Minister for External Affairs. He was met at the airport by the cabinet and a wide variety of public officials. He expressed confidence that the information he had gained and the impressions he had obtained during his visit would prove of great benefit in formulating national policy in connection with the United Nations. He declared that "Ireland is a Christian country. Hers is a Christian past and as all Ireland is Christian, her future, if it is to be significant must be Christian also. Her part will not be played by preaching Christianity at foreigners, while failing to apply it to ourselves in the solution of the Irish problems by patient, united and honest study of these problems". This was the 30th speech the Taoiseach gave since his departure[4].

Yale University USA, where John A Costello stayed for a few days during his trip.

(L-R) Patrick Lindsay, John A. Costello, Sean T. O'Kelly, R. Mulcahy, 1956.

Archbishop John Charles McQuaid (centre).

CHAPTER 20

FATEFUL YEAR OF 1956
PERSONAL - POLITICAL - FINANCIAL

While the Taoiseach was in the USA, his wife became ill in Dublin. She died shortly after his return home from America. Her death notice read:
Costello – April 20 1956 at St. Vincent's Private Nursing Home. Ida, deeply beloved wife of John A Costello S.C. T.D. Taoiseach, Herbert Park Ballsbridge, Dublin. Deeply regretted R.I.P. Funeral (Private) Today (Saturday), After 10 oclock Mass at Sacred Heart Church Donnybrook, to Deans Grange Cemetery.
Mrs Costello had been a member of several charitable organisations including the Council of the Women's National Health Association and the Peamount After Care Guild. Though she had been ill, her death was sudden. Her son, Declan TD, had been in Strasbourg at the Council of Europe that same day. The Government, in a message to their leader said: "The news of Mrs Costello's death has been received by your colleagues in government with the deepest regret. We offer to you and to all the members of your family our most heartfull sympathy. We pray that God will give you strength and consolation in your great sorrow. May she rest in peace. – William Norton. Tánaiste". Cardinal d'Alton, who was in Washington, sent a message which included reference to "the quite unexpected" death. Eamon deValera called personally to the Taoiseach's home to express his sympathy. Richard Nixon, the American Vice-President, and John McCormack, the House Majority Leader, both sent messages of sympathy. John Conway, the Irish Consul-General in New York, who had met Mrs Costello when she had accompanied her husband on his 1948 visit to New York said, "I am horrified. This is a tremendous shock. I have known Mary since 1917, she visited the USA in 1948 and made many friends". The Earl of Home, British Secretary of State for Commonwealth Affairs, sent a personal letter to the Taoiseach.

Archbishop John Charles McQuaid presided at the funeral mass. The President Sean T O'Kelly and his wife attended, as did members of the government and both Houses of the Oireachtas and Diplomatic corps. The leaders of all the major religious orders were present along with leaders of commercial, professional and civic life. Chancellor Alibrandi represented the Papal Nuncio, Dr. Levame. Mrs Costello's five children were the chief mourners along with their father. Her three sisters were also present. Among the vast congregation were WT Cosgrave, Eamon deValera, Ernest Blythe, Sean MacEntee, PS Doyle and PJ Lindsay.

On 27 April Costello wrote a personal letter to Archbishop McQuaid thanking him
"On my own behalf and on behalf of my family for presiding at the Requiem Mass for the repose of my wife's soul. I could not give adequate expression to my feeling of gratitude to Your Grace. My children and I have suffered a grievous loss. We have been greatly comforted by the kindness of so many friends, by the many Masses that

have been offered for the repose of her soul and by the conviction of our Christian faith that God has her in his kind hands"[1]
Some of his political colleagues felt, not surprisingly, that much of the life force left the Taoiseach after his wife's death, and that, his heart was not in the enormous task facing him.

In May 1956, Labour lost a seat in Laois-Offaly that it had held since the 1920's, when, apparently, Fine Gael voters did not transfer their votes to Labour. Worse was to happen when, in July, a Clann na Talmhan TD from Kerry, Patrick Finnucane, again decided that his support for the Government was conditional on local issues in his constituency. At a by-election in Cork in August, Fianna Fáil retained its seat easily with the Fine Gael vote down substantially. In September another front opened with severe criticism from the Labour TD James Larkin. He complained at a Labour Party meeting that government economic policy was engrossed in making cuts rather than making capital investment. He urged the party to join with the Trade Union movement in forcing the government to a policy of progress against retrogression and decline. He said "The advice is given to produce more while thousands are rendered unemployed and lose all possibility of producing anything at all. Agriculture is in a backward state"[2]. The government was shaken by this criticism as it seriously threatened its Labour base and held dangers for the isolation of its Labour members.

This spurred the Government to action. Tom O'Higgins, and significantly not Gerard Sweetman, argued in cabinet, through a memorandum, that a new policy for development was necessary.

FINANCIAL CRISIS 1956

Sweetman, as Minister of Finance, had continued to be most concerned about budgetary matters. There had been a deficit of £35 million in 1955, while the external assets of the banks fell towards that same figure. On 13 March 1956, under the Emergency Imposition of Duties Act, he introduced taxes on sixty-eight 'luxury' imports. His object was to make those imports dearer so that less of them would be bought. His budget in May increased tax on petrol, cigarettes, betting and entertainment taxes. Sweetman said that the estimates had been cut to the maximum, consistent with the provision of services, the maintenance of employment and the development of our resources. It was during this crisis on 30 May 1956 that Ken Whitaker became Secretary of the Department of Finance on the retirement of the previous incumbent. This appointment was unusual in that Whittaker bypassed more senior officials. He was a contemporary of Sweetman's and according to himself, this fact made for an easier relationship between them. Whitaker was also, "the one executive in Finance who could talk the Minister's language"[3]. In July Sweetman again increased taxes on imports. He told the Dáil the country was then fighting for its economic independence. He said that "without a radical change in the situation we cannot enjoy much longer the artificial standards to which we have become accustomed, since our external reserves to which we owe these standards are steadily running out. Unless our present purchasing power is upheld by an immediate increase in production, we must accept a temporary reduction in that purchasing power now, or suffer a wholesale and drastic reduction in imports in a very short time, with dire effects on industry, trade and employment"[4]. He also cut Government spending by £5 million. The Labour Party Conference earlier that summer was fiercely critical of government policy. After Larkin's broadside something dramatic had to be done. Sweetman felt somewhat isolated in cabinet and he particularly felt that he should have had clear support from Costello in the problems that confronted him, and that he did not get it[5]. Tom O'Higgins adds, that "Sweetman had many sterling qualities. He was highly intelligent and full of integrity and courage, but he was intensely proud and at times displayed an intolerance for the views of others which often led him to unnecessary confrontation". O'Higgins, as Minister of Health, was asked by Cabinet to prepare an economic plan. This took him many weeks to complete. When the cabinet saw it, they were willing to back it, if he could secure the support of Sean MacBride and his two Clann na Poblachta TD's, who alone among those opposed to Fianna Fáil remained outside the government. O'Higgins went to MacBride's home at Roebuck House in Clonskeagh and they discussed his proposals. These envisaged a new declaration of policies before a joint meeting of all their Oireachtas members. MacBride agreed to attend such a meeting and propose a vote of confidence in the Government. At a joint meeting of the hundred or so Inter-Party's TD's and Senators in the Engineer's Hall, Costello outlined a new economic policy on Friday 5 October 1956. He spoke for two hours in great detail about the whole gamut of economic life, for which he received a standing ovation[6].

The plan had six principles:

To favour investment in Agriculture over all forms of investment
To favour and encourage private investment, to supplement and relieve the pressure on public investment.
To favour home investment rather than foreign investment
To favour higher investment in Ireland based on Irish savings.
To encourage all kinds of exports.
To achieve the results desired, by cooperation rather than by compulsion.

He spoke at some length on the following issues:

£50,000 Grants for New Factories: Industrial Advisory Council: Immediate establishment of Agricultural Institute and Capital Investment Programme: Independence for Radio Éireann: Bovine TB campaign: Stable Agricultural Prices: More Fertilisers: Oil Refineries: Mineral Reserves: Briquette Factories: Tax Concessions for Coal Production: Income Tax Relief: Stock Exchange: USA Grants: Pulp Industries: Gaeltarra Éireann; Marketing; Health Insurance.

James Larkin and Sean MacBride, who had been among the chief critics of the Government in recent times, also spoke. MacBride said that the programme had been too long delayed, but it was better late than never. Other speakers included James Dillon, Dan Morrissey, James Tully, Tom Kyne and Declan Costello. A vote of confidence in the Government was proposed by Tom Kyne [Labour] and seconded by Dan Morrissey [FG]. This was supported by Mr. O'Hara [Clann na Talmhan] and Sean MacBride [Clann na Poblachta]

The *Irish Times* wrote in an editorial, "The plan that Mr. Costello announced yesterday is the one that ought to have been put before the country thirty years ago. The pity is that we have had to wait for a moment of 'crisis' when the spending which it necessarily involves, looks more formidable than it would have appeared in more normal times". Costello's speech left Mr. McElligot, Governor of the Central Bank since 1953, with a "sense of disappointment", since it was silent on the two "major questions" of economic and public expenditure and bank interest rates. He wrote to his Minister, "that the path of economic salvation in the long run may lie upon the lines suggested on 5th October, but the emergency is upon us and we are at present bereft of means to deal with it"[7]. Gerard Sweetman instructed his new Secretary at Finance, Ken Whitaker, to begin immediate implementation of certain aspects of the plan. These included tax concessions to encourage coal production, an export tax incentive, new factory building grants, new industrial building tax allowances and the creation and issuing of prize bonds by the Minister for Finance. Sweetman also set up a capital investment committee, with John Leyden in the Chair. General M. J.Costello, [Agriculture] Kevin McCourt [Industry], Ruaidhri Roberts, [Trade Unions] Patrick Lynch, Louden Ryan, CF Carter, [Queens University] William Bland, [ACC] CK Mill [Guinness] sat on the committee. No member of the Department of Finance was a member. An air of optimism permeated the Government, as deValera alone proved negative to the plan. Sweetman asked the committee to assist the government in framing the capital budget 1957-8. The committee reported on 22 January 1957. It issued a favourable report on Sweetman's 1956 measures, but advised against a reduction in the capital programme. It favoured a reduction in current Exchequer spending through the abolition of subsidies on butter, flour and wheatmeal. Ken Whitaker was later to say that Sweetman was a singularly unfortunate Minister of Finance, in as much as his Government was overthrown before the " ideas which he implemented could bear fruit"[8].

INTERNATIONAL CRISES

The euphoria within Government was very short lived, due to a combination of international factors. In October 1956 the Uprising in Hungary against Soviet occupation took place. It was put down by Russian troops with Cardinal Mindszenty fleeing to the American Embassy in Budapest. Later, Hungarian refugees arrived in Ireland. This was followed by the invasion of Egypt to sieze the Suez Canal, by English and French forces. Both these events caused international instability. This latter invasion soon led to petrol rationing and price increases of three and a half pence a gallon, completely outside Governmental control. A supply of a tank full of petrol per month was envisaged for private cars and some garages closed for four days a week.

Two by-elections occurred in November. Peadar Doyle of Fine Gael had died and his seat in Dublin South West became vacant. A Fianna Fáil seat in Carlow-Kilkenny was also vacant. In a small turnout Noel Lemass took the Fine Gael seat in Dublin.

The votes in the bye-election were:

Dublin South West:		Carlow-Kilkenny:
Lemass F.F	14,416	F.F. - 23,782
Power FG	9,682	F.G. -11,752

Buoyed by the two victories, deValera demanded an immediate general election. Clann na Poblachta now held the balance of power in the Dáil. MacBride intimated that he would continue to promote the policies he had advocated in the first Inter-Party Government, long-term planning, forestation and credit. This appeared to indicate that he intended to honour his recent vote of confidence in the Taoiseach. The *Irish Times* editorial said, " The star of the Inter-Party Government is setting. There is increasing evidence that the country is weary of Mr. Costello and his curiously assorted colleagues. There is little sign that it wishes to see their place taken by Mr. deValera and his associates". The Dáil adjournment debate of the 13 December 1956 was on the economic situation. Sean MacBride, under personal insults from Sean MacEntee, was very critical of, " this kind of childish, irresponsible crossfire, as precluding those who take part in it from appreciating the actual problems and the basis on which we have to deal". He said that they had failed to build an Ireland in which people could live and work. He identified the starvation of capital and a sound investment policy and a lack of planning as the main reasons for failure. When questioned by Neil Blaney as to why he then supported the present government, MacBride replied, "The answer is extremely simple. We know that the alternative to Deputy Sweetman as Minister for Finance is Deputy MacEntee and we all know that not only would you have a credit squeeze now, but also in addition, subsidies would probably be removed to reduce the consumer's purchasing power, because that is exactly what he did in 1951-52". He acknowledged progress in the ESB, Irish Shipping and Bórd na Móna. MacBride praised the Government for its new investment committee. The debate ended with what turned out to be Costello's final words as Taoiseach. He declared that "We believe that we have done a hard and thankless but necessary job. We face the future not with any complacency but knowing that we have even more formidable difficulties to overcome that we had before. We are going to do that job in our own time and, when we have done it and when we have had time to bring our policy into operation, we shall face the country with confidence knowing that Fianna Fáil will never disgrace these benches again". Sean Lemass countered by asking, "that is the way the Taoiseach asks for cooperation?" Costello replied, "I have long since ceased to hope for it". The vote resulted in 72 votes for the Government and 65 against. Neither Sean MacBride nor Jack McQuillan voted. The Dáil adjourned to 13 February 1957.

Eamonn deValera kisses the ring of Archbishop Angelo Roncalli,
while Sean MacBride, Archbishop McQuaid, and John A, Costello look on.
Luxeil Columbanus Congress 1950.

T.K. Whitaker, Secretary the Department of Finance mid 1950's.

CHAPTER 21

IRA RE-ORGANISES IN THE 1950's

Costello said of his governments, "Our biggest achievement I would say was the Declaration of the Republic: that was my aim since 1926 and I was glad of the opportunity to secure peace in old Ireland once more"[1]. He had also hoped to take the gun out of Irish politics. However the reality was somewhat different. To use a phrase that has a current resonance, the IRA had not gone away, as Costello had hoped. It almost had, but not quite!

In 1948 the IRA had intended to draw up plans for a military campaign in the North. This did not materialise as the organisation became almost moribund. However it did succeed in infiltrating Sinn Féin, which became its political front. The fact that Clann na Poblachta had gone into government and with Fine Gael had alienated many IRA personnel. Some decided to wait and see, while others became disillusioned and abandoned the IRA. The results of 'going political' and participating in the Anti-Partition campaign produced no tangible results for the IRA. As Conor Cruise O'Brien has written "Hardline Republicans (i.e. the IRA) could not possibly be satisfied by the Costello-MacBride Republic: the old Irish Free State under a new name. But they were ready to welcome the new name as a step in the right direction, achieved by their friends in office and not achieved by Fianna Fáil. It did not suit them to grab a claimed national achievement of a coalition with Sean MacBride in it"[2]. O'Brien says that the IRA knew that a government with Sean MacBride could never get as rough with them as deValera's governments had.

The IRA again decided in 1951 to plan for another military campaign. If they were to be realistic, this required weapons and training of volunteers. As Bowyer Bell writes, "Five years after the war, in 1950, the IRA had only a shadow of its former strength. The claim by the new Taoiseach John Costello that he had taken the gun out of politics seemed justified. Yet, in 1951, the IRA Army Convention ratified the decision of the Army Council to undertake a campaign in the North against the British, while remaining quiescent in the South"[3]. At that stage the IRA was a fragile structure incapable of the grand action but gradually getting stronger.

In October 1951 the IRA expelled one of its members, Liam Kelly of Pomeroy, for planning unauthorised raids. He then set up his own military and political groups. He recognised the legitimacy of the Dáil and in 1953 was elected to Stormont as MP for mid Tyrone. He was then arrested and jailed for sedition in the North, Sean MacBride asked Costello in the Dáil, "I wonder could the Taoiseach say, as far as he is aware, whether there is any elected representative of the people in prison in any democratic country in Europe, out side the present case?"[4]. MacBride engineered a Senate seat for Kelly in June 1954, hopeful that the IRA would become more politically aware. Jack McQuillan proposed that all elected parliamentary representatives of the people of the occupied counties should be granted audience in the Dáil and Senate. MacBride supported this motion saying, "Listening both to the Leader of the Opposition and the Leader of the Government, it is quite clear that neither has any policy in regard to the end of partition after thirty years"[5].

Twenty-one TD's supported Jack McQuillan's motion. These were a cross section of the members of the smaller parties, which remarkably included Government Ministers, and the Tánaiste William Norton. Both Fine Gael and Fianna Fáil imposed a party whip on their members, which with a few T.D's from the smaller parties, brought those who voted against up to one hundred. It was one of the rare occasions that Fine Gael and Fianna Fáil joined forces to vote together.

Speaking to the motion, Costello acknowledged the sincerity of McQuillan and "my former colleague Deputy MacBride". He said that, while previously there had been a free vote on such a matter, his colleagues in Fine Gael had decided that they would now vote as a Party against the motion. He added, "They do so, having gravely and seriously considered the matter and not being obsessed by the fact that on a previous occasion they voted for the motion. The matter is too serious now". He said that if he thought that giving the right of audience to elected representatives of the Six Counties would in the slightest help to solve the partition problem, he would vote for the motion. deValera agreed with Costello but added that the question should be a matter of definite Government policy, and, irrespective of how the Parties may vote, he took it that what the Taoiseach had said was Government policy. He declared his certainty that any Irish Government would make every possible effort to solve Partition. The reason progress had not been made by any government was because the problem is in itself "an extremely difficult one. It is a tantalising problem. It is an exasperating problem"

Sean MacBride said that isolated acts of violence in the Six Counties were not likely to further the ultimate aim of unity. He blamed to a large extent "ourselves in this House, if young men actuated by patriotic motives take it upon themselves to act". There was a lack of leadership over the last thirty years, he added. He felt that the motion could give that leadership on Partition. He asked that if Ireland was a nation and the Dáil was the national Parliament, on what basis could they refuse the elected representatives of the Six Counties to be heard?.

The IRA began to carry out raids on military installations both in the North and in England, collecting arms and ammunition. Among the targets were Derry in 1951, Felstead in Essex in 1953, Armagh in 1954 and Arborfield in Berkshire in 1955. This action was certainly popular in the North as Sein Féin polled very well in various elections. Two jailed IRA prisoners were elected MP's in 1955. All this activity brought more recruits into the IRA, and afforded it the opportunity to train a series of its units for a sustained military campaign within the North. A series of operational schedules and attack procedures were drawn up by Sean Cronin, an ex-Irish army officer for the IRA[6]. The Northern authorities naturally reacted to this IRA activity with great force from its armed police and para-military B-Specials, arresting and interning known Republicans.

The Taoiseach felt obliged to make a statement in the Dáil in November 1955 clearly outlining the Government's position on Partition and the unlawful use of force. He said that the situation was so potentially grave that it was necessary that the Government pronounce in the interest of the nation as a whole. He acknowledged that Partition was forced on the nation by "a more powerful state, a champion of freedom" and sustained by its military and financial power. He recognised that the nationalists of the North were discriminated against in many ways. "Men of power there offer no hope of peaceful redress". He did not find it surprising that some "of our people" should turn to force as a means of ending Partition. The subordinate rulers of the Six Counties also bore responsibility for refusing all attempts to work out a constitutional solution of Partition and to safeguard the rights of nationalists there. He reiterated his statement of 28 October 1954 that no real solution to the Partition problem could be found by force. That would lead to civil war. He said that the recent raids on British military posts in the Six Counties and Britain were attributed to the IRA. He rejected the right of any such organisation to that name, save for the Irish army of today, maintained by the Oireachtas. "We have" he said, "a sovereign, independent, democratic Irish State".

He said that one such group arrogating the right to use force does not recognise the legitimacy of the Oireachtas. They have no right to make decisions for the Irish people. He recognised that the numbers involved in violence were small but they had the power to do great damage to the life and liberty of the nation itself. He acknowledged that there was a small minority of public representatives who supported violence. He called on them to choose democracy and to cease applauding those who defy the Oireachtas by word and deed. He again accepted that the use of force was created by the actions of the British government and the " unrelenting opposition of the Six Counties authorities to any reasonable approach to the ending of Partition". He admitted that the execution of warrants between the Six Counties and Saorstat Éireann had ceased, except in one instance, since the High Court in 1929 held that there was no authority to execute such warrants. While Costello saw room for manoeuvre in this area, he made it clear that, "there can be no question of the handing over to the British or to the Six-County authorities, persons whom they may accuse of armed political activities in Britain or in the Six Counties". The Taoiseach referred to his hope in 1948 that he could take the gun out of Irish politics. He had thought that this was done by 1951. When in recent times force again reared its head, he and his colleagues had been patient and hoped that with forbearance, public opinion and the conscience of those involved would see that it would not be tolerated. In that light he appealed to public opinion and to those involved to determine that the Oireachtas alone must uphold authority. He declared that if his request was not responded to, the Government was bound to use all the power and force at its disposal, to ensure that unlawful military activities should cease. Mr. deValera spoke briefly expressing the hope that the appeal of the Taoiseach would be heeded.

Sean MacBride described Costello's speech as, "Statesmanlike and constructive". He went on: "The Partition of Ireland is a clear infringement of the sovereign rights of the Irish people. It is inevitable that there will be an attitude of open revolt on the part of the people separated from their motherland. The real solution is to remedy the wrong and that is primarily Britain's responsibility. Only this Parliament has the right to wage war. I do not believe that acts of violence, unsupported by the resources of the State can achieve the goal. If I did, I would say so and I would participate in or lead any movement engaged in such a policy. I join with the Taoiseach in urging those who speak on these questions to refrain from making inflammatory speeches. I have little sympathy with those, who from a safe distance, would encourage young men actuated by patriotic motives to endanger their lives and liberty. There is a special responsibility on the Government and on Dáil Éireann to provide active leadership. In my view, an Irish government is entitled to use, if needs be, the armed force of the State. There is a clear responsibility on an Irish government and on Dáil Éireann to provide clear leadership. The first logical step is to provide an all-Ireland Parliament where representatives of the Six Counties could come". Costello had written to Dr. McQuaid on that same afternoon, sending him a copy of the fifteen-page statement he intended to make "tonight in Dáil Éireann on the subject of Partition and the unlawful use of force"[7].

The following month, on 15 December 1955, Senator Eoin Sheehy Skeffington spoke on Senator Roger McHugh's motion calling for access for Northern parliamentary representatives to the Dáil and Senate. He welcomed the Taoiseach's statement, but regretted the Government's failure, as yet, to take any active steps to stop open recruitment, drilling and the possession of arms by private military organisations". Sheehy Skeffington praised the economic and social conditions in the North. When he proposed three amendments to the motion he found no seconder[8].

In January of 1956 the government received an *aide-memoire* from the British government, pressing strongly for the co-operation of the Gardai against the IRA. It alleged "a total unwillingness on the part of the Civil Guard to assist the RUC with information or to co-operate in identifying the raiders on the RUC Barracks at Roslea in County Fermanagh". The *aide-memoire* refers to the fact that in March 1955, IRA training activities were going on at Scotstown, County Monaghan. This information was given to the Gárdai and the Irish Government, "yet it appears that the men were allowed to continue with their illegal activities without interference"[9].

The Department of External Affairs replied, in a remarkable fashion, in February, telling the British quite starkly that they could expect little co-operation from the Irish authorities on subversive activity. It said "Briefly, the attitude is that the Irish Government could not allow information to be furnished about Irishmen already apprehended, or being actively sought in connection with armed political activities and could not accept any responsibility or commitment in regard to the intentions of unlawful organisations which are, of their nature, secret". Conor Cruise O'Brien contended that "this document clearly reflects the influence of the late Sean MacBride, on whom that Government depended for its continued existence. It represents what was to remain the high water-mark (until 1969-70) of Irish government collusion with the IRA. The deValera-Lemass government dropped this policy when it came to power in 1957"[10].

The IRA paid little heed to these political statements and continued to plan for further successive armed attacks against non-military installations within the North. The IRA believed that due to their quiescence in the South, the government there would tolerate the campaign, as the raids resumed in late 1956 with Flying Columns in action in Antrim, Derry and Fermanagh. The IRA issued a campaign proclamation on 12 December saying that, "Spearheaded by Ireland's freedom fighters, our people in the Six counties have carried the fight to the enemy. Out of this national liberation struggle a new Ireland will emerge, upright and free. In that new Ireland we shall build a country fit for all our people to live in. That then is our aim: an independent, united, democratic Irish republic. For this we shall fight until the invader is driven from our soil and victory is ours"[11]. On the night of 12 December the IRA destroyed bridges and attacked a barracks in Fermanagh. The Unionist people were fuming as Lord Brookeborough went to London to see the Prime Minister, Anthony Eden, in order to have pressure put on Costello's government. This visit resulted in the British ambassador in Dublin visiting the Department of External Affairs, demanding immediate action. In the House of Commons, Eden declared his intention to uphold order in the North. He said, "In the Ireland Act of 1949, the Parliament of Westminster declared Northern Ireland to be an integral part of the United Kingdom. This is a Declaration, which all parties in this House are pledged to support. The safety of Northern Ireland and its inhabitants is, therefore a direct responsibility of Her Majesty's Government, which, they will, of course, discharge".

The North did not really need the British army to protect it, as it had its own formidable forces in 2,800 police, 1,000 fulltime B-Specials and 11,600 part-timers[12]. The Governments of Northern Ireland and of the Republic, together with the British were most concerned that the flying columns should be contained and isolated. They feared that the wider communities of Unionists and Nationalists might become directly involved in communal strife. This was especially Costello's fear. If the Nationalists came under widespread attack, he feared that he would not be able to restrain Southern nationalists from going to the aid of their fellow countrymen. As Taoiseach Jack Lynch was to say in later years, neither would the Irish government be able to stand by. Sinn Féin was banned in the North and many Republicans were interned. There was a cessation of incursions during the Christmas season, but the campaign was renewed on 31 December with a raid on Brookeborough Barracks in Fermanagh. During the retreat two IRA men were fatally wounded and abandoned by their retreating colleagues, who were arrested and subsequently jailed in the Republic. One hundred Gardaí were deployed at the border. The newspapers headlined the deaths of the two men, Sean South and Fergal O'Hanlon. Within a few days, the funerals of both men gave vent to a massive outpouring of grief and anger all over the Republic. A Republican rally at

College Green addressed by Tomas MacCurtain, drew a massive attendance. Many public bodies, including Dublin Corporation, passed votes of sympathy for the men and their cause. Both young men were exemplary characters. Many thousands honoured the funeral cortege as it travelled from Dublin to Limerick of Sean South. In Limerick, 20,000 people awaited the cortege, including the city's mayor[13]. Jack McQuillan, an Independent TD and Patrick Finnucane of Clan na Talmhan, demanded an early recall of the Dáil to debate the motion, "That Dáil Éireann is of the opinion that as the situation in the Six counties is on a parallel with that obtaining in Hungary, Egypt and Cyprus, our permanent delegate at the United Nations should be instructed to demand of the Secretary-General the immediate despatch of UN observers to the occupied part of the National territory. That Dáil Éireann is of the opinion that the government should discontinue immediately the use of the Irish Army and the Gardaí Síochana as instruments of British policy, in helping maintain partition, and that the men recently taken into custody as a result of such use should be released forthwith"[14]. [Ireland had finally been admitted to the United Nations on 13 December 1955, in the company of sixteen other countries] Costello feared the worst and knew that his leadership was crucial and required immediately. He went on Radio Éireann on Sunday night, 6 January, to address the people. He acknowledged the tragic deaths of the week, but declared again that there was only one government, one parliament and one army in Ireland. He said, "There should be no word, act or gesture that would give the men responsible for the raids in Northern Ireland a pretext for claiming that they had popular approval or support. It is because of the duty that we owe to the people, the duty to avert the evils that follow, when men take the law into their own hands, that the government decided to instruct the Gárda Síochana and the Defence Forces to take the necessary action. I cannot too strongly condemn the wicked misrepresentations that our Irish Forces are being used to help partition. They are, on the contrary, acting on the instructions of an Irish Government, responsible to a freely elected Parliament, a Government which is working for Ireland and for Ireland alone". Mr deValera declared, "I am entirely in agreement with what the Taoiseach has said". On 10 January Anthony Eden resigned as Prime Minister, to be replaced by Harold Macmillan. The leadership of the IRA were quickly arrested and charged. However, on 12 January a huge rally supporting the IRA was held at College Green. Tomas MacCurtain said that the IRA would not return fire on Irish soldiers, and that they were no threat to the Government. More arrests followed, including that of MacCurtain. The raids in the North continued. An electricity transformer in Derry was bombed. Two bombs destroyed the Territorial Army Barracks in Dungannon and a barracks in Tyrone was blasted.

The main IRA strategist, Sean Cronin, was arrested, and a document entitled, 'General Directive for Guerilla Campaign' was read in court.

Costello was later to say of this period, "I applied the ordinary processes of the law but did not use emergency legislation and would not do so"[15].

On the political front, the Dublin Regional Council of the Labour Party called for the Labour Party to withdraw from government due to the unemployment situation. James Everett, Minister for Justice, deemed the raids on Northern Ireland 'national suicide'. The Minister for Home Affairs in the North, Mr. Topping welcomed the Southern government's actions against the IRA. At a party meeting of Clann na Poblachta, Sean MacBride called for a positive policy to undo partition. He said that, "no amount of self sacrificing courage could replace such a policy". Pressures within Clann na Poblachta had been mounting due to the IRA campaign and the economic situation. The census of June 1956 had recorded the population at 2,894,822, the lowest ever recorded in the State. Net emigration between 1951-1956 was 200,394. The *Irish Times* editorialised under the heading "The Vanishing Irish".

The attitude to emigration by the 'possessing classes' was very much a harsh fact of political life, with some, such as James Dillon, viewing emigration as possibly unpatriotic. That the standard of living in our nearest neighbour was so high naturally acted as a magnet for those who wanted to better themselves and get away from a 'frugal' society. Alexis Fitzgerald, a humane and successful lawyer, who played such an integral part in Irish political life, particularly with John A Costello's governments, said on the subject in 1954, "I cannot accept either the view that a high rate of emigration is necessarily a sign of national decline or that policy should be over-anxiously framed to reduce it. It seems more important to preserve and improve the quality of Irish life. High emigration excess granted a population releases from social tensions, which would otherwise explode. It makes possible a stability of manners and customs which would otherwise be the subject of radical change. It is a national advantage that it is easy for emigrants to establish their lives in other parts of the world"[16].

The National Executive of Clann na Poblachta instructed its three TD's to cease supporting the Government. MacBride argued against this but his influence had diminished greatly. Eventually the Party decided to introduce a motion of no confidence in the government and MacBride proposed this on 28 January 1957. This was a shattering blow to Costello, who received no prior warning from MacBride[17]. deValera deemed, "Mr. MacBride's gyrations amusing, but the situation, in the creation of which he has played a full part, is not so amusing". Initially, deValera decided to introduce his own motion of no confidence, but when he later made the tactical decision to support MacBride's motion, the end was nigh for the Government. Tom O'Higgins, who had so lately negotiated MacBride's support for the new economic departure, was completely shocked with MacBride's action. O'Higgins later said of MacBride, "When he was with you, he was forceful and charming, but when the sun went in, he was a different man"[18]. The death of Tom Derrig meant that the position in the Dáil was tied at 72 votes for each side. While the Ceann Comhairle would support the status quo, the government could not be guaranteed that all its own 'supporters' would support the government. There was still two weeks to go to the return of the Dáil. Both Dillon and

O'Higgins favoured taking their chance in the Dáil vote. Despite the favourable economic planning then in train, Costello feared a Dáil defeat and thought it better to fight in the country. Dillon believed that if MacBride had forseen this outcome, he would have withdrawn his motion.

James Dillon also believed that Costello had grown weary of the business of governing, and that after the death of his wife, "his heart was no longer in the business"[19]. Many people had remained suspicious of MacBride's conversion to constitutional means. This move by him added to that distrust. The *Irish Times* editorial of 31 January 1957, reflected this when it wrote, "His motives sound good, largely based on the Government's inability to correct an economic decline which would have occurred whatever government had been in power. What is bound to make him suspect – not for the first time – in the eyes of the ordinary Irish public is the spurious and obviously studied opportunism of his schism. It coincides just too nicely with the operation of the illegal organisations against the Six Counties: it fits in just too comfortably with the wave of sentiment, whipped up or traditional, which was for a time, seen to be overcoming the decent people of the Twenty Six Counties and their less decent representatives in the local councils. One finds it hard to avoid the conclusion that Mr. MacBride is not exactly as disinterested a politician as a man of his stature ought to be".

On 4 January Costello advised President Sean T O'Kelly to disolve the Dáil on 12 February and called a General Election on 5 March.

Many commentators have written that the economic portents were good at that time, with signs that the balance of payments already improving.[20] Joe Lee's verdict was that there had been little sign of any revival in Fianna Fáil's electoral prospects. He regarded the 1957 defeat as self-inflicted by Sweetman's squeeze. He said, "Had Fine Gael been cleverer, or luckier, the implications for Fianna Fáil could have been unsettling. Whether through misjudgement or through misfortune Fine Gael forfeited the chance to overtake Fianna Fáil"[21]. Costello's second government, like deValera's 1951-54 government, is seen as having been an inconsiderate one. It's recovery programme, which was later developed to great success, came too late. Its termination is seen as a failure, lacking in confidence. It damaged the notion of coalition government for many years and led to an unbroken term of sixteen years of uninterrupted Fianna Fáil rule.

※※※※

CHAPTER 22

FINE GAEL DOLDRUMS
1957-1973

The Taoiseach told the electorate that his government deserved to be returned. He outlined sixteen reasons why this was so[1]. The public did not listen to him. The IRA raids in the North continued. deValera concentrated on convincing the electorate that coalition government was a bad thing. During the electoral campaign Sean MacBride again called for a national government. Fine Gael, too, put out feelers for a possible understanding between them and Fianna Fáil. However, deValera rejected such ideas saying that there was little talk of a national government when Fine Gael was in a majority. He argued that any such cooperation or amalgamation would inevitably lead in the long run to a Left-Right division in Irish politics. He rejected that concept as being bad for the country as it would probably entail swings from one side to the other on a regular basis. He favoured two broadly-based political parties, composed of a wide range on national opinion as best for the country[2]. The *Irish Times* wrote about this in an editorial after the election. It said; "We would have preferred an inconclusive verdict which would have forced the two major parties to first merge and then regroup on the elements of a clearly defined RIGHT-LEFT. Fine Gael at various times during the election campaign has made the offer of a merger or a coalition with Fianna Fáil. Although the offer was rejected roughly, our hope is in that Fine Gael will retain the spirit in which it was made".

The truth seems to have been that the Government had more or less lost confidence in itself, and was somewhat relieved at the outlook of leaving office. The election campaign was notable mainly for the reluctance of Fine Gael and Labour to say whether they were campaigning for the return of the government. Costello's suggestion that Fine Gael voters vote "all the way through", was the only call from any party for an exchange of transfers with its coalition partners[3]. Niamh Puirseil writes that "Labour was distinctively ambiguous about whether or not it was on an Inter Party ticket during the 1957 General election"[4]. The election result was a near disaster for the out-going Government Parties and for Sean MacBride and his party. It was a massive success for Fianna Fáil. The detailed results, with the previous election results in parenthesis, became clear on 8 March.

They were:

FF	FG	LAB	CP	Sein Féin	CT	IND
78	40	12	1	4	3	9
(65)	(50)	(19)	(3)	(0)	(5)	(5)

Fianna Fáil had its greatest ever electoral success, with a clear overall majority of nine. The Inter-Party group had lost eighteen seats. Four Sein Féin candidates were elected; Rory Brady in Longford-Westmeath, Einachan O'Hanlon in Monaghan, JJ Rice in Kerry and John Joe McGirl in Sligo-Leitrim. They refused to take their seats in the Dáil. The total Sein Féin vote was 65,640. McGirl was in jail during the election serving a two-month sentence for membership of an illegal organisation. On his release he said that he heard the result of his election on the radio.

In the Taoiseach's constituency of Dublin South East, the first preference results were:
Costello J. FG, 6,918
Browne N. IND, 6,035
MacEntee S. FF, 5,916
Moore S. FF, 2,473
O'Donovan J. FG, 1,332
Bermingham. Ratepayers, 1,291
Callanan. CP, 396

The first three were elected. Noel Browne, who had earlier joined Fianna Fáil, was refused a nomination by that party to run in Dublin South East. He subsequently took the courageous decision to run as an Independent on 20 February. Sean MacBride was a casualty in the election.

The result of the first preference count in his constituency of Dublin South-West was:

Briscoe R.	FF,	8,162
Lemass N.	FF,	5,436
O'Higgins MJ.	FG,	4,830
Carroll J.	IND,	3,878
MacBride S.	CP,	2,677
Butler B.	FF,	2,543
Dixon B.	IND,	2,488
Dearle S.	SF,	2,442
Colgan JB.	LAB,	2,045
Power E.	FF,	1,866
ffrench-O'Carroll.	FF,	1,854
O'Keeffe J.	FG,	1,397

On the 11th count, in the early hours of the morning, Butler of Fianna Fáil defeated MacBride for the last seat by 6,008 votes to 5,391, the top four having already been elected. It was an ignominious end for a man who at best had a dearth of political skill. Brian Feeney writes that, "MacBride's opportunism, besides ruining his own party, had resulted with the return of deValera, who would have no hesitation in treating harshly with republicans. By July internment was also introduced in the South. This, with the activities of the Special Branch, soon led to a termination of the IRA campaign" [5].

Patrick Lindsay has recounted a story about the outgoing Minister's journey to Áras an Uachtárain to hand in their seals of office. He travelled with Costello, Dillon and Maurice Moynihan Secretary of the Government. He describes Costello "with his head down and looking totally unlike the kind of man he was – he looked gruff whereas he was the kindest of men". As they passed the quaint Irish House public house, Dillon remarked on the beauty of the architecture. Dillon then said that he was never in a public house in his life except his own in Ballaghadereen in County Mayo. He added that he had sold it because of his objection to all the money people spent on drink. Lindsay continues, "then, to my consternation Jack Costello said that he was in a public house only once in his life, in Terenure, and was nearly choked by a bottle of orange. I was totally appalled by this state of affairs and I expressed my feelings as follows;"*****, I now know why we are going in this direction today and why we are out of touch with the people". Lindsay then goes on to say how the public house was the focal point of much social and commercial activity of the country and anybody who did not frequent public houses had to be out of touch with the people. In this state of affairs he asks, "how could we be going in any other direction?" Lindsay, a most sociable man, also recalls that when he visited the President to receive his seal of office, Sean T. O'Kelly offered them a drink. But on this occasion he noted that the President's manner was quite different and no drink was offered. Lindsay concludes with, "It was a bleak day"[6].

Archbishop McQuaid wrote to Costello commiserating on his electoral defeat. Costello replied on 11 March. He wrote that, "There are many compensations in my defeat. There is however the regret that we have been judged at the worst possible time in the most adverse circumstances. I am thankful for Your Grace's most kind and comforting letter. The fact that Your Grace thought of me at this time is something that I will always treasure". However, some few days later on 15 March Costello felt obliged to refuse an invitation to attend a High Mass on the 18 March. His excuse was that he had promised his daughter in Cork that he would "spend the last few days with her". He assured McQuaid that, "all the Ministers have been informed of the Mass. General Mulcahy will represent me and Mr. Cosgrave will also be present"[7].

On 20 March Sean Lemass proposed Eamon deValera as Taoiseach, with Sean MacEntee seconding. Costello on behalf of the Fine Gael Party opposed this. He did so not in any spirit of animosity towards deValera, but rather because he believed that Fianna Fáil was not equipped to provide the kind of Government the country needed.

The new Taoiseach Eamon deValera nominated his Ministers as follows;
Sean Lemass –   Tánaiste and Industry and Commerce.
Sean MacEntee – Health.
James Ryan –   Finance.
Frank Aiken –   External Affairs, and Agriculture (temporarily).
Oscar Traynor – Justice.
Paddy Smith –   Local Government and Social Welfare.

Erskine Childers – Lands
Jack Lynch –   Education and the Gaeltacht.
Neil Blaney –   Posts and Telegraphs.
Kevin Boland –   Defence
Sean Moylan –   Agriculture

Costello, speaking for Fine Gael, said that he realised that the new Government faced serious economic, financial and political difficulties. He acknowledged that the Opposition also had a high duty and responsibility to be constructive in the national interest. He believed that his new policy programme of October last would give positive results for the country. He asserted that they had taken their decisions in disregard for their own political fortunes. He said it was a very serious situation when some elected Deputies refused to take their seats and denied the validity of the institutions of the State. He called for respect for the organs of State from all quarters In reply, the Taoiseach said he appreciated the speech made by the Leader of the Opposition.

Tom O'Higgins has written about the aftermath of a sudden defeat for a government. He says that for ordinary backbenchers a concentration on constituency business to ensure that one would be re-elected next time out became paramount. Ex-Ministers had a major readjustment to make to a new way of life and probably the quest for "securing a new source of income". He had been a minister for two years and ten months and missed out on a ministerial pension by a matter of weeks. Not having any income, he relied on a friendly bank manager until such time as he re-established himself at the Bar. He said that when first elected as a TD, the allowance "was £52 a month, with no frills such as free post or telephone". He found it essential to carry on his practice at the Bar. The system of 'friendly pairing' facilitated this[8].

Within Fine Gael an enveloping air of hopelessness and despondency permeated the party. It was clear that the party could never envisage forming a government on its own. Patrick Lindsay described the party as "depressed and demoralised" at that time. Yet Gerard Sweetman in particular, began to articulate dogged antagonism to the idea of future coalitions. O'Higgins wrote that "At times this antagonism was directed towards Costello, who, although not leader of Fine Gael, was accorded the title of leader of the Opposition and thus personified the continuance of the inter-party idea. The relationship between the two men in government had been anything but cordial; particularly in 1956"[9]. Very soon the Fine Gael front bench had only three full-time politicians, Dillon, Mulcahy and Cosgrave. This placed an enormous workload and responsibility on these Deputies. Costello, through parliamentary party leader, had resumed his career at the Bar. Michael Gallagher writes that Costello devoted as much time to his legal work as to politics[10].

In 1958 the civil service through Ken Whitaker produced the *First Programme for Economic Expansion*, which had its genesis in Costello's October 1956 policy initiative. At the initiative of Tom O'Higgins, Michael O'Higgins, Declan Costello and Alexis Fitzgerald, Fine Gael set up a Fine Gael Research and Information Centre to modernise and develop social and economic policies. Gerard Sweetman particularly distrusted Declan Costello's 'left wing' tendencies, particularly his support for state involvement and social investment in the economy.

1959 PRESIDENTIAL ELECTION & REFERENDUM

deValera was in his mid-seventies and nearly blind. He was being urged to consider retirement, but did not appreciate this pressure from his colleagues. The impending retirement of Sean T O'Kelly from the Presidency offered a satisfactory solution where he could succeed his old colleague. This party decision was conveyed to deValera by Oscar Traynor[12]. The Fine Gael front bench initially intended not to contest the election at all. However, Sean MacEoin changed that when he declared that while he did not wish to contest the election, that if he did not do so, he would be betraying his old friend and colleague, Michael Collins. Patrick Lindsay writes that, "Suddenly the whole scene changed and Fine Gael were in the contest"[13].

At its October 1958 Ard Fheis, Fianna Fáil decided that as well as electing deValera as President, they would also use his vote-gathering power to ask the people in a referendum to abolish the proportional representation [PR] method of conducting elections. It was a sort of re-insurance for the Party against the departure of the 'Chief'. Fianna Fáil would then be assured of large majorities even with less than half the popular vote. It was a repeat of the successful tactic of holding a general election and a referendum on the same day as in 1937. A Constitutional Bill was introduced in the Dáil.

Arthur Griffith had been a founder member of the Proportional Representation Society of Ireland in April 1911. Sein Féin adopted PR to ensure that the Unionist minority would be represented in parliament. The 'principles of PR' were enshrined in the Free State Constitution of 1922, leaving certain flexibility for the parliament. The rather narrow general election victories of 1923 and 1927 created a feeling within Cumann na nGaedheal that PR would not deliver stable government. Ernest Blythe argued in cabinet for a change to the system of single transferable vote used in Britain. deValera'a 1937 Constitution actually mentioned the single transferable voting system. Costello had argued against this as a mistaken restriction. He said as in the 1922 Constitution, the voting system should be open to change by the parliament. A section of Fine Gael remained opposed to PR and made several unsuccessful attempts to make that party policy. As deValera was so opposed to PR, Fine Gael resisted any such temptation, as the single transferable vote always favoured the biggest party. Fianna Fáil had hoped to tempt Fine Gael to support the referendum or even to adopt a passive role. The temptation was that, at some time in the future, Fine Gael might come to be able to form a government on its own. This did not work, as, as Tom O'Higgins wrote, "Co-operation was easily arranged with other parties and with various Independent deputies, whose seats were also endangered"[14].

Costello led for Fine Gael when he spoke in the Dáil on 26 November 1958. He said that the abolition of PR could lead to a lessening of the rights of minorities, be anti-democratic, assist arrogant and unrepresentative government, and make unification more difficult. He also alluded to a possible re-orientation of political structures as the Treaty politicians departed.

He said; " We are coming to the end of an era. We do not know how the parties will split up. There may very well be what I might describe, with not any overemphasis, as a Radical Party. Certainly, in a few years there will be a break-up of the present political parties. God alone knows what will be the result".

deValera had referred extensively to previous statements by Costello on PR, implying that he had been against PR. Costello asserted that he had held a consistent view. deValera had quoted from advertisements by Cumann na nGaedheal on PR in 1927, and assigned the arguments therein to Costello. The latter denied this saying, "I was not responsible for them. I was in Geneva during the course of that General Election after the murder of Kevin O'Higgins". He said that WT Cosgrave's government, which had a sufficient Dáil majority, could have abolished PR under the then Constitution had it so wished. Costello agreed that during the debate on the draft Constitution in 1936, he put forward a possible case for PR, but that he had told deValera then, that the system of election should be left open to change by legislation if necessary, rather than included rigidly in the Constitution. He had said that, "elections should be based on the principles of PR". He declared that, unfortunately, in 1959, the Taoiseach was taking the opposite course. Costello admitted that PR did tend to assist small parties to get parliamentary representation, but said that was a good thing and had not militated against stable government. He questioned whether the object in hand was "to murder the Labour Party or to eliminate the Fine Gael Party, or a combination of both". In exchanges with deValera, the latter agreed that it was "probably right" to say that in 1927 he would have supported any combination of parties that would have put Cosgrave out, that he would support a Coalition, though he would not form it. Costello said that deValera was so prepared to act again in 1951. He said that it was the duty of any Parliament to form a Government, no matter what the position was, after a general election. Costello said that because deValera was defeated twice since he put PR into the 1937 Constitution, he now wished to change his mind and remove it. He said that deValera was wrong in 1936 and he was wrong in 1959. The Taoiseach did not suffer from political humility. Costello said that deValera wanted the British system, where the Conservatives and Labour did not like PR. Those two parties went in and out of office on the swing of a small section of political opinion.

The Bill was passed in the Dáil but was narrowly defeated in the Senate. The Government introduced a motion in the Dáil to pass the Bill unchanged. It became law after 90 days.

At this time deValera had been under severe pressure in the Dáil from Deputies Noel Browne and Jack McQuillan on his relationship to the ownership of *Irish Press* shares. In 1958 McQuillan had received shares in the *Irish Press*. He gave one of them to Browne who then had "the right to inspect the books in head office" Browne saw that deValera had systematically over a period of years become a majority shareholder of *Irish Press* newspapers[15]. In the Dáil, he declared that deValera "had used his joint position to create a very prosperous commercial entity, a very solid egg for the day of his retirement". The motion criticising deValera was defeated by 71 votes to 49. Some people believe it was this issue that finally convinced deValera to leave politics. On the day after this vote, 15 January, deValera announced his decision to run for the Presidency. The story of the *Irish Press* shares was allowed to rest until recent times, when it was again investigated.

The blatant attempt to run the referendum on the same day as the Presidential election, added to the opposition's determination against the measure. At the final Fine Gael rally at the GPO, Costello said "that there was no demand for this revolutionary proposal, other than to secure party political advantage for themselves, Fianna Fáil had given no reason whatsoever for this change in PR"[16]. The *Irish Times* editorialised that same day, "Two issues are being put before the electorate today. There should only have been one. It is to the discredit of the Fianna Fáil party. Mr deValera has blemished his reputation by allowing his name to be associated with the campaign to abolish PR". Polling day was the 17 June 1959. deValera was elected President by 538,000 votes to 417,636 for Sean MacEoin. The voters rejected Fianna Fáil's attempt to abolish PR. This was seen as a very sophisticated operation by the electorate, which voted for deValera, while rejecting his referendum proposal by 487,00 to 453,00. Sean Lemass was proposed as Taoiseach on 23 June. Costello opposed the motion, emphasising that he was doing so on purely political grounds. He said that the previous Government had been elected to carry out a difficult economic task, but that it had used the past nine months and much public money, trying to change the electoral system, a matter not mentioned during the election two and a half years previously. He added that it had suffered a serious defeat on an issue of major public policy, despite the Party harnessing all the old loyalties and allegiances linked to the former Taoiseach. He accused Lemass of insulting the electorate by asserting in response to the defeat of PR, that he would redraw the constituencies in an effort to thwart the will of the voters.

COSTELLO FAILS TO SUCCEED MULCAHY

Lemass, unlike deValera, was a hands-on operator in the Dáil. He was eager to put his own mark on proceedings in the Dáil and the country, and he did so energetically. This soon contrasted with the operation of Fine Gael with its split leadership. Mulcahy had always been a distant persona with little popular appeal. He had given forty-four years of active political service and was then aged seventy-two years. In the Dáil, Costello was a competent operator, and could be excellent on important issues. But at least half his time was spent on his legal practice and his front bench role was not effective. There was little new life or ideas within the party of contentedly well-off men to challenge Lemass and a reinvigorated Fianna Fáil. Gradually though, unease arose from the few full-time politicians who were carrying the bulk of the party work. Fine Gael always had difficulty in being loyal to its leader.

On 17 October Mulcahy informed his front bench of his decision to resign as party leader. Costello told the front bench meeting that the dual leadership should be terminated. The general feeling though, was also for a fulltime leader. Costello was surprised at this condition. He would have become the almost automatic leader, had he so agreed. He wanted to remain as a part-time leader though continuing his practice at the Bar. Mulcahy's view was that the party required a single full-time leader. At the next meeting of the parliamentary party, Mulcahy formally resigned. Costello was not present. A letter from him was read, indicating his view that he could properly lead the party in a part-time capacity. He wrote, "My carefully considered opinion was, and is, that it is wrong in principle in a small democracy, where average incomes are low, that a leader of a party in opposition should necessarily be a person whose economic circumstances permits him to devote his whole time to party and parliamentary work. Others may legitimately hold different views, but it is not a matter on which to make a serious issue. My own circumstances are such as not to permit withdrawal from my professional practice". Costello, acknowledging that most frontbenchers felt otherwise on the matter, added, "I should, as I do now, relinquish my position as leader of the opposition. The decision is final". He hoped to continue "in the dignified if unaccustomed position of a backbencher".

Liam Cosgrave and James Dillon were both proposed as leaders but the voting was postponed to the following day, when Dillon, with Gerard Sweetman acting as his manager, emerged as the victor. Mulcahy, after counting the votes alone, made the announcement in somewhat confusing circumstances. It appeared that Costello had received votes. Maurice Manning writes, "What is intriguing, at least from Mulcahy's figures, is that a substantial section of the party still favoured a Costello leadership – even on his own terms"[17]. It appears that McGillligan, the O'Higginses, and Declan Costello did not vote for Dillon. Tom O'Higgins wrote, "For the first time, what was basically a Sein Féin party had a leader from an entirely different tradition. It was inevitable that such a change, even if its full significance was not immediately realised, would tend to alter the party's outlook"[18]. Dillon was further isolated by not being able to choose his own frontbench, as that was the prerogative of the parliamentary party. Sean Lemass, almost immediately was recognised as the politician best equipped to press foward with the new economic and social programmes. This also meant that effectively there was little difference between Fianna Fáil and Fine Gael, except that they took different sides in the civil war. Early in 1960 William Norton resigned as Labour Party leader. He was replaced by Brendan Corish, who was dedicated to taking Labour on an anti-coalition path, which was to afford Fianna Fáil an unbroken run in government for more than a decade.

Dillon appeared and was a conservative man, with more in common with the old Irish Parliamentary Party, which had been led by his father, than with a modern Ireland. Fianna Fáil played on this. Dillon meanwhile complained that he had no party back-up as Leader. He often had to go into the Dáil himself to speak or call in Liam Cosgrave or Gerard Sweetman to do so. He wrote, "I was saddled with a number of gentlemen whom I certainly would not have chosen, they were no good, and it was not possible to get them to turn up to deal with the business falling within their sphere of responsibility"[19]. It appeared to be traditional within Fine Gael, that as soon as a new leader was appointed, elements within the party began to work against the leader.

In 1959, Declan Costello felt that Fine Gael should not be afraid to use new techniques traditionally associated with the parties of the left. He said, "We should be prepared to jettison motives and concepts which belong to the hey-day of nineteenth century liberalism: we should try to bring about conditions where there is genuine equality for all, irrespective of the level of society in which they have been born. I believe Fine Gael should move openly and firmly to the left"[20]. Dillon was never convinced of the efficacy, or the need for this new departure. The old problem of being effective in the Dáil continued. The predominance of lawyers on the front bench created such a problem that Dillon considered appointing one of the lawyer TD's act as an informal Whip in the Law Library. On the occasion of his retirement, Mulcahy described the situation as "a disgrace and could not go on. The time has come for Deputies to consider retiring, the present position imposed a task on a small minority that cannot be performed"[21].

This was a very frustrating time for those in Fine Gael, like John A Costello and his son Declan, who had hoped to lead Irish society into a new age. John A. spoke about realignment in Irish politics. In May 1961, he talked of the possibility of sections of the two major parties breaking away to join Labour[22]. This did not happen, though some years later in 1967-68 serious consideration was given to an alliance or amalgamation between Fine Gael and Labour. Many parliamentarians from both parties favoured a merger. Liam Cosgrave raised the possibility with Brendan Corish in January 1968. This was put to the Labour front bench, which turned the proposal down, as it would be very difficult. Labour remained very happy to have certain Fine Gael Deputies join the party. Garret Fitzgerald, who was directly involved in these discussions, has written, "And so Fine Gael and Labour went their separate paths as parties. Had this move succeeded, the political history of the succeeding years would surely have been very different"[23].

During the general election of 1961, Dillon said that his party had no objection in principle to working with others. He was also less attractive a prospective Taoiseach in Labour'e eyes as Costello had been[24]. Fine Gael did well in the October general election recovering ground. It won an extra seven seats and its vote was up by over 5%. The absence of high transfers hurt both Fine Gael and Labour. Fianna Fáil lost eight seats.

Declan Costello and those in Fine Gael who supported his vision of a new departure for the Party were somewhat sceptical of making much headway within such a conservative party. Declan Costello contemplated leaving Fine Gael and joining Labour. However, his father advised him that before doing so he should, "give Fine Gael a chance to decide where it stood by putting to the party the issues that he wished them to adopt as policy, so that he could make a clear decision for or against. Accordingly, he had listed eight points, and was waiting the party's reaction"

Fine Gael accepted Costello's social democratic ideas at its Ard Fheis on 26 May 1964. This was not easily achieved as James Dillon condemned "young men in a hurry" and Gerard Sweetman opposed the new ideas. However Liam Cosgrave's intervention in favour of Costello's ideas won the day for the new policy. Dillon and Sweetman continued to describe Fine Gael as a centrist party, a party of enterprise. Garret Fitzgerald believes that Fine Gael accepted the new ideas due to its being, "fearful of the effect of Declan's departure"[25]. Fine Gael won two by-elections in late 1964.

A committee had been established under the chairmanship of Liam Cosgrave, to outline in detail the new Fine Gael policy, but it had not completed its work when a general election was called for March 1965. Garret Fitzgerald joined this group "out of admiration for Declan Costello and for his effort to give a new contemporary relevance to Irish politics". Fitzgerald writes that Declan Costello still remained somewhat sceptical of Fine Gael's real commitment to his ideas. This was shared by Fitzgerald who was supposed to stand for the Party alongside John A Costello in Dublin South East. After initially agreeing to stand, Fitzgerald later withdrew.

Fine Gael's attempt to become a *catch-all* party like Fianna Fáil was not quite agreed. Gerard Sweetman and James Dillon still seeking to conceal the liberal implications of the new policy The 1965 election results were disappointing in that Fine Gael increased its vote, but did not secure any extra seats. When the new Dáil met, Dillon resigned as party leader and Liam Cosgrave was elected leader. Cosgrave had been in agreement with the new departure and intended to drop Sweetman from the front bench entirely, but was persuaded to retain him as spokesman in agriculture by Tom and Michael O'Higgins[26]. Garret Fitzgerald writes that he and others assumed that there would be an interval between the resignation of James Dillon and the election of a new leader. He had hoped that, "in those circumstances Declan Costello would have had a good chance of being elected by the parliamentary party"[27].

THE SUCCESSION BILL 1964

The Succession Bill had been in preparation for several years to tackle a system which militated against married women in particular, but also against children. John A Costello made a major contribution to the very lengthy Bill in December 1964. He said that a few sections of it caused problems. The fact of the matter was that up to 50% of men did not make wills and left it to the courts to decide. He acknowledged that nothing caused more problems in families than where some members felt hard done by in the distribution of the estate. He forecast that the debate on the "controversial matters", would be "long and bitter". He said the Bill had received a hostile reception, as it would affect every member of the community's private interests; it was therefore, unlike what Deputy Tully called for, a truly political matter. He allowed that it might also become an election issue. He rejected Deputy Corish's sentimental call that they should repudiate the notion that the Irish people do not recognise their obligations towards their wives and families. There was no use in shirking the issue, he said. He then told a true story to illustrate peoples thinking.

"There was a man who had seven daughters and finally a son was born and the son was the apple of his eye". He explained "as this boy grew up, what he was going to do for him; he would send him to the best school and then to the university, and his attitude was summed up when he said 'You would like to do the best you could for the one child you have'. The seven daughters were in the halfpenny place. He recounted cases where women, wives, were badly treated by husbands, after a lifetime of service, and only left with the fortune she brought into the place. He spoke of instances where men tried to control their families behaviour from the grave. He felt that the Minister must make a very much stronger case for the provisions of the Bill. The kind of farmer who settles on one particular son, with the widow relegated to the use of one room, the grass of a cow etc, find the Bill a shock. But he maintained that the Bill did not go far enough and that the people had to be prepared and educated for it. The Minister had to bring the people with him. Costello favoured a rigid system, which had a forced contribution from the testator, but recognised that there were other systems which offered more judicial discretion. He wanted the Minister to make his case on the best system, before the Dáil, and not in Committee Stage. He said that many people could not be talked out of going to court, even by their legal advisors; and that they would fight a will suit to the last ditch, if there was any chance at all.

The Bill did go into Committee Stage in the spring and summer of 1965, when the new Minister of Justice, Brian Lenihan, also a barrister, was very receptive to the views of Costello. Much of the interchange between them as they considered various sections of the Bill appears as that between a wise student and a schoolmaster. This was one among many fundamental contributions Costello made to the institution of new legislation in his lengthy career as a constitutional and legal expert. A flavour of this debate can be gleaned from this extract from the official Dáil record.

Costello: *That is precisely the point. The trustee has no power to do anything to interfere with the widow's right to one-third. That is hers absolutely under a previous section.*

Lenihan: *This is to meet the situation where the spouse is regarded as incapable of managing the estate.*

Costello: *That may be so, but it does not do that. The testator cannot reach down after his death and try to control her, even if he thought she was not a good business person. He cannot do that. There is nothing in the section that enables him to do it.*

Lenihan: *I will have another look at this section. I should like to have the Deputy's views as to whether we should spell out more precisely what the position of the trustees should be.*

Costello: *That is an entirely different matter. We have not approached that at all. If we decide that the widow is entitled to a legal share, we should not go back on that, and should not interfere with it at all. However we can debate that matter afterwards. At the moment this section does not do anything.*

Lenihan: *I will have a full look at the section between now and Report Stage. There are two negatives. It should be put positively. Anyway, I have an open mind as to whether this section should be there at all*

Costello: *Now the Minister is talking. If we take up the position that the person is entitled to one-third, we should not interfere with that at all.*

MJ Higgins: *I am sorry I did not have the assistance of Deputy Costello earlier in the day when I was dealing with that section.*

Costello: *Logically we could leave it alone.*

Lenihan: *We may do that between now and Report Stage.*

Question put and agreed to.

Section 117

Question proposed: "That section 117 stand part of the Bill".

Costello: I am looking forward to arguing the question of moral right if this Bill becomes law and I am still alive

Section 118 agreed to.[28]

A NEW MEMBER

Declan Costello and Alexis Fitzgerald approached Garret Fitzgerald to run for the Senate after the 1965 general election. This he did successfully and was appointed to the Seanate front bench by Liam Cosgrave. As the 1966 Presidential election loomed, Fitzgerald realised that in fact he had never formally joined the Fine Gael party. He knew that this had to be done at local level. He approached his local Fine Gael TD, John A Costello. Fitzgerald found Costello's response, "was as usual, forceful, blunt, and idiosyncratic". Costello said, "forty years in politics; twice Taoiseach; never joined Fine Gael". Fitzgerald timorously suggested that they were in different times, and Costello's example might not be the best one to follow. He thought that the older man may have been disappointed with such a conventional attitude to politics. Costello then admitted that, indeed, there was a local Fine Gael organisation in Dublin South East. He directed the aspirant member to an executive committee meeting on the following Thursday at the Morehampton Hotel. Fitzgerald duly attended and found a small group of elderly people present[29].

SWEETMAN'S REVENGE
PRESIDENTIAL ELECTION 1966

The 50th anniversary of the 1916 Rising was to be commemorated in some splendour during 1966. Detailed plans were being made to mark the occasion. Both Fine Gael and Fianna Fáil each had a notable who had fought in the Rising and had been sentenced to death, deValera and WT Cosgrave. Unfortunately for Fine Gael, the latter died on 16 November of 1965. That very same day saw the Fianna Fáil Ard Fheis hear from Sean Lemass that deValera had agreed to stand again for President in 1966. This placed Fine Gael in a difficult position. When Sean T. O'Kelly stood for a second time in 1952, Fine Gael had agreed not to oppose him. Now amid the national solidarity emanating from the commemoration of the Rising, many in the Fine Gael front bench, including its leader, felt that it might not oppose deValera. However the party grassroots opposed this, in some anger, as indicating another lack of serious resolve to fight Fianna Fáil. The *Irish Times* editorial got in on the act on 31 January, challenging Fine Gael to take on deValera. Tom O'Higgins says, "an agreed nomination would have been possible with any other candidate, but to the grassroots Fine Gael supporter, agreement on Eamon deValera was unthinkable"[30].

The parliamentary party met and agreed that they had to fight the election. Liam Cosgrave warned the members "Remember Presidential candidates don't hang like apples on trees, waiting to be picked when you want one". The meeting just after Christmas left it up to the front bench to select the candidate.

Tom O'Higgins then took soundings on a possible candidate, including Sean MacEoin, James Dillon and Sean MacBride, but all were ruled out for various reasons. O'Higgins then settled in his own mind on John A Costello as the best candidate possible, though he envisaged some difficulty in persuading him to run. O'Higgins decided not to approach Costello, who would not be at the meeting as he had retired from the front bench some years previously, but to wait and hear the reaction from the meeting. O'Higgins formally proposed Costello and gave his detailed reasons for doing so. A few members nodded assent but then there was silence as Cosgrave looked around the table for other contributions. Sweetman, who was sitting directly opposite O'Higgins, then spoke. He was vehemently opposed to O'Higgins' proposal, claiming that sentiment had no place in their discussion. He opposed Costello's nomination on the basis that, Fine Gael could not oppose on the 50th anniversary of the Easter Rising, a person who had fought in that Rising, "with a man who had been old enough in 1916 to have fought in the Rising and had not". Sweetman added that it would lead to a humiliating defeat for Costello, and he could not understand how one who claimed to admire him would wish to expose him to a most humiliating defeat. O'Higgins was flabbergasted at Sweetman's remarks. Paddy Lindsay spoke next, saying that they should get away entirely from 1916, and run someone who could not have been there in 1916. Lindsay then proposed O'Higgins himself as their candidate.

This appeared to get unanimous backing and Liam Cosgrave stood up and almost implored O'Higgins, asking, "Will you do it Tom". O'Higgins assented[31]. With Gerard Sweetman acting as an enthusiastic campaign manager, and with his cousin Roger Sweetman acting as a policy advisor and speech writer, O'Higgins won 49.5% of the popular vote and gave Fine Gael a great national fillip. deValera got 558,861 votes to O'Higgins' 548,144, a majority of 10,617.

The shafting of Costello at the Fine Gael front bench meeting was the culmination of Gerard Sweetman's revenge on Costello, whom he believed had treated him poorly over several years as Taoiseach. Sweetman acted as judge and jury on Costello's lack of involvement in the 1916 Rising. The suspicion must remain that Sweetman was not the only frontbencher happy to see Costello demeaned in such a fashion.

Despite an initial coolness between Liam Cosgrave and Gerard Sweetman, due to some disagreement about his treatment of Cosgrave's father, WT Cosgrave, a decade earlier, Sweetman then became party organiser, a position for which Garret Fitzgerald says "his forceful personality well fitted him". Fitzgerald adds that Sweetman "was not an ideological right-winger but rather a politician with a business orientation and a practical interest in winning power for his party. He was tough, and had little instinctive sympathy with the younger generation, least of all with the liberal youth of the 1960's He had no malice in him and did not bear grudges, but in what he conceived to be the interests of the party, he could be quite ruthless"[32].

Fianna Fáil made another attempt to abolish Proportional Representation in 1968, with the debate in Dáil Éireann ending on 3 April. The electorate again rejected this. John A Costello did not contest the June1969 General Election and neither did his son Declan. However Alexis Fitzgerald was elected to the Senate, and was immediately invited to join the Fine Gael front bench by Liam Cosgrave.

In 1972 John A Costello was the guest speaker at the Michael Collins commemoration at Béal na Bláth. He was speaking some years into the most recent episode of the northern troubles, which earlier that year had seen the wilful murder of twelve people in Derry by British soldiers and the retaliatory burning of the British Embassy in Dublin. He still ascribed the main responsibility to the British Government, but as he had when Taoiseach, said that violence was not the way forward. He said: "Irish unity may be bought at too great a price if bought at the price of shame and sin. We no longer required the heroic qualities of the days of Collins and it was not by arms that what remained to be done could be done. The British people had a serious responsibility in relation to the North. Their Government created the problem and maintained or acquiesced in the injustices" [33].

In 1973 Fine Gael was returned to government with the Labour Party. Liam Cosgrave became Taoiseach and chose Declan Costello as his Attorney General.

CHAPTER 23

THE COSTELLO INTERVIEW AFTERMATH

DAN O'DONOVAN, JOSEPH BRENNAN, CHARLES HAUGHEY

Costello gave an interview to Michael McInerney of the *Irish Times* in 1967. Joseph Brennan, an ex-secretary of the Department of Finance and an ex-Govenor of the Central Bank, took great umbrage from a comment by Costello, which he felt was directed against himself. Brennan already had several old scores to settle with Costello.

Costello's Inter-party Government had dismissed a cousin of Brennan's, Dan O'Donovan, who had been Secretary of the Department of Social Welfare, from his post in February 1951. Mr. O'Donovan was the accounting officer of the Department and had suspended another officer, Mr. J O'Driscoll, a member of the Labour Party, on the grounds that such discipline was necessary. His minister William Norton and the Government ordered him to lift the suspension. The Taoiseach later ordered him on five occasions to carry out the Minister's instruction and also informed him that it had become a matter of ministerial and governmental authority. O'Donovan held that the Taoiseach and the Government did not have the authority to so direct him, as accounting officer. When Mr. O'Donovan declined to reinstate the official, he was removed from his post. O'Donovan was one of the original Dáil staff under Michael Collins in 1919 and had a long and distinguished career in the civil service. Costello gave a detailed reply to a Private Notice Question from Mr. deValera in the Dáil on the matter, where an acrimonious exchange took place between Captain Cowan and members of Fianna Fail[1].

Joseph Brennan, Governor of the Central Bank, backed O'Donovan as being technically correct in his stance. He deemed Costello's action as "a scandalous piece of bullying which had no *locus standi* whatsoever for overruling or otherwise directing you in your capacity as Accounting Officer"[2]. Brennan's position was that only the Dáil had authority to so direct O'Donovan. Sean MacEntee attacked Norton in the Dáil on the issue claiming that Norton was trying to promote a Labour Party member in place of O'Donovan[3].

Brennan also nursed a personal grievance against Costello since the St Patrick's Day parade in 1949. After the military parade, Brennan entertained the Taoiseach and some of his Ministers in the Bank on College Green. He though Costello was ill mannered in talking all the time with his colleagues "without troubling to address a remark to me"[4]. Tom Garvin comments on the incident: "Costello was possibly more worried about the economic theories of the voter than about those of the Governor of the Central Bank. The former had more power. In some ways the Inter-Party economic and social policies were rather like deValera's, still intellectually pre-economic. The difference was that Costello was more afraid of the voters than was deValera.

The latter watched the Irish voter as a hunter stalks his prey, and understood the voter as perhaps no one else of his generation did"[5]. When Fianna Fáil came back into office in 1951 Dan O'Donovan was reinstated into the civil service as a ministerial advisor at Social Welfare. In 1953 the then Secretary at Social Welfare retired, and O'Donovan got his old job back When returned to office in 1954, Costello's second cabinet considered the situation and transferred O'Donovan to the post of secretary to the President, which was acceptable to all[6].

Joseph Brennan had been a thorn in the eyes of many politicians during his lengthy career as a public servant. It may be worthwhile to look briefly at his career. He was another Cork man, also linked with Michael Collins. He had worked in the Chief Secretary's office in Dublin Castle from 1912-1922 and had provided Collins with vital information for the Treaty negotiations. Collins had been instrumental in him being appointed as Controller and Auditor General in the Provisional Government in 1922. He was appointed Secretary of the Department of Finance in 1923 at the age of thirty-six. Joe Lee writes that Brennan's insistence on rigorous accountability came as a culture shock to many of the heroes of the revolution. His image of the politician appears to have been that of a pig with his snout permanently stuck in the trough. There was a certain cold grandeur about his cherished image of the public service, a body of incorruptible state servants valiantly resisting the rush of the Gadarene swine to the flesh pots of public money[7]. He held that position until 1927. Brennan was an arch-conservative, determined that Finance should control the whole of the civil service[8]. This he was able to do for a short period as the government ministers were engaged on nation building. After the August 1923 general election, WT Cosgrave appointed Ernest Blythe as Minister of Finance. He and Brennan did not get along at all. Brennan alienated the cabinet over his bitter criticism on aspects of the Shannon Scheme[9].

Brennan was effectively sacked in 1927 by being appointed Chairman of the new Currency Commission. His successor JJ McElligott was also a conservative like WT Cosgrave and Blythe. When Fianna Fáil came to power in 1932, it appointed a commission to investigate the civil service. It made Brennan chairman and he duly brought in a conservative report. The report said that civil servants were responsible to Parliament, by which he certainly meant the Department of Finance. When the Banking Commission was set up by MacEntee in 1934 to report in 1938, Brennan was again Chairman. His report naturally came down on the conservative *status quo* pursued by Cosgrave's governments and the early Fianna Fáil one in economic and social policies. It criticised the increase of the national debt and called for a policy of debt redemption. When Frank Aiken as Minister of Finance came under financial pressure and sought credit from the banks, the banks resisted, as did Aiken's own Secretary McElligott, and Joseph Brennan then Governor of the Central Bank. When Aiken asserted that the Constitution favoured his powers in the matter for the welfare of the people, McElligott pointed out that it was only the Central Bank, which could determine action against the banks. Brennan also came out strongly against Paddy McGilligan's expansive budgets, and wrote a very critical report in 1951 provoking a public furore[10]. Fianna Fáil under MacEntee was pushed into de-inflationary measures. The Opposition made vituperative references to the malign influence of Brennan. Brennan and McElligott mistakenly assumed that exports would increase if domestic demand were dampend. The deflationary policies led to stagnation in trade and discouraged investment in manufacturing industry. By 1953 Brennan was no politicians friend and the Government accepted his resignation in March 1953.

The Costello interview with Michael McInerney appeared in a series of lengthy articles in the *Irish Times*. In one of these published on 6 September 1967, Costello spoke in some detail about the Shannon Scheme. He said that some newspapers, businessmen, Department of Finance officials and financiers opposed it. He said, " We were denounced as latter-day pirates and 'young men in a hurry'. We were also pioneers in the Shannon Scheme, as WT Cosgrave, Mr. Blythe and many other 'conservatives' stood up to the assault and put the Scheme through in spite of the uproar". Joseph Brennan took umbrage at the reference to the criticism of Department of Finance officials who opposed the Shannon Scheme. He wrote to Costello on 15 September 1967, accusing him of a diatribe against him. He wrote:

"As Secretary of the Department of Finance at that time I must, if only for myself, strongly repudiate this allegation and do not believe that it can apply to any of my colleagues. Apart from the too common impropriety of casting aspersions on civil servants in matters where responsibility rests with the minister, I regret that you should give currency to these allegations and I hope that you will take proper steps immediately to withdraw it at least insofar as it may concern myself".

Costello replied robustly writing:

I had not known what views, other than your own, any particular official of the Department of Finance held in reference to this matter. I understand that you were strongly of the opinion and persistently adhered to it, that you as Secretary of the DOF, was entitled, both as a duty and a right, to be given ample opportunity for examining in detail the proposals of the Shannon Scheme: that you expressed the view that such an examination would take a very long time- at least a year and perhaps more than that. You persisted in your claims in spite of submissions that were put to you that there were no valid grounds for postponing the scheme pending your prolonged investigation. In view of your insistence on your right and duty the matter had to become one for government decision. The decision was that the minister should proceed immediately, notwithstanding that you had threatened to resign from your post as head of the Department, if your demands were not acceded to. I have no doubt that you acted on sincere motives and deep conviction. However I do not think that the description of the opposition, was an unreasonable description of your attitude, which must of course be taken to be the official Departmental opinion. You will understand of course that I do not wish that the matters that I have mentioned herein in reference to your attitude should be given any publicity".

Brennan replied to Costello's put-down letter and Costello then told him that if the interview were re-printed the reference to 'Departmental of Finance officials' would be omitted. He declined to furnish Brennan with documentation on which he had based his interview. Almost immediately Brennan decided to write to the current incumbent Minister of Finance, Charles J. Haughey He outlined the details of his grievance and hoped that the files concerning the Shannon Scheme could be made available to him.

He wrote that: *"The Minister of Finance and their officials are not unused to unfair sniping from irresponsible quarters and have to tolerate it up to a point but it is another matter when the ex-Taoiseach attacks a civil servant. As you are now the Minister of the Department whose officials have been attacked, I should be greatly obliged if you would allow me a short interview about the present case".*

Mr. Haughey replied saying, *"I should be happy to see you as you suggest".* In the event those files could not be located. The last letter in Joseph Brennan's file is to Mr. Costello and dated 17 February 1968. It is a long rambling letter in which Brennan outlines his unhappy experience working with Ernest Blythe and his eventual resignation as Secretary on 20 September 1927.

However he does tell the ex-Taoiseach that; *"There is nothing in your remarks to indicate that you have any authentic knowledge of how the affairs of the Department of Finance were administered at the period in question by the then Minister"*[11].

In the same interview with the *Irish Tmes* Costello spoke briefly about his colleagues in government. He described Norton as *"a wonderful man, unequalled as a politician".* He said that Norton and Noel Browne never got on. MacBride, he said, was always loyal. Dillon was *"magnificent".* Murphy *"did a great job on housing".* Of Browne, he said, *"he was a very hard-working minister until the disaster of the Health plan".* He said Patrick Lynch and Maurice Moynihan *"were helpful and cooperative".* Everett cooperated with Norton to reunite the Labour Party. Alexis Fitzgerald *"had a brilliant mind which he used almost entirely for the Government".* Of Sean Lemass, Costello noted *"a most able, but a ruthless politician who worked hard, harder than most".* When asked for his views on deValera, he refused to comment.

Costello went on *"Our biggest achievement I would say was the Declaration of the Republic; that was my aim since 1926 and I was glad of the great opportunity to secure peace in old Ireland once again"*[12].

❀❀❀❀

CHAPTER 24

FREEMEN OF DUBLIN

In 1975, it was pointed out by devotees of ex President deValera that the one honour that had not been bestowed on him was that of the Freedom of Dublin city. This was raised among the elected Councillors. Agreement was reached unanimously, when it was decided that on the same occasion John A Costello would be similarly honoured. Thus, on 7 March 1975, the assembled City Councillors and about one hundred invited guests gathered at the Mansion House. The Lord Mayor, James O'Keeffe, conferred the Freedom of the city on both men. deValera responded with a short formal statement. However Costello took the opportunity to make a wider address. He said that the honour had come as a complete surprise to him and it was unsought. He described himself as a citizen of Dublin. Though born in the city, he adjudged himself not of sufficient ancestry to make him a "Jackeen". He had represented Dublin constituencies in the Dáil for over thirty years, having had long association with City Hall. He then referred to his father, whom he said, had been a City Councillor, and had been devoted to trying to get houses for the people, and to helping the poor. He told the gathering that one of the reasons he had been acceptable to the Labour Party as Taoiseach in the Coalition Government was that his father had been a friend of Jim Larkin.

Costello then said that he and deValera had been political opponents, adding "We fought many a fight, sometimes we agreed and sometimes we didn't. Mr. deValera he said jokingly, "did not like Fine Gael lawyers, and he was one of the more prominent of these. However we did get on well together and I think he had a secret admiration for lawyers in general". Costello said that the lawyers eventually won the day when they made Mr. deValera an honorary lawyer. Costello went on to say that he and Mr. deValera had fought the Constitution in the Dáil almost word for word. However he never heard a wrong word from him during that time. "Both in and out of office I received nothing but the utmost courtesy from him. I have great pleasure tonight to be on this neutral ground with him"[1].

After the formal ceremony deValera's and Costello's guests were invited to the Lord Mayor's drawing room. deValera's guests far outnumbered Costello's. Among the latter was Tom O'Higgins. He was persuaded by Sean MacEntee to meet deValera, and a remarkable exchange took place. MacEntee introduced him as the Chief Justice. As O'Higgins sat beside deValera, the latter said, "Oh; you opposed me". "Yes sir, I did", O'Higgins agreed. "You have to admit that had I been able to campaign, the result would have been quite different", deValera responded. O'Higgins answered, "I'm sure you are right". "I'm very glad to hear you say so" deValera replied. O'Higgins commented that he had made deValera happy and "no harm had been done"[2].

COSTELLO ON DEVALERA

deValera died later in that same year of 1975. His passing at the age of 87 was marked by great state formalities, despite the fact that a coalition government under Liam Cosgrave was in office. Costello spoke on RTE that same evening, in a very forthright way about deValera. He said he was a man capable of creating in others tremendous loyalty and even excessive devotion, and also very practical hatreds, which even then existed in their children's children. .

Costello believed that on the day deValera was elected President and entered the Park on his duties, his influence on the country as a parliamentary democrat and politician, ceased for all time. Then he made the surprising comment, "In my opinion he has left nothing of permanent value, although he did a remarkable series of practical demonstrations of what his policy was during his time. Particularly I would like to emphasise in keeping this country out of the war. Nevertheless his influence was widespread during his life. I think his influence is now at an end". Mr. deValera was undoubtedly a most controversial figure and perhaps in future years he will develop as being one of the most controversial figures in Irish history. Whatever views people may have about the quality of his policies or his actions, there is no doubt that he impressed his personality and ideals upon the people of the country and the country as a whole.

To a considerable extent, he navigated the ship of state in the direction in which he wished it to go for up to 50 years, and formed the basis of the building up of the State. I have had the privilege of being in the Dáil for a large number of years and have had many discussions with him in debate on all sorts of topics. I have had an opportunity of watching him. I had an opportunity of listening to the not always flattering observations of my colleagues in the Fine Gael party on his actions, from Easter Week onwards, and especially during the period of the Civil War. In my opinion one of the worst characteristics of his personality was his pertinacity in adhering to principles or ideals, which he had convinced himself were the proper principles or the ideals he sought after. He thought very deeply and for a very long time, changed his mind frequently, but if he eventually came to the conclusion that what his view then was the proper one, nothing could convince him that he was wrong or get him to change. To that extent he was a difficult man to argue with in the course of a committee stage in the Dáil. One of the extraordinary things that he did when he came into office in 1932 and in 1933, he firmly and fully adopted the principles of the British Government and the British people in Parliamentary democracy, especially cabinet responsibility".

Costello himself felt that the principle of parliamentary responsibility and unity in Cabinet and policy was rather overworked and inclined to damage the country. He defended the working of Inter-Party governments where a measure of unity and a very considerable marriage of policy could be achieved, rather than having total agreement on every point of detail. Costello acknowledged that deValera was totally against the idea of coalition government, and wondered whether his influence on parliamentary democracy would outlive him. Costello said that clearly deValera had dominated all aspects of Fianna Fáil, thus getting his views accepted in cabinet and thereby in the parliamentary party. He always wanted a parliamentary majority to ensure that his views were paramount, and could never understand that any other system of government could work.

This assessment of deValera hurt members of the deValera family, particularly Terry deValera. Terry was the lawyer son of Eamon deValera and a legal colleague of Costello's. In his *Memoir* Terry deValera says of his good solicitor friend, Tommy Robinson: "One of Tommy Robinson's closest friends was John A Costello. He was always briefed in major cases as Robinson's leading senior counsel. I came to know Mr. Costello well, and from the day I was introduced to him, he showed me nothing but kindness and consideration. My master even entrusted me to carry personal messages and to work for the Costello family. I was once allowed to attend a pre-trial consultation in a very important case in which John A Costello was the leading counsel. The clients and witnesses were present and some discussion came up regarding a document to be filed in court. Robinson was somewhat uptight about the case and became quite excited, wrongly accusing me of failing to file the document. Mr. Costello knew that I had and he roared at his friend, springing to my defence, despite the other parties being present. Robinson felt quite chastened by the 'attack' of his friend. In later years, I myself briefed John A Costello as my leading senior counsel, and a more learned, loyal and conscientious leader one could not have. When leading in a case, he had a rather fatherly approach which I found both helpful and encouraging".

Terry deValera recalled one important case when Costello was for the opposition. Despite losing, Costello applied for and won a portion of the costs abated or disallowed. Afterwards Costello apologised privately to deValera saying, "I'm sorry about the costs, Terry, but you know I had to do my duty". deValera continued, "This was a gracious remark from an esteemed adversary. While I know that he was quite different in his political views, he privately had a wholesome respect for my father as my father had for him. I will therefore never understand the reason, which prompted him to speak on television in such a disparaging way, the night my father died. Perhaps the lawyer in him came out and he was simply speaking to what he regarded as his brief. At heart he was a lawyer first and perhaps a somewhat reluctant politician, although a dedicated one. He would have made an outstanding Chief Justice, if such had been his wish"[3].

✻✻✻✻

Eamonn deValera and John A. Costello, chat at the Mansion House,
on the occasion of the conferring of the Freedom of Dublin on them.

DEATH

The Irish newspapers carried the death notice of John A Costello on 6 January 1976. It read:

"Costello (Dublin) January 5 1976. At his residence 20 Herbert Park John A. Costello S.C. husband of the late Ida Costello. Beloved father and Grandfather. May he rest in peace. Funeral arriving at church of Sacred Heart Donnybrook 4.30 this [Tues] evening. Requiem mass at 11 o'clock tomorrow [Wed] Internment will take place at Deans Grange cemetery".

Liam Cosgrave, then Taoiseach of a Coalition Government, almost under siege from economic pressures and a murderous IRA campaign, spoke of his predecessor saying:

"He was in the fullest sense a true Christian gentleman. This quality he displayed in his distinguished legal career to the advantage of his clients and to the people of the legal profession. This quality he also displayed in his political career to serve the nation with an impartial fairness seldom if ever equalled. The same Christian approach was even more obvious in his dedication to his family to whom I offer my deepest sympathy.

Mr Costello's greatest contribution to the Irish nation was in the constitutional sphere. He drafted many of the original Public Safety Acts and in any constitutional decision, his views were never reversed"[4].

The Irish Times editorialised, that same day, *"John A Costello's origins were legal not combatitive. He came of a constitutionalist Nationalist stock and his appearance in Fine Gael was through the good offices of a former Chief Justice, Hugh Kennedy. Loyalty was his forte. No man ever had so misleading a manner. He breathed belligerence, but it was the armour he put on against his sensitive and compassionate disposition. He was without blarney and neither sought or won cheap popularity. Those who knew him liked him most. In personal and private life he was without enemy".*

There was no State funeral at the request of the family. President Cearbhall Ó'Dálaigh, Tánaiste Brendan Corish, Jack Lynch, leader of Fianna Fáil, and government ministers, attended the removal.

Tom O'Higgins said, *"Costello was a forceful and successful advocate at the Bar: an excellent examiner of witnesses and advocate. He broke not once but twice, what had always been considered the harsh and inflexible rule of the Bar – namely that you could not leave and return to it successfully".*

On 13 January 1976 the legal profession paid formal tribute to their dead colleague.

The grave of John A, and Ida Costello, in Dean's Grange Cemetery Dublin.

FOOTNOTES

Introduction

1. Jordan Anthony, WT Cosgrave 1880-1965, Founder of Modern Ireland,Westport Books 2006.
2. Feeney Brian, Sein Féin O'Brien 2002 p. 192
3. McInerney Michael, Irish Times interviews with JA Costello, 4-7 September 1967.
4. Irish Times 4 September 1967.

Chapter 1

1. Mulcahy Papers P7/ C/116.
2. ibid P/7/C/122.
3. Irish Times 9/2/1948.
4. ibid 10/2/1948.
5. ibid 14/2/1948.
7. Mulcahy Papers. P/7/D/116.
8. Browne Noel, Against the Tide Gill & MacMillan p. 125.
9. Lawlor Caitriona Sean MacBride Remembers Curragh 2006 p. 145.
10. Browne op. cit . p. 107.
11. Lynch & Meeenan (Eds) Pages From a Memoir p. 37.
12. McCullagh David, A Makeshift Majority-
    The first Inter-Party Government, 1948- 51 IPA 1998 p. 274.
13. Manning, Maurice, Dillon. Gill and Macmillan 2004, p. 226.
14. Mulcahy Papers ibid.
15. Lawlor op. cit p. 148.
16. McInerney op. cit.
17. Lynch & Meenan op. cit p. 37.
18. McCullagh op. cit. p. 275 note 168.
18a. Costello was a long-time member of the exclusive Portmarnock Golf Club, being Captain in 1947. While he was not interested in the strife and tension of club competition, the outcome of his Sunday morning match mattered greatly to him. On one occasion his son John recalls his father's indignation when RF Browne refused to play again after lunch. John also recalls Seamus O'Connor wading across the estuary from Baldoyle rather than be late for his date on the tee. John has vivid memories of his father's high spirits before he set out for his Sunday game. John A was also a member of Milltown Golf Club. He played there, generally alone, in the evenings after work. Silence was something Jack Costello valued and practised. [Information from TM Healy, a member at Portmarnock since 1941].
19. Costello Papers.
20. McInerney.
21. Mulcahy Papers P/7/D/116.
22. McInerney ibid.
23. Mulcahy Papers P/7/D/116.
24. Irish Times 17/2/'48.
25. McCullagh p. 36.
26. ibid p. 37.
27. Puirseil Niamh, The Irish Labour Party 1922-1970 UCD 2007 p.212.
28. Irish Times 23/2 '48.
29. ibid 15/6/'49.
30. deValera Terry, Memoir p. 234.
31. McDermott Eithne, Clan na Poblachta, Cork University Press 1998 p. 71.
32. S 14169 NAI. 18/2/'48 Moynihan's notes for Taoiseach with new Attorney General.
33. Irish Times 25/2/48.
34. Ms. 22,586. NLI.
35. Bew Paul & Patterson Henry, Sean Lemass, Gill & MacMillan 1982. p. 50.

Chapter 2

1. Irish Independent 19/2/'48.
2. McInermey op. cit.
3. McCagne Eugene, Arthur Cox, Gill & Macmillan 1994. p. 29.
4. McInerney op. cit.
5. Meenan James, George O'Brien, Gill & MacMillan 1980 p. 32.
6. ibid. p. 37.
7. Costello Kevin, The Law of Habeas Corpus in Ireland, Four Courts 2006 passim.
8. McInerney op. cit.
9. Jordan Anthony, Sean – A biography of Sean MacBride, Blackwater 1993 p. 117.
10. Martin Peter, Censorship in Two Irelands, Irish Academic Press 2006 p. 70.
    And The Right of Public Meetings, Justice Department 8/4/1938.

Chapter 3

1. Lawlor op. cit. p. 117
2. Attorney General Memo 55/7/1929 NAI.
3. O'Halloran Clare, Partition and the Limits of Irish Nationalism, Dublin 1987, pp. 122-124.
4. ibid.
4a. NAI Cab. 189 4/7/50.
4b. Irish Times 7/2/'51.
4c. deVere White Terence, Kevin O'Higgins Tralee, p. 237.
4d. NAI. S 3332 15, Sept 1922.
5. Fitzgerald Desmond Papers.P/80/5127.
6. Kennedy Michael, Ireland and the League of Nations IAP 1996 p. 30.
7. NAI 1194/2.
8. Public Record Office London, Co. 739/4/49361 Curtis to Devonshire, 5-10 September 1923.
9. Dáil Debates, Volume 4 Column 139.
10. Kennedy op. cit. pp. 60-63.
11. Dáil Debates, Vol. 33. vol 2050-2167 and 2195-2330.
12. McInerney.
13. Dáil Debates, Vol 28 Col. 277-320 & 334-374.
14. NAI. S 6051 17 July 1930.
15. O'Sullivan Donal, The Irish Free State and its Senate London 1939 p. 250-1.
16. Report of the Delegation of the Irish Free State to the League of Nations Assembly, Stationary Office Dublin 1930.
17. Kennedy, op. cit. p. 256.
18. Lawlor op. cit . p. 50.
19. Jordan Anthony WT Cosgrave Founder of Modern Ireland, Westport Books 2006 p. 140.
20. Dáil Debates, Vol. 36. col. 2290-2332 & 2334-2362.
21. House of Commons Debates, CLIX 1193-4 & 1205.
22. Gilbert Martin, Churchill Vol 5. Heinmann 1981 p. 375.
23. House of Commons op. cit. 311.
24. Gilbert op. cit. p.420.
25. Jordan Anthony, Churchill A Founder of Modern Ireland, Westportbooks 1995 p.160-2.
26. Senate Debates, Vol 15. Col. 938.
27. McInerney.
28. ibid.
29. Dáil Debates, External Relations Act, December 1936.
30. McInerney.
31. ibid.
33. McInerney.

Chapter 4
1. NAI. DT/S 5708A.

Chapter 5
1. Lindsay Patrick, Memories, Blackwater, 1992 p.5.
2. Cruise O'Brien Conor, Passion & Cunning, Paladin 1990. pp. 54-5.
3. Irish Independent 9/1/1933.
4. Irish Independent 13 /1 1933.
5. Mulcahy Papers P/79B/96/13
6. Manning, Maurice, The Blueshirts, Gill & MacMillan, 1987 p. 115.
7. Irish Independent 21/12/1933.
8. McInerney.
9. Dáil Debates, 25/2/1937 col. 1116.

Chapter 6
1. Dáil Debates, Vol 64. col. 1293ff 11 December 1936.
2. Longford & O'Neill, deValera, Dublin 1970. p.290.
3. Ward Margaret, Maud Gonne, Pandora 1990. p. 173. For a modern defence of the Constitution .cf "deValera, The Contitution and the Historians" by Gerard Hogan in "The Irish Jurist" vol. xl new series 2005
4. Manning, Dillon p. 138.
5. Lee Joseph, Ireland 1912-1985 Cambridge 1989 p.202
6. Dáil Debates 27/7/1941 col. 1878.

Chapter 7
1. Manning, Dillon p. 186.
2. Irish Independent 4/6/1943 & 21/6/1943.
3. ibid 15/6/1943.
4. ibid 24/6/1943.
5. Dáil Debates, 1/7/1943 col. 26-39.
6. McGilligan Papers 35/207.
7. Manning, Dillon p.190.
8. Irish Independent.
9. ibid 20/5/1944.
10. Dáil Debates.

Chapter 8
1. Gallagher Michael, Economic & Social Review, Vol. 10 No. 1 Oct 1978 Party Solidarity and Exclusivity and Inter Party Relationships in Ireland 1922-1977, p. 15-17.
2. Whyte JH, Church & State in Modern Ireland 1923-1979. Gill & MacMillan, p.113 & 379.
3. Irish Times 4&5 April 1947.
4. Mulcahy Papers, P/7/D/123; 14/5//1947.
5. ibid 3/7/1947.
6. Manning, Dillon p. 220.
7. Manning Maurice, In The Farmer, Lee, [Ed]1979 p. 52.
8. Irish Press 27/7/1944.
9. The Leader Editorial 3/1/1948.
10. Gallagher op. cit. p. 54.
11. Dáil Debates, 7/11/1947.
12. O'Connor, Emmet, A Labour History of Ireland 1824-1960, Gill & MacMillan, 1992. p. 164.
13. McCarthy C, Trade Unions in Ireland, Dublin 1977 1894-1960. p. 253-259. & Gaughan Anthony, Thomas Johnston, Dublin 1980 pp. 376-381.
14. O'Connor Emmet, A History of Labour, Gill & MacMillan 1992. p 504.

Chapter 9
1. Irish Times, 28/1/1948.
2. ibid 15/1/1948.
3. ibid 19/1/1948.
4. Irish Independent 6/2/1948.
5. Browne Noel, Against the Tide, Gill & MacMillan 1986. p. 103.
6. Fitzgerald Garret, All In a Life, Gill & MacMillan 1991. p. 45.

Chapter 10
1. Dolan Anne, Commemorating The Irish Civil War, Cambridge 2003 p.26
1a. Jordan Anthony, WT Cosgrave Founder of Modern Irelamd,
    Westport Books 2006 pp. 168-170.
2. NAI Minute of OPW to Minister of Finance 31 July.
3. Dolan, p.48.
4. Dáil Debates, 21 May 1946. col. 448.
5. Dáil Debates, 12/5/1948. col. 1323.
6. Dept. Taoiseach, 4 & 9 Feb. 1949.
7. Taoiseach to OPW 27/2/1950.
8. Dolan op. cit . p. 51.

Chapter 11
1. Jordan, MacBride op. cit. pp. 96-7.
2. Irish Independent, 10/3/1948.
3. Feeney, op. cit. p. 194.
4. Boyer Bell, J., p. 249.
5. Irish Independent.
6. Fanning Ronan, The Irish Department of Finance IPA 1922-1968.
7. ibid. p. 457.
8. Moynihan Maurice, Currency and Banking in Modern Ireland, 1922-1960. 1975.
9. Dáil Debates, Vol. 120 col. 1629 & 1631-32.
10. O'Brien, Conor Cruise, Memories Profile 1998. p. 136.
11. Jordan, MacBride op. cit. p. 98.
12. NAI S 1646/4 17/2/1949.
13. Jordan, MacBride p. 98.
14. Dáil Debates, Vol 126 June-July 1951.
15. NAI S14106A GC 5/4 2/3/1948.
16. Fanning, op. cit. p. 407-8.
17. Browne, op. cit. p. 128.
18. Cruise O'Brien, op. cit. p. 136-7.
19. Dáil Debates, Vol. 127. col. 931-2.
20. ibid vol 127 col. 1087-1088.
21. Fanning p. 390.
22. Farrell Brian, 'Coalitions and Political Institutions' in Bodganor's [Ed]
    An Irish Experience 1983. p. 254.
23. O'Broin Leon, 1982 pp. 157-8.
24. Irish Times, 17/3/1951.
24. Browne op. cit . p. 203.
25. Irish Times 7/12/1950.
26. ibid 14/12/1950.
27. Gorry Paul, Baltinglass Chronicle 1851-20001.
28. RTE 13.30 News 5/3/1973.
29. Manning, Dillon, p. 233.
30. Patterson Henry, Ireland Since 1939, Penguin 2006 p. 87.
31. Corish Patrick, Maynooth College 1795-1995 Gill & MacMillan 1995. p. 332.
32. Dunleavy J & G, Douglas Hyde, University of California 1991 p. 434.

Chapter 12

1. Akenson Donald Harman, Conor, McGill Queens Universitry, 1994. pp. 129-130.
2. Lawlor op. cit. p. 174.
3. PRO UK. DO/130/ 97 27/1/1948.
4. Dáil Debates, 18/2/1948 col. 25.
5. Irish Times 22/7/1948.
6. Mansergh Nicholsa, The Unresolved Question Yale 1991. p. 326.
7. McGilligan Papers, P/35/215.
8. Mansergh ibid.
9. McInerney.
10. Dáil Debates 6/8/1948. col. 2440-1.
11. McCabe Ian, A Diplomatic History of Ireland 1948-49, IAP 1991 p. 35.
12. RTE Archives 4184.
13. Ibid to Bruce Arnold.
14. McInerney.
15. PRO, UK., DO/130/93.
16. Irish Times 10/7/1962.
17. McCabe op. cit. p. 149-150.
18. McDermott Eithne op. cit. p. 118.
19. Manning, Dillon p. 240.
20. RTE , This Week 27/4/1969.
21. Ottawa Journal 7/9/1948.
22. Canadian DEA 50021 sub 199'5 9/9/1948.
23. Manning, Dillon p. 244.
24. Lawlor op.cit p. 180.
25. Keatinge Patrick, The Formulation of Irish Foreign Policy IAP 1973
26. Fitzgerald op. cit. p. 45.
27. Mulcahy Richard, A Family Memoir Dublin 1999. p.250.
28. Irish Times 3/1/1979.
29. ibid 17/1/1979.
30. NAI Cabinet, 35 9/8/1948.
31. NAI S 14470 , Nolan note & Legge's Letter, Irish Times 15/1/1976 & McCullagh p. 90.
32. NAI Cab. 38 11/10/1948.
33. NAI Cab. 41. 20/10/1948.
34. Irish Times 23/!0/1948 & 26/!0/1948.
35. Cooney John, John Charles McQuaid O'Brien 200 [Maffey Report 1948] p. 224.
36. PRO UK DO 130/93 15/10/1948 To Secretary of State.
37. Kennedy Michael & Skelly, Joseph Morrison (eds) Irish Foreign Policy,
    Four Courts 2000 p.185.
38. O'Brien, Conor Cruise, Memories op. cit p.141.
39. PRO UK 128/13/143-4.
40. Browne p. 133.
41. Irish Times 25/11/1948.
42. Browne p. 133.
42. Dáil Debates Vol. CXV col. 786 & Irish Times 14/5/1949.
43. PRO UK DO/13099 19/5/1949.
44. Irish Times 11/3/1948.
45. Cruise O'Brien, States of Ireland, Panther 1974 p. 133.
46. Irish Times 18/3 1948.
47. Irish Times 24/7/1948.
48. Jordan, Sean op. cit.
49. Laithwaite Gilbert, to Commonwealth Relations Office 1950 & Irish Times
    1+2 January 1981.

50. Irish Press 4/3/1949.
51. Dáil Debates Vol 102. col. 1374. 24/7/1946.
52. Irish Press 20/3/1951.
53. S 9361 22/3/1951 NAI.
54. McCullagh p. 255.
55. Jordan, Sean p. 115.
56. S 14261 12/6/1948. NAI.
57. Browne p. 191.
58. McDermott, Clann na Poblachta p.138-9.
59. McGilligan Papers P/35/B/75 13/12/1948 . Dept. Finance Memo..
60. Lee p.312.
61. Irish Times 20/11/1949.
62. Quinn G, The changing pattern of Irish Society 1838-1951,
    in "War Years and After" Nolan & Williams p. 132.
63. Irish Press 19/10/1949.

Chapter 13

1. Irish Times 6/7/1950,
2. Dáil Debates, 11/7/1950.
3. McCullagh p. 217.
4. Irish Times 14/11/1950.
5. Irish Times 7/3/1951.
6. Lee p. 325.
7. Round Table 43. Dec 1952. p. 73.
8. Mission Outlook 1973 Kimmage Manor.
9. Jordan, Sean p. 126-7.
10. ibid.
11. NAI S 9469A.
12. Jordan, Sean p. 129.
13. NAI S 14997 21/3/1951.
14. Irish Times [McQuaid quoted by John Cooney] 6/4/1998.
15. Browne p. 176-7.
16. ibid p. 167.
17. ibid p. 177.
18. NAI S 10719 b 11/4 1951.
19. McInerney.
20. The theologian was Dr. Francis Cremin of St Patrick's College Maynooth. He was still not happy to have his name revealed when Noel Browne published his autobiography.
21. Jordan Anthony, WT Cosgrave 1880-1965, Founder of Modern Ireland. Westport Books. 2006 p. 91.
22. Lee, p. 318.
23. McDermott, p.146.
24. RTE, 'Seven Days' 24/6/1969.
25. Lee p. 317.
26. O'Brien, Conor, Cruise Memories p. 155.
27. Browne p. 218-9.
28. Irish Times 2/12/1950.
29. McCullagh p. 256.
30. McInerney.
31. Mulcahy Papers, P/7/C/151 20/11/1959.
32. Mission Outlook op. cit.

Chapter 14
1. Irish Times 8/5/1948.
2. Ibid 14/5/1948.
3. ibid.
4. ibid 29/5/1948.
5. Jordan, Sean p. 137.
6. Manning, Dillon p. 280.
7. Irish Times 14/6/1948.
8. RTE 11/2 'This Week'. 1973.
9. Irish Times 17/5/1954.

Chapter 15
1. Quinn Antoinette, Patrick Kavanagh A Biography. Gill & MacMillan 2001 p. 323.
1a. Kavanagh Peter, Patrick Kavanagh 1902-1967, A Life Chronicle, the Peter Kavanagh Hand Press New York 2000 p. X11.
2. Quinn p. p. 328.
3. Kavanagh Peter, Patrick Kavanagh p.265.
4. ibid p. 273.
5. ibid.
6. Quinn p. 339.
7. Lynch Brendan, Parson's Bookshop Liffey Press 2006. p. 63.
8. Quinn p. 348.
9. ibid p. 340.
10. ibid p. 273.
11. ibid p. 340.
12. Kavanagh Peter, Patrick Kavanagh Sacred Keeper, Goldsmith Press 1980 p. 287-8.
13. Kavanagh Peter, Patrick Kavanagh A Life Chronicle 1902-1967.
   Hand Press New York 2000 p.282.
14. Quinn p. 435.
15. Kavanagh Peter, Patrick Kavanagh 1902-1967, A Life Chronicle. p. 386.

Chapter 16
1. O'Higgins Tom, All in a Life, Gill & MacMillan, 2001, p.156.
2. ibid p. 157.
3. Puirseil Niamh, The Irish Labour Party, 1922-1970. 2007. p 179.
4. Irish Times 2/6/1954.
5. Jordan, Sean p. 146.
7. Manning, Dillon p. 293.
8. O'Higgins p. 186.
9. Lindsay p. 157.
10. Dáil Debates 11/6/1954.
11. NAI F 200/6/54.
12. Keogh Dermot, Twentieth Century Ireland, Gill & MacMillan, 1994 p. 150.
13. Kennedy & Skelly p. 287.
14. ibid p. 322.
15. NAI DT S 13750 30/4/1956.
16. Fanning Ronan, Independent Ireland, Dublin 1983, p. 202.
17. Dáil Debates 11/7/1956.
18. Jordan, Sean p. 165.
19. Dáil Debates Vol. 164. 23/10/1967. Oral Answers.
20. NAI DFA S 14330 To Costello 8/3/1955.
21. Wylie Paula, Ireland and the Cold War 2006 IAP p. 224.

Chapter 17

1. Whyte James, Church and State in Modern Ireland Gill & MacMillan 1980. p. 308.
2. NAI 1485/A/C 19/1/1955.
3. Irish Times 13/4/1955.
4. NAI S 14815 F.
5. NAI S 14815 E.
6. ibid 29/7/1955.
7. Irish Times 23/7/1955.
8. NAI S 14815 E.
9. McDowell RB & Webb DA, Trinity College Dublin 1592-1992, Red Press 2004. p. 475.
10. ibid pp. 475-480.
11. Manning, Dillon, p. 301.
12. NAI S 14815 F.
13. NAI S 14815 G.
14. ibid.
15. ibid. The Agricultural Institute, now called Teagasc employs 1500 people, has 8 research centres and 8 colleges.
16. McDowell & Webb pp 470-1.
18. NAI S 2321 B 16/8/1955.

Chapter 18

1. Dáil Debates Vol. 55 Col. 2033.
2. Dáil Debates 25/4/1951.
3. Cooney, p. 319.
4. Harmon Maurice, A Life Constable 1994 pp. 209-210.
5. NAI S 9979.
6. NAI S 9984.
7. NAI S 9988 F
8. NAI S 9979
10. NAI S 9981 G.
11. NAI S 9987
12. NAI S 9981
13. ibid
14. NAI S 2533
15. NAI S 2531.
16. O'Byrne Robert, Hugh Lane, Lilliput 2000 p. 238. Mary Kelligher, librarian at the RDS showed this elegant volume to me.
17. McInerney
18. ibid
19. ibid
20. Bodkin Thomas, Hugh Lane and His Pictures, Arts Council 1956 p. 95.
21. ibid p. 86.
22. Irish Times 2/1/1990.
23. NAI S 9988 E

Chapter 19

1. NAI S 16021 A.
2. Bradford Sarah, America's Queen, A Life of Jacqueline Kennedy Viking 2000 p. 61.
4. Irish Times 15/3 1956.

Chapter 20

1. Archives Archbishop's House Drumcondra.
2. Irish Times 27/9 1956.
3. Fanning p. 504.

[4]. Dáil Debates, Vol. 159 col 1591-94 25/7 1956.
[5]. O'Higgins p 186.
[6]. Irish Times 5/10/1956.
[7]. Moynihan Maurice, Currency and Banking in Ireland Gill 7 MacMillan 1975.
[8]. Fanning p. 511.

Chapter 21
[1]. McInerney.
[2]. Cruise O'Brien, Memories p. 140.
[3]. Boyer Bell J, The Gun in Irish Politics, Transaction New Jersey, 1991 p. 105
[4]. Dáil Debates 19/4 1954.
[5]. Dáil Debates Vol. 147 27/10/1954.
[6] Boyer Bell, The Secret Army, Poolbeg 1989 p. 276.
[7]. Dublin Diocesan Archives.
[8]. Sheehy Skeffington Andre, Skeff, Lillput 1991 pp. 170-1.
[9]. Jordan Sean p. 151.
[10]. Irish Independent 1-2 1990.
[11]. United Irishman July 1957.
[12]. Boyter Bell, The Secret Army p. 293.
[13]. Irish Times 8/1/!957.
[14]. Irish Times 4/1/1957.
[15]. McInerney.
[16]. Report of the Commission on Emigration and other Problems, 1956 Dublin 1956 p. 222
Reservation No. 2 Alexis Fitzgerald.
[17]. McInerney
[18]. Irish Times 7/10/1991.
[19]. Manning p. 311
[20]. Kennedy & Dowling, Economic Growth in Ireland; Since 1947, Dublin 1975 p. 220.
[21]. Lee, p. 328.

Chapter 22
[1]. Irish Times 1/3/1957.
[2]. ibid 25/3 1957.
[3]. Garvin Tom, p. 45.
[4]. Puirseil p. 198.
[5]. Feeney p. 206.
[6]. Lindsay, pp. 171-2.
[7]. Dublin Diocesan Archives.
[8]. O'Higgins p. 138 & 184.
[9]. ibid p. 186.
[10]. Gallagher Michael, Political Parties in the Irish Republic,
Manchester University Press, 1958.
[12]. Longford & O'Neill, Dublin 1970, p. 447.
[13]. Lindsay p.157.
[14]. O'Higgins p. 187.
[15]. Browne p. 234.
[16]. Irish Times 17/6/1959.
[17]. Manning p.327.
[18]. O'Higgins p. 188.
[19]. Dillon James, Memoir p. 88
[20]. Maye Brian, Fine Gael p.114.
[21]. Manning, Dillon p.342.
[22]. Irish Times 2/5/1961.

[23]. Fitzgerald, p. 79.
[24]. Garvin. p. 163.
[25]. Fitzgerald, p. 68.
[26]. O'Higgins, p. 191.
[27]. Fitzgerald, p. 70.
[28]. Dáil Debates April 1965. On the occasion of the death of John A Costello in 1976, Brian Lenihan, speaking in a tribute in the Senate after the Leader MJ O'Higgins, said, "In the course of my professional and political career, I was the recipient of much of the learned advice of which the Leader of the House has spoken"
[29]. Fitzgerald p. 74.
[30]. O'Higgins, p. 194.
[31]. ibid.
[32]. Fitzgerald, p. 76-7.
[33]. Irish Times 23/8/1972.

Chapter 23
[1]. Dáil Debates 21/2/1951.
[2]. O'Broin Leon, No Man's Man, Memoir of Joseph Brennan IPA 1982. P. 131.
[3]. Irish Times 9/3/1951.
[4]. O'Broin p. 156.
[5]. Garvin Tom, Preventing the Future Gill & MacMillan 2004 p. 85.
[6]. NAI S 9404 26/8/1954.
[7]. Lee, p. 107.
[8]. Fanning p. 39.
[9]. O'Broin Leon in 'Studies' Spring 1977, Joseph Brennan Civil Servant Extraordinary pp. 34-7.
[10]. Lee p. 313.
[11]. Brennan Papers Ms. 26402. NLI
[12]. McInerney.

Chapter 24
[1]. Irish Times 8/3/1975.
[2]. O'Higgins p. 288-9.
[3]. deValera Terry, Memoir Curragh Press 2004 pp. 205-6.
[4]. Irish Times 6/1/1976

SELECT BIBLIOGRAPHY
Bew Paul & Patterson Henry, "Sean Lemass" Gill & MacMillan 1982.
Bodkin Thomas, "Hugh Lane and His Pictures" Arts Council 1956.
Boyer Bell J. "The Secret Army: a History of the IRA,1916-1979" Dublin 1980.
Browne Noel, "Against the Tide" Gill & MacMillan 1986.
Coogan Tim Pat, "DeValera" London 1995. "The IRA" London 1980.
Cooney John, "John Charles McQuaid Ruler of Catholic Ireland" O'Brien 1999.
deVere White Terence, "Kevin O'Higgins" Tralee, 1966.
Dolan Anne, "Commemorating the Civil War", Cambridge 2003.
Fanning Ronan, "The Irish Department of Finance" 1922-68 " IPA 1978.
                Independent Ireland" Helicon Press 1983.
Fitzgerald Garret, "All In A Life" Gill & MacMillan 1991.
Garvin Tom, "Preventing the Future" Gill & MacMillan 2004.
Jordan Anthony, "Churchill – A Founder of Modern Ireland" Westport Books 1995.
                "Sean – A Biography of Sean MacBride" Blackwater 1993.
                "To Laugh Or To Weep - A Biography of Conor Cruise O'Brien"
                Blackwater 1993.
                "WT Cosgrave 1880-1965, Founder of Modern Ireland"
                Westport Books 2006.
Kavanagh Peter, "Patrick Kavanagh 1902-1967 A Life Chronicle",
                Peter Kavanagh Hand Press New York 2000.
Keatinge Patrick, "The Formulation of Irish Foreign Policy", IPA 1973.
Kennedy Michael, "Ireland and the League of Nations" IAP 1996.
Lawlor Caitriona [Ed] "Sean MacBride Remembers" Curragh 2006.
Lee JJ, "Ireland 1912-1985 Politics and Society" Cambridge 1989.
Lindsay Patrick, "Memories" Blackwater 1992.
Manning Maurice, "The Blueshirts" Dublin 1970.
Manning Maurice, "James Dillon" Gill & MacMillan 1998.
McCauge Eugene, "Arthur Cox" Gill & MacMillan 1994.
McCullagh David, "A Makeshift Majority- The First Inter-Party Government 1948-1951"
                IPA 1998.
McDermott Eithne, "Clann na Poblachta" Cork University Press 1998.
O'Connor Emmet, "A Labour History of Ireland 1824-1960" Gill & MacMillan 1992.
O'Higgins Tom, "A Double Life" Gill & MacMillan 2003.
O'Neill TP & Longford, "Eamon DeValera" Dublin 1970.
Puirseil Niamh, " The Irish Labour Party 1922-1970" UCD 2007.
Quinn Antoinette, "Patrick Kavanagh A Biography" Gill & MacMillan 2001.
Ryle Dwyer T. "Eamon DeValera" Dublin 1980.
Whyte JH, "Church and State in Modern Ireland 1923-1970" Dublin 1971.

INDEX

A

Abbey Theatre, 140
Abdication of King, 41
Abrahamson Leonard, 118
Acheson Dean, 85
Act of Union, 33
Arborfield, 150
Achonry, Bishop of, 37, 123
Aer Lingus, 110
Afforestation, 67,87.
Africa, 117.
Agricultural Bill, 123.
Agricultural Institute, 7, 119-124.
Agricultural Sciences, 123.
Aide Memoire 1956, 152
Aiken Frank, 53,118,159, 172.
Akenson Donald, 73.
Albert College, 119
Alton Dr, 121.
Alexander Lord, 76.
All Party Committee on Constitution 1998, 33
All Party Committee on Senate, 44
Amery LS, 132.
Anglo-Irish Trade Agreement, 44,74.
Anglo-Irish Treaty, 23-4.
Anti-Partition Campaign, 83-4, 149.
Antrim, 153.
America, 116,131.
American Dollars, 77
American Embassy Budapest, 146
American Foreign Service, 120.
American State Department, 85,117,139.
American War of Independence, 139.
Aras an Uachtarain, 18,91, 159.
Archictectural Association, 131
Arklow, 99.
Army Comrades Association, 7,35-7, 39.
Arts Council, 7. 110, 129-130, 133.
Atkinson George, 61.
Atlee Clement, 74, 113.
Atomic Centre Brookhaven, 139
Attorney General, 6,11,15,19,21-3,44,50,71,125-6,131,135-6.
Auchinloss Hugh, 140.
Auden WH, 108.
Australia, 25,28,31,42,70,80,83.

B

Baggot St. Bridge, 111.
Baldwin Stanley, 26-7.
Balfour Declaration, 24
Ballaghadereen, 159
Ballsbrige, 143.
Ballsbridge Terrace, 49.
Ballymena Presbyterian, 122.
Baltinglass, 69-70.
Banking Commission, 114.
Barber Institute Birmingham, 133.
Bar The, 15,18,35,101,179.

Barrett Dick, 62
Béal na Bláth, 63.
Beatty Chester, 129.
Beavan Aneurin, 133
Behan Brendan, 108.
Belmont Ave, 49.
Bennet Mr. 30.
Berehaven, 27.
Berkeley George, 139.
Berlin, 23.
Betjamen John, 34,108.
Beyers General, 30.
Blackmore CH, 21
Blackshirts The, 38
Blackrock College, 90,134.
Bland William, 146.
Blaney Neil, 147, 160.
Blessed Trinty, 126.
Blasphemy, 126.
Bloody Sunday Derry 1972, 170.
Blowick Joe, 13,51-2,57,85, 113.
Blueshirts The, 7,35,38,62.
Blythe Ernest, 31,143,161,172.
Bobbio, 23.
Bodenstown, 39,65.
Bodkin Thomas, 17,129,130, 132-3, 135-6.
Bog of Allen, 42.
Boland Freddy, 75,116.
Boland Gerry, 53.
Boland Kevin, 16
Book of Kells, 139.
Bord na Mona, 144,147
Boswell Papers, 139
Boundary Commission Report, 21.
Bouvier [Kennedy] Jacqueline, 139-141.
Boycott in Baltinglass, 69-70.
Boyer Bell J., 149
Brady Rory, 158.
Brady Sean, 36.
Brennan Joseph, 69,86,139,171-4.
Brennan Mr. [Australia], 31.
British Army, 18,139.
British Embassy Riot, 170.
British Empire, 30.
British Government, 21-2, 33,41-2,132.
British Markets, 47
British Nationality Bill, 74.
Brookborough Barracks, 153.
Brookborough Lord, 153.
Brooke Basil, 84.
Browne Bishop, 90,120-1.
Browne Noel, 7,10,11,14,54,57,67,68.73,75,79-82,85,89-92,95,99,101-3,122,158,163,174.
Browne RF, 11
Brugha Cathal, 62.
Bruton John, 63.
B Specials, 150, 153.
Buckingham Palace, 31.
Budapest, 146.
Budget 1950, 85-6

Budget 1951-2, 146.
Burke Liam, 16.
Byrne Alfie, 11,115.

C
Cabinet Estimates Committee, 85
Cabot Lodge Henry, 140.
Callaghan Rose, 17.
Canada, 6,23-5,28,30,42,73,76-80,99,116.
Capital Budget First, 66.
Capital Investment Committee 1956, 146.
Carlow-Kilkenny, 55,147.
Carlow Sugar Beet Factory, 31.
Carson Edward, 109, 131.
Carter CF., 146.
Cash for Honours, 33.
Catholics, 17
Catholic Bishops,7.
Catholic Church, 23
Catholic Country, 124.
Catholic Hierarchy, 89,119,120.
Catholic Moral Teaching,95.
Catholic Social Teaching, 91,92.
Cavan, 90,100.
Ceann Comhairle,101,113,155.
Cenotaph on Leinster Lawn, 58-63.
Central Bank, 69,86,120, 171.
Centre Party, 35,37.
Chamberlain Austen, 24,27.
Chamberlain Neville, 45.
Chief Justice, 175.
Children of Lir, 62.
Christian Country, 141
Christian Gentleman, 179.
Christian Civilisation, 116.
Christmas Present, 110.
Civil Servants 67, 160.
Claidheamh Solais, 61.
Charter of Equality, 31.
Charisma, 8.
Chequers, 80,83.
Chief Justice, 15,21.
Childers Erskine, 32, 160.
China, 118.
Christies, 134.
Christian Brothers, 140.
Christus Rex Congress, 120.
Churchill Winston, 26-8, 31,45.
City Hall, 175.
Civil War, 6,7,11,61-2,69,133,151,176.
Clare, 18,119,125.
Clarke Austin, 72,107.
Clann na Poblachta, 7,9,10,13,52,74-5, 80,84-5,90-1,96-7,101,114,149,155.
Clan na Talun, 9,15,47-8,50-3,55,91,144,149,155.
Clery Arthur, 18.
Clonlara, 119,125-128
Clonskeagh,145.
Coalition First Mooted, 51.
Coalition Government, 7,55,99,157,165-6,171.

Cobh, 76.
Cockburn CJ, 19.
Coburn James. 102.
Codicil of Hugh Lane's Will, 137.
Codification of International Law, 25-6.
Collective Responsibility, 69.
College Green 153-4, 171.
Colley Harry, 61-2.
Collins Sean, 16
Collins Michael, 21,28,31,42,44,58-61,63,75,161,170-1.
Colonial Laws Validity Act, 26.
Commonwealth British, 6-7,23-4,28,30,41,43,73-6,78,102.
Commonwealth Prime Ministers Conference, 80.
Communism, 55,116,118
Connemara, 99
Connolly James, 133.
Connolly Thomas, 105-6.
Constitution 1937, 43-5.
Controller & Auditor General, 172.
Conway John, 143.
Coogan Eamon, 55.
Cogan Patrick, 70,102.
Constitution Bill, 6
Cooke Helen, 69.
Cooke Katie, 69.
Cope Alfred, 22
Corish Brendan, 15,100,113,164-5,167,179.
Corish Patrick, 71
Cork, 35,159.
Cosgrave Liam, 15,51,63,67,85,113,116,118,141,159,164-5,168,176,179.
Cosgrave WT., 6,8,19,22-4,27,31-3,35,37,44-5,47-8,51,59,65,69,84,119,131-2,138,143,169,172.
Costello Declan, 52,103,141,143,160,164-6,175.
Costello Grace, 13
Costello Ida Mary, 143.
Costello John, 17.
Costello John A.,
    Anti-Partition, 117.
    Appoints Arthur Cox to Senate,
    Arts Council, 130.
    Attorney General, 21-32.
    Bar Returns To, 101.
    Beal na Blath, Speaks At, 1972, 170.
    Blueshirts Defends, 38.
    Bodkin Thomas, Praises, 129,137.
    Boundary Commission On, 32.
    Bouvier-Kennedy Jacqueline, 140.
    Brennan Joseph Castigates, 173.
    Browne Noel On, 174.
    Canada Events In 1948, 76-7.
    Catholic Hierarchy Rebukes, 119-124.
    Cenotaph Defends, 61-2.
    Chosen as Taoiseach, 1948, 9-16.
    Coalition, 48,49,55..
    Collective Responsibility, 69.
    Completes Cenotaph, 60-63,
    Confirms Revocation-
    of External Relations Act, 76

Constitution 1937 On, 43-4.
Cosgrave WT On, 32.
Death of, 179.
Death of Wife, 143-4.
Defends Role in-
Mother & Child Scheme, 92-5.
Defends Archbishop McQuaid, 98.
Defends TCD & Protestant Citizens-
to Catholic Bishops, 123.
Department of Finance, 68.
Description Of In 1967, 8.
DeValera Eamon, On, 175-7.
Dillon James On, 174.
Disliked by Gerard Sweetman, 114.
Economic Policy Declaration 1956, 144-5
Education, 17.
Elected to Dail, 36.
Emergency Legislation, 50.
Everett James On, 12.
Execution of Rory O'Connor, 32
External Relations Act, 41-2.
Father Speaks of, 175.
Family, 20.
Fitzgerald Alexis On, 174.
Freedom of Dublin, 175.
Free State Government Defeat On, 32.
Golfing Enthusiast, 11.
IRA, Condemns, 151, 154
Kavanagh Patrick-
Interaction With, 105-112,
Keynesian Economics, 6,65-6.
Labour Party, 20.
Lane Pictures, 130-8.
League of Youth, 38.
Lemas Sean On, 174.
Letter to Bishop Rodgers
re. Clonlara Incident,, 127-8.
Loses Dail Seat, 47.
MacBride Sean On,174
Marriage, 20.
Interview Complaint, 171-4.
McGilligan Patrick On, 32.
Mulcahy Richard On, 32.
National Gallery London,-
Trustees, Criticises, 135.
National government, 47.
Norton William On, 174.
O'Faolain Sean, Appoints-
to Chair of Arts Council, 129-130.
O'Higgins Kevin On, 32.
Order of St. Patrick, 33.
Political Realignment, 157,165-6.
Proportional Representation-
Defends, 162.
Recovers Dail Seat, 49.
Renewal of IRA Camapign,149.
Resigns as Parliamentary Leader, 164.
Republic Legislation-
Personal Control, 81-2.
Seeks Mulcahy's Recollection of 1948-

For Interview, 9-12.
State Visit to USA, 138-141.
Succession Bill, 166-8.
Costello MJ, 146.
Costello's Folly, 63
Council of Education, 12.
Courtmartial, 19.
Council of Europe, 84, 143.
Council of State, 89.
Court of International Justice, 25.
Courts of Justice Bill, 19.
Cox Arthur, 11-12,17-8,114.
Cowan Peadar, 74-5,97,101,171.
Craig James,131.
Cremin Francis Fr., 186.
Cronin Sean, 150,154.
Crosbie James, 16.
Cruise O'Brien Conor, 35,67-8,80,85,96,149,152.
Cumann na nGael, 21,23,35-7,39,59,63,161.
Curator Post, 109.
Curran Lancelot, 22
Currency Commission, 141,172.
Curtis Lionel, 33
Cyprus, 154.

D
D'Alton Cardinal, 114,120,143.
Dail Eireann, 6,9,11,25-6,36,41,44,49,52,68-
9,81,97,102,113,115,152,156,165.
Dalymount Park, 125.
Davitt Cahir, 17.
Dean's Grange Cemetery, 143
Declaration of Republic, 7,63,73-83, 99,149,174.
Defence of the Realm Act, 19.
Dempsey Alan, 16.
Department of External Affairs, 43.77,117,152-3.
Department of Defence, 14.
Department Finance, 65-8,86-7,119,146,171-2,174.
Department of Health, 92.
Department of Justice, 125.
Derry Catholics, 122.
Department of Taoiseach, 110,139.
Derrig Tom, 13,155.
Derry Siege of, 76.
Derry, 83,150, 153.
'Deserted Village', 105.
DeValera-Collins Pact, 20.
DeValerian Dictatorship, 35.
DeValera, Eamon, 7,9,10,13,27-8,31,38,41-2,44,50,52-
4,57,59,61-2,65,74-5,82-
3,96,100,102,11,119,121,123,132,135,143,146,151,157,16
1,174,176.
DeValera-Lemas Government, 153.
DeValera Terry, 13,177.
Devaluation, 87
Dictatorship Powers, 43..
Dignam Bishop, 94
Dillon James, 7,11,13-4,45,48,50-1,66,71,76,82,87,89,92-
3, 96-7,102,113,119,121,145,155,158,164-5,169.
Dillon John, 17.

Diplomatic Advances, 22-32,
Dockrell HM, 36.
Dolan Anne, 59,62-3.
Dominican College Eccles St., 20.
Dominions, 24-6,28,33.
Dominion Status, 26.
Donegal, 97.
Donegal Fishermen, 22.
Donnellan Michael, 15,52.
Donnybrook, 143.
Douglas James, 16.
Doyle Thomas, 105.
Downing St., 30,74.
Dual Monarchist, 63
Dublin, 77,105,152-3.
Dublin Castle, 33.
Dublin County, 36.
Dublin Corporation, 17.
Dublin South East, 10,55,101-2, 158.
Dublin South West, 158.
Dublin Townships, 48-9, 57.
Duke of Gloucester, 34.
Duke of Windsor, 33
Dungarvan, 37.
Dunmore, 52.

E
Earl of Home, 143.
Earl of Selkirk, 134.
Easter Week, 176.
Economic Planning, 7.
Economic Policy, 85-6.
Eden Anthony, 153-4.
Edward VII, 2,33.
Edward VIII, 38,41.
Egan V. Macready, 18.
Egypt, 154.
Eire, 73,77.
Eisenhower President, 139.
Elections General, 9 [1948], 9, [1932], 35 [1933], 36
[1937], 44 [1943], 47[1944], 49-50 [1944], 55-7 [1948],
99 [1952], 109 [1954], 157-8 [1957].
Electoral Amendment Act 1947, 53.
Electricity Supply Board, 147.
Emergency Legislation, 154.
Emergency The, 47,62.
Emigration, 155.
Emmet's Epitaph, 82.
Ennis, 125.
Erne River, 22.
Esmonde John Sir, 10,97,105-6.
Estimates Committee, 115.
Evatt Dr., 81.
Everett James, 12-13,48,69,85,113,155.
European Recovery Programme, 65,77.
Examination results, 18.
Ex-Ministers, 160.
External Affairs, 10,22,67.
External Relations Act 1936, 6,10,13,41-2, 55,73-4, 76-80.

F
Fahy Frank, 36,111.
Fanning Ronan, 65,67,116.
Farmer's Party, 37.
Farmington Connecticut, 138.
Farrell Michael, 69.
Farren Robert, 107.
Fascist Model, 35,39.
Feeney Brian, 65.
Felstead, 150.
Feminists, 6,43.
Fergus bishop, 121,123.
Fermanagh, 83,152-3.
Ffrench O'Carroll Michael, 101-2.
Financial Crisis 1956, 144.
Fianna Fail, 6-7,9,12-
3,15,24,26,35,38,49,52,55,61,63,73,77,96,99,105,120,124
,165.
Fiftieth Anniversary of Easter Rising, 169.
Fine Gael, 6,7,9,10,14,37-9,45,47-9,51-2,55-
6,61,63,73,84,99,101,157-170.
Fine Gael's Heroes, 68.
Fine Gael Research Centre, 161.
Fine Gael Government, 114.
Finucane Patrick, 144, 154.
First Programme of Economic Expansion, 169.
Fiscal Policy, 85.
Fitzgerald Alexis, 13,52,57,63,66,90,139,155,161,
168,170,174.
Fitzgerald Desmond, 22,24,28,59.
Fitzgerald Garret, 57,79,165-6,168,170.
Fitzgerald Joan, 57.
Fitzpatrick Richard, 139.
Flanagan Oliver J., 11,53,102.
Flying Columns, 153.
Flynn John, 101.
Football Association Ireland, 125.
Forbes Bernard, 33.
Foreign Policy, 116-7.
Four Courts, 113.
Foxrock, 98
Foyle River, 22..
Frazer Peter, 81.
Freedom Fighters, 153.
Freedom of Dublin, 175.
Freeman Edward, 17.
Freeman of Dublin, 7.
Free State, 18,21-3,25-8,30,38,59,65,73,131-2,149.
Free State Government, 8,20-1.
'From A Prelude', 110.
Full Time Politicians,160

G
Gadarene Swine, 172.
Garda Siochana, 126,154.
Garden of Remembrance, 61-2.
Gallagher Michael, 160.
Garden Party, 76..
Garvin Tom, 171.
Genealogical Office, 33.

'General Directive for Guerilla Campaign', 154.
Geneva, 22-5,42,162.
George VI, 31.
George VIII, 33.
George Lloyd, 22,33-4.
Germany, 38.
Gleeson Judge, 125.
Glenamaddy, 20.
Government of Ireland Act, 21,27.
Goldsmith Oliver, 105.
Gonne Maud, 43,45,52.
Governor General, 41,76.
GPO., 102,163.
Grand Central Station, 76.
Great Britain, 99,116.
Great Dublin Lock-Out, 17.
'Great Hunger The', 105,107.
Great Northern Railway, 22.
Gregory Lady, 130-3, 138.
Griffith Arthur, 8, 22, 28, 31, 44, 58, 60-1, 63,75,113,161.
Groome Joe, 49.
'Gurrier', 105.
Guthrie Mr [Canada], 31.
Gwynn Aubrey, 17.
Gwynn Denis, 17.

H
Habeas Corpus, 18-9,38.
Hacket John, 76.
Haddington Road, 49,73,111.
Hague Court of Justice, 62.
Hammarskjold Dag, 140.
Hanly Daithi, 62.
Harmon Maurice, 130.
Hartnet Noel, 52.
Harolds Cross, 49.
Haughey Charles, 115,174.
Hayes Michael, 15,59.
Health Act 1947, 89,92-3.
Hearne John, 76,139.
Herbert Park, 143.
Hertzog General, 24.
High Commissioner, 23,75-6.
High Court, 105.
Hitler Shirts, 38.
Hist Society TCD., 17.
Hogan Patrick, 15,17,31, 35, 101.
Home Rule, 17.
Honours System Ireland, 33.
Hospital Sweepstakes, 67.
Holy Year 1950, 71.
Hoover Herbert, 139
Horgan John, 76.
Horse Show Dublin,140.
House of Commons, 17, 133.
House of Lords, 17,131,134.
House of Representatives, 139.
Hungary, 154.
Hungarian Refugees, 146.
Hungarian rising, 146.

Hurley Judge, 125.
Hyde Douglas, 45,49,72.

I
Incorporated Law Society,19.
Imperial Conferences, 1923,23. 1926, 24,30. 1929, 30. 1930, 30.
Imperial Parliament, 30.
Independents, 10-13,101.
India, 26,99.
Institute of Bankers, 66.
Intellectual Standards, 122.
Inter-Party Government, 7,11-12, 113-156,
Industrial Development Authority, 7,86.
International Monetary Fund [IMF], 68.
Internment, 150,158.
Iona College, New Rochelle, 140.
Ireland Act 1949, 83.
Irish Association for Civil Liberty, 130
Irish Crown Jewels, 33.
Irish House The, 159.
Irish Insurrection, 18.
Irish Language, 23.
Irish Life Assurance 114.
Irish Medical Association [IMA], 88,93.
Irish Missionaries, 117.
Irish News Agency, 84.
Irish Press Shares, 163.
IRA, 7,35,39,50,52,63,65,149-155,157,179.
Irish Shipping, 147.
Irish Trade Unions, 10.
Irish Universities Act, 1908,17.
ITGWU, 12,53.
Israel, 118.

J
Jammets' Restaurant,140.
Jehovah Witnesses, 125-6.
Johnson Judge, 37.
Joyce James, 17.
Judas, 91.

K
Kavavagh Libel Case, 105-111.
Kavanagh Peter, 109-111.
Kavanagh Patrick, 7,103-111.
Keating Sean, 138.
Keatinge Patrick, 78.
Kelly Liam, 149.
Kelly Oisin, 62.
Kennedy Hugh, 17,21,26,179.
Kennedy Jack, 140.
Kennedy Michael, 24,26.
Kerry, 115.
Kettle Tom, 17.
Keyes Michael, 113.
Keynes Lord, 66.
Keynesian Economics, 7,65-6,86.
Killaloe, 125.
Killarney, 140.

King Function of, 26,30.
Kitt Tom, 62.
Knights of St. Columbanus, 71.
Knights of the Order of St. Patrick, 33.
Korean War, 87.
Kyne Tom, 146.

L

Labour Government, 114
Labour Party in 1920's, On, 20.
Labour Party, 7,9,12,20,44,48-9,53-5,102,144,155,157,164-5.
Labour Party Conference 1956, 145.
Labour Party Split, 48,53-4.
Laithwaithe Gilbert, 83.
'Lane Hugh & His Pictures', 134.
Land Acts, 31.
'L and H' The, 17-8.
Land Registry, 21.
Land Rehabilitation Programme,
Lane Hugh Paintings, 130-8.
Laois-Offaly, 99,144.
Larkin Jim, 11,17,53-4.
Larkin Jim Young, 13,114,133,140,144-5,175.
Latin High Mass, 98.
Lavery Cecil, 14-5,17,22,38,89.
Lavery Lady, 132.
Law Library, 10,113,165.
Law Term, 98.
Lawyers in Dail, 48.
Leader The, 7,103,105,107.
League of Nations, 22-5, 31,116.
League of Nations Council, 25
League of Nations Treaty Bureau, 23.
League of Youth, 38.
Lecturer in Poetry, 110.
Lee Joe, 86,90,96,156.
Legge Hector, 76,78-9.
Lehane Con, 62
Leinster House, 10,53,113.
Leinster Lawn, 61-2.
Lemass Noel, 147.
Lemass Sean, 13-4,38,44,53,55,68,96,191,118,136-7,147,159,174
Lenihan Brian, 167.
Leonard Joseph Fr., 139-140.
Lewis Sheldon Wilmarth, 139-140.
Leyden John, 146.
Library of Congress, 139.
Limerick, 140.
Limerick District Court, 125.
Limerick Prison, 19.
Lindsay Patrick, 35,115,143,158,160-1,169.
Local Government Acts, 31.
Locke's Distillery Dispute, 53.
London, 83,1105,109,111,132.
Longford, 10.
Longford-Westmeath, 158.
Lord Chancellor, 11.
Lough Foyle Dispute, 22.

Louth, 102.
Lucey Bishop, 119-121.
Lusitania, 130.
Luzio Monsignor, 94.
Lynch Brendan, 109.
Lynch Jack, 153,160,179.
Lynch Patrick, 10-11,34,65-6,65-6,86,146,174.

M

MacBride John Major, 28,52,82.
Sean MacBride,
7,9,11,11,13,21,26,52,55,57,63,65,67,71,77,80,85,90,101,
114,116,118,145,151-2,155,157,169,174.
MacCurtain Tomas, 65,153-4.
MacDermott Eithne, 14,86.
MacDonald Ramsay, 132.
MacDunphy Michael, 21.
MacEntee, Sean, 36,47,53,61-2,90,99101,114-5,143,147,158-9,171,173.
MacEoin Sean, 10-11,14,42,65,113,161,169.
Machievellian Leader, 9.
Mackenzie-King, 24,76-7,81.
MacManus Deirdre, 80.
MacMillan Harold, 134,137.
MacNeill James, 131,
Macready General 18-9.
Maffey John Sir, 80.
Magee & Hillman, 71.
Magenis Jim, 17.
Maguire Conor, 17.
Manning Maurice, 47-8,71,77,114,123,164..
Mansion House, 11-2, 84,175.
Mansion House Committee, 84.
Marinelli Foundry Florence, 62.
Marshall Aid, 67,86,119-120.
Martin Alec Sir, 133.
Mater Hospital, 110.
Mauretania The, 76.
McCabe Ian, 76.
McCann Hugh, 134,136.
McCarthy Niall, 105.
McCaughey Sean, 52
McColl Ds., 132,137,
McConnell AJ., 121.
McCormack John Speaker, 139,143.
McCourt Kevin, 146.
McCracken W., 49.
McCullagh David, 97.
McElligot JJ., 67,145,172-3.
'McGilligan's Charter', 31.
McGilligan Patrick, 11,14,16-7,25-6,30-1,35,42,44,46,66,68-9,71,70-80,86,89,114,122,173.
McGirl John Joe, 158.
McGrath Raymond, 62
McHugh Roger,
McInerney Michael, 8-9, 39, 171,173..
McQuaid John Charles Archbishop, 43,80,90-1,93-5,98,110,120-1, 124-5,143, 151,159.
McQuillan Jack, 97,147,149-150,154,163.
Mellowes Liam, 62.

Metropole, 23.
Military Tribunals, 38-9.
Mill CK., 146.
Millar Stephen, 126-7.
Milltown Golf Club, 180.
Milk Price of 1951, 97.
Milroy Sean, 28.
Mindsenty Cardinal, 146.
Monaghan 105,158.
Montgomery Hyde H., 137.
Montreal, 76.
Moore Sean, 158.
Morrissey Dan, 9,14,114,145.
Moscow, 99.
Mother & Child Scheme, 89-98.
Mother Ireland, 84.
Mountjoy Jail, 35,37.
Moylan Sean, 59,160.
Moyne Lord [Brian Guiness],134,136-7.
Mulcahy Richard, 6,9-15,35,37,47-
8,51,55,57,61,73,79,86,113,160,163-4.
Mulvill Michael, 92.
Murphy TJ., 14.
Murray Charles, 139.
'My Bleeding Heart', 96.

N

NATO, 6,77,79,8-5,97,139.
National College of Art, 129.
National Drainage Plan, 12.
National Farmers' Association, 120.
National Gallery, 129.
National Gallery London, 130-4,137.
National Government, 47,114,157,165-6.
National Guard, 36.
National Labour, 9,10,11-3,48,53-4,57.
National Loans, 86.
National Museum, 129.
National Press club, 85,116,139.
Nazi, 39.
Nelson's Pillar, 130.
Neutrality, 45,48.
Newfoundland, 28.
Newman Cardinal, 129.
New York, 76,139-140,143.
New Zealand, 28,80,89.
Nixon Richard, 139,143.
Nolan Nicholas, 74.
Northern Ireland, 33,82,122,133,155.
Norton William, 9-12, 39,44,
53-4,57,72,75,79,84,90,99,113,125,143,150,164.
NUI., 17,119,121.

O

Oath of Allegiance, 27.
O'Brien George, 17-8.
O'Brien Louie, 67,77-8.
O'Brien William, 53.
O'Caoimh Aindreas, 136.
O'Ceallaigh MR. 59.

O'Connell Ginger, 17.
O'Connell Schools, 17
O'Connor Charles Sir,19.
O'Connor Rory, 62..
O'Connor Seamus, 11.
O'Dalaigh Cearbhall, 74,179.
O'Donnell Patrick, 114.
O'Donovan Dan, 171-2.
O'Donovan John, 102,115.
O'Driscoll J., 171.
O'Dwyer Mayor, 76.
O'Duffy Eoin, 36-7, 39.
OEEC., 84,100.
O'Faoileain Sean, 130.
Office of Public Works, 59,61-2.
O'Grady Mr, 60.
O'Hanlon Eineachan, 158.
O'Hanlon ferghal, 153.
O'Hegarty Diarmaid, 21.
O'Higgins Kevin, 11,17,22,24,30,35,42,44,58-
61,63,79,164.
O'Higgins, Michael, 16,160.
TF O'Higgins, 11,14-5,51-2,55,73,90,92, 102.
O'Higgins Tom, 102,113-4, 144-5,155,160,169,175,179.
O'Keeffe Michael, 175.
O'Kelly Sean T. President,
13,71,125,143,156,159.161,169.
O'Leary John, 16.
Olympian Standards, 107.
O'Brien George, On Costello's Prospects,18.
O'Malley, David, Dr., 20.
O'Malley Ida Mary, 20.
O'Rahilly Alfred, 24.
Order of St. Patrick, 33-4.
O'Regan John Fr., 125.
Ottawa, 23,73,76-7,79.

P

Pacelli Cardinal, 152.
Pakenham Lord, 28,134-7.
Papal Nuncio, 143.
Paris, 23,81.
Parliamentary Democracy, 176.
Parnell Sq., 61-2.
Parson's Bookshop, 111.
Part Time Politicians, 101.
Partition, 84, 117,144,150-1.
Patterson Henry, 71.
Pearse Margaret, 36.
Pearse Patrick, 8,113.
Pearson Mr, 81.
Personal & Confidential, 110.
Pernicious Minority, 108.
Picadilly, 42.
Pius Pope XII, 91.
Polish Delegation, 25.
Political Murders, 39.
Pomeroy, 149.
Poor Clares, 69.
Pontius Pilate, 35.

Portlaoise Jail, 65.
Portmarnock Golf Club, 11,180.
Power Albert, 61.
President, 43-4.
Presidential Election, [1959],161,163. [1966], 168-170.
Press Conference in Canada, 76.
Prince of Wales, 32.
'Prison Bars', 43.
Privy Council, 25,31.
Proportional Representation, 161-3,170.
Protestants, 119-121,123-4.
Public Houses, 159.
Public Record Office Belfast, 21.
Public Safety Act, 38, 171.
Puirseil Niamh, 157.

Q
Quebec, 24.
Queenstown, 27
Queens University, 17.
'Question Time', 52.
Quinn Antoniette,107-8,110.

R
Radical Party, 162.
Radio Eireann, 15,52,107-8,145,154.
Rathmines, 49,99.
Referendum on Constitution, 44.
Renunciation of War Pact, 24.
Republic, 13,63.
Republican Courts, 19.
Republic of Ireland Bill,
Requiem Mass, 143.
Restoration of Order in Ireland Act, 19.
Rialto Hospital, 107.
Rice JJ., 158.
Rice Richard, 11.
Rice Vincent, 37.
Right of Public Meetings, 20.
Ringsend, 47.
Rising 1916, 19.
'Roaring Meg', 76.
Roberts Ruaidhri, 146.
Robinson Tommy, 177.
Roche Dick, 11.
Rodgers Bishop, 125-7.
Roebuck House,
Rome, 107.
Roslea, 152.65.
Ross John Sir, 19.
Rosslare, 70.
Royal British Legion, 59.
Royal Irish Academy, 131.
RTE, 176.
Royal University,17.
RUC., 152.
Rugby Lord, 16,55,74-5,80.
Russia, 85,116.
Russian UN Veto, 85.
Russell Hotel, 78.
Russell Mayor, 120.

Rutteledge Patrick, 13,35,38.
Ryan Frank, 35.
Ryan James, 14,89,92,95,159.
Ryan Louden, 146.
Ryan Patrick CC., 125-7.

S
Sandymount Green, 49,55.
Saorstat Eireann, 151.
Scotland, 69.
Scotstown, 152.
Scullen Mr., 31.
Senate, 47,131,150,152,162,168.
Senate American, 139.
Sex Disqualification Act, 18.
Shannon Airport, 141.
Shannon Electrification Scheme, 31,66,114,173-4.
Sheehy Skeffington Eoin, 152.
Sheldon William, 97.
Shelly Morrison Joseph, 116.
Shine Ruth, 131.
Sinecures, 111.
Sinn Fein, 22,65,149,150,158,161.
Sinn Fein, Party, 164.
Six Counties, 150-1.
Skelton OD., 24.
Sligo-Leitrim, 158.
Smith James, 65.
Soccer Match, 125.
Social Security plan, 12.
'Sore Thumb on Partition', 141.
South Africa, 24,28,30,42,81,99.
South Armagh, 83.
South Down, 83.
South Sean, 153-4.
Soviet Support, 141.
Special Branch, 158.
Spellman Cardinal, 140.
Spring Dan,12.
Stamp Duty, 1102.
Standing Committee of Hierarchy, 123.
Strasbourg, 143.
St. Columbanus, 23.
St. Laurent Louis, 76,81.
St. Patrick's Cathedral, 72.
St. Patrick's Maynooth, 71,121.
St. Vincent's Private Hospital, 143.
State Funeral, 179.
Status of Women in Constitution 1937, 43.
Statute of Westminster, 24,26,28,30,35.
Staunton Bishop, 90.
Sterling Area, 68,87.
Stormont, 149.
Succession Bill, 166-8.
Suez Canal Invasion, 146.
Sunday independent, 77.
Supreme Court, 21,37,89,100.
Sweetman Gerard, 16,68,114-5,144-7,156, 160-1,164-5,170.
Sweetman's Revenge, 169
Sweetman Roger, 169.

T

Taft William H., 120,140.
Taoiseach, 11,13,48.
'Tarry Flynn', 108.
Tate & Wallace Collections, 132.
TCD, 7,119-123.
TD's Allowance 160.
Teevan Judge, 105,107.
Temperment, 76.
Templeogue, 35.
Terenure, 159.
Territorial Army Barracks Dungannon, 154.
Thompson WJ., 132.
Thorncastle St., 149.
Tiernary Professor, 110-111,120.
Tokyo, 23.
Tone Wolfe, 39.
Topping Mr., 155.
Traynor Oscar, 159,161.
Treaty, 20.
Treatry Ports, 45.
Tribunal of Inquiry, 53.
Truman President, 82-3,85.
Tuam, 121.
Tuberculosis, 12,77,87,89.
Tullamore, 99.
Tully John, 101,146,167.

U

University College Cork, 119.
University College Dublin, 17,108, 119.
University Grants, 122.
Unionists, 153, 161.
United Nations, 26,85,117-8,140-1,154.
United Nations Charter, 118.
United States of America, 23,76-7,80,85,116,139,143
USA State Visit 1956, 139-141.

V

Vanishing Irish, 155.
Vatican, 23,71.
Vetinary College, 119
Victoria Prize, 18
Volunteers Irish, 17.
Volunteers Ulster, 17.

W

Wagner Collection, 139.
Waldorf Astoria, 140.
Walpole Horace, 140.
Walsh Archbishop, 121.
Walshe Joe, 22,24.
War Memorial Islandbridge, 59.
Washington, 85,116,139-140.
Watercolour Association, 131.
Waterford Corporation, 131.
Waterloo Road, 57.
Wearing of Uniforms Bill, 38.
Wellington Duke of, 134.
Westminster, 153.

Westport, 37.
Wexford, 10.
Whitaker TK., 68,86,144,146,160.
White Henry, 65.
Wilde Oscar, 109.
Wilson Committee, 132.
Wilson Harold, 133.
Witt Robert Sir, 132.

Y

Yale University, 139,141.
Yeats WB, 130-1.
Yugoslavia, 139,141.